SUPER SONS
VOL.3 PARENT TRAP

PETER J. TOMASI
writer

CARLO BARBERI
PAUL PELLETIER
BRENT PEEPLES
pencillers

ART THIBERT
CAM SMITH
SCOTT HANNA
inkers

GABE ELTAEB * PROTOBUNKER * HI-FI
colorists

ROB LEIGH * DAVE SHARPE
CARLOS M. MANGUAL * TRAVIS LANHAM
letterers

JORGE JIMENEZ and **ALEJANDRO SANCHEZ**
collection cover artists

SUPERMAN created by **JERRY SIEGEL** and **JOE SHUSTER**
SUPERBOY created by **JERRY SIEGEL**
By special arrangement with the Jerry Siegel family

PAUL KAMINSKI Editor - Original Series * **ANDREA SHEA** Assistant Editor - Original Series
JEB WOODARD Group Editor - Collected Editions * **ERIKA ROTHBERG** Editor - Collected Edition
STEVE COOK Design Director - Books * **MONIQUE NARBONETA** Publication Design

BOB HARRAS Senior VP - Editor-in-Chief, DC Comics
PAT McCALLUM Executive Editor, DC Comics

DIANE NELSON President * **DAN DiDIO** Publisher * **JIM LEE** Publisher * **GEOFF JOHNS** President & Chief Creative Officer
AMIT DESAI Executive VP - Business & Marketing Strategy, Direct to Consumer & Global Franchise Management
SAM ADES Senior VP & General Manager, Digital Services * **BOBBIE CHASE** VP & Executive Editor, Young Reader & Talent Development
MARK CHIARELLO Senior VP - Art, Design & Collected Editions * **JOHN CUNNINGHAM** Senior VP - Sales & Trade Marketing
ANNE DePIES Senior VP - Business Strategy, Finance & Administration * **DON FALLETTI** VP - Manufacturing Operations
LAWRENCE GANEM VP - Editorial Administration & Talent Relations * **ALISON GILL** Senior VP - Manufacturing & Operations
HANK KANALZ Senior VP - Editorial Strategy & Administration * **JAY KOGAN** VP - Legal Affairs * **JACK MAHAN** VP - Business Affairs
NICK J. NAPOLITANO VP - Manufacturing Administration * **EDDIE SCANNELL** VP - Consumer Marketing
COURTNEY SIMMONS Senior VP - Publicity & Communications * **JIM (SKI) SOKOLOWSKI** VP - Comic Book Specialty Sales & Trade Marketing
NANCY SPEARS VP - Mass, Book, Digital Sales & Trade Marketing * **MICHELE R. WELLS** VP - Content Strategy

SUPER SONS VOL. 3: PARENT TRAP

DC Comics, 2900 West Alameda Ave., Burbank, CA 91505
Printed by LSC Communications, Kendallville, IN, USA. 8/24/18. First Printing.
ISBN: 978-1-4012-8446-6

Library of Congress Cataloging-in-Publication Data is available.

PEFC Certified

Printed on paper from
sustainably managed
forests, controlled
sources

PEFC

PEFC/29-31-337   www.pefc.org

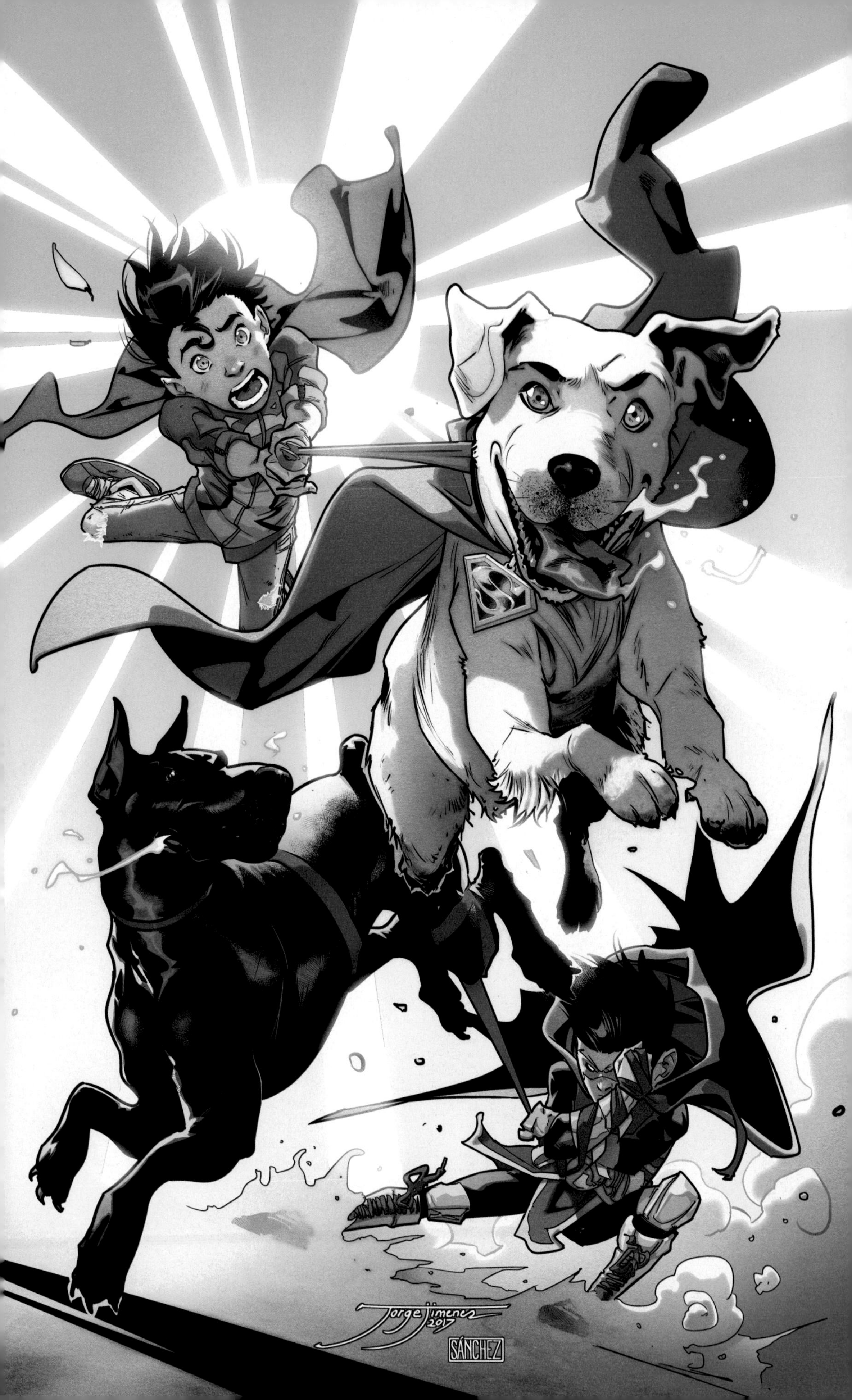
Jorge Jimenez 2017
SÁNCHEZ

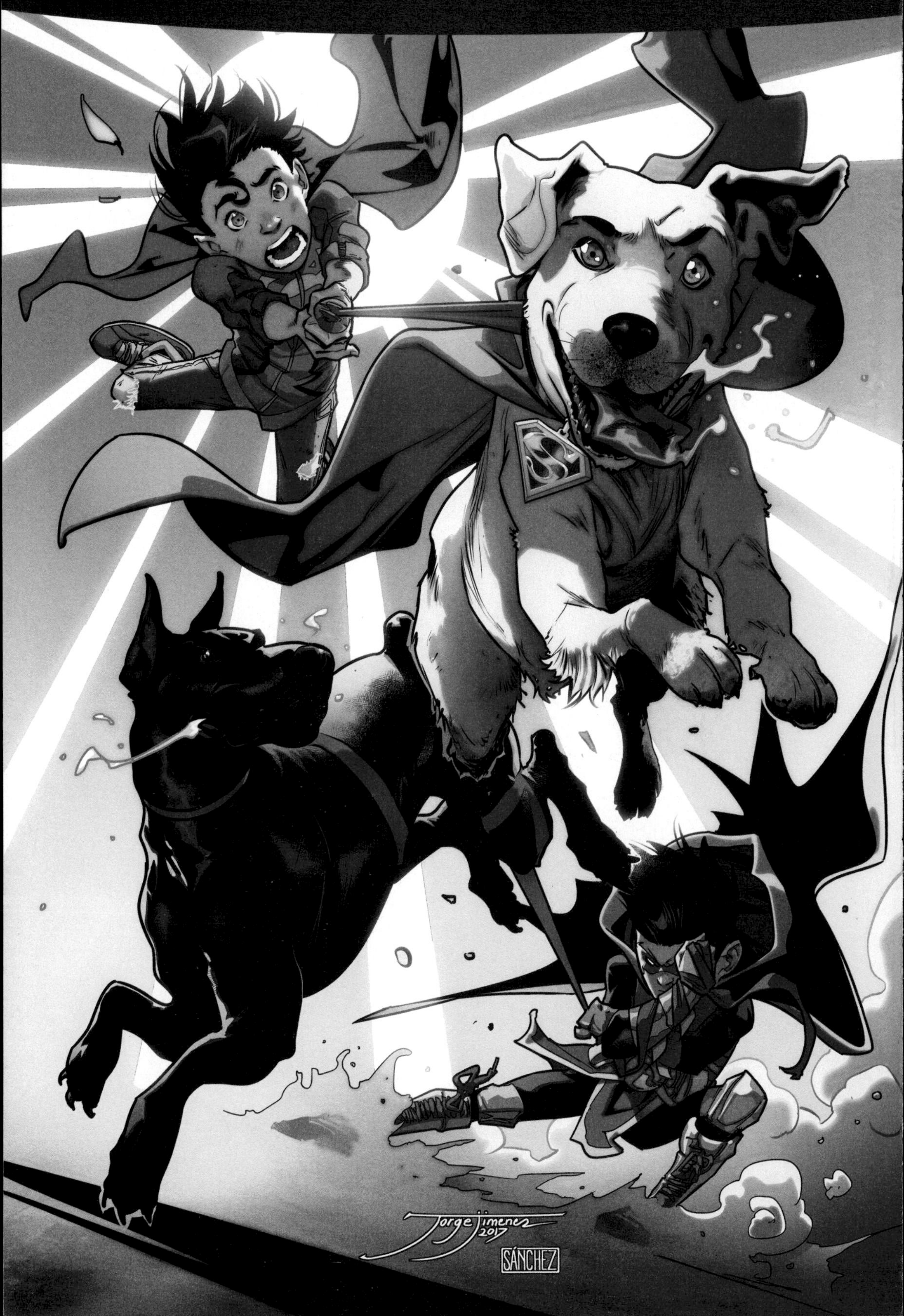
Jorge Jimenez
2017
SÁNCHEZ

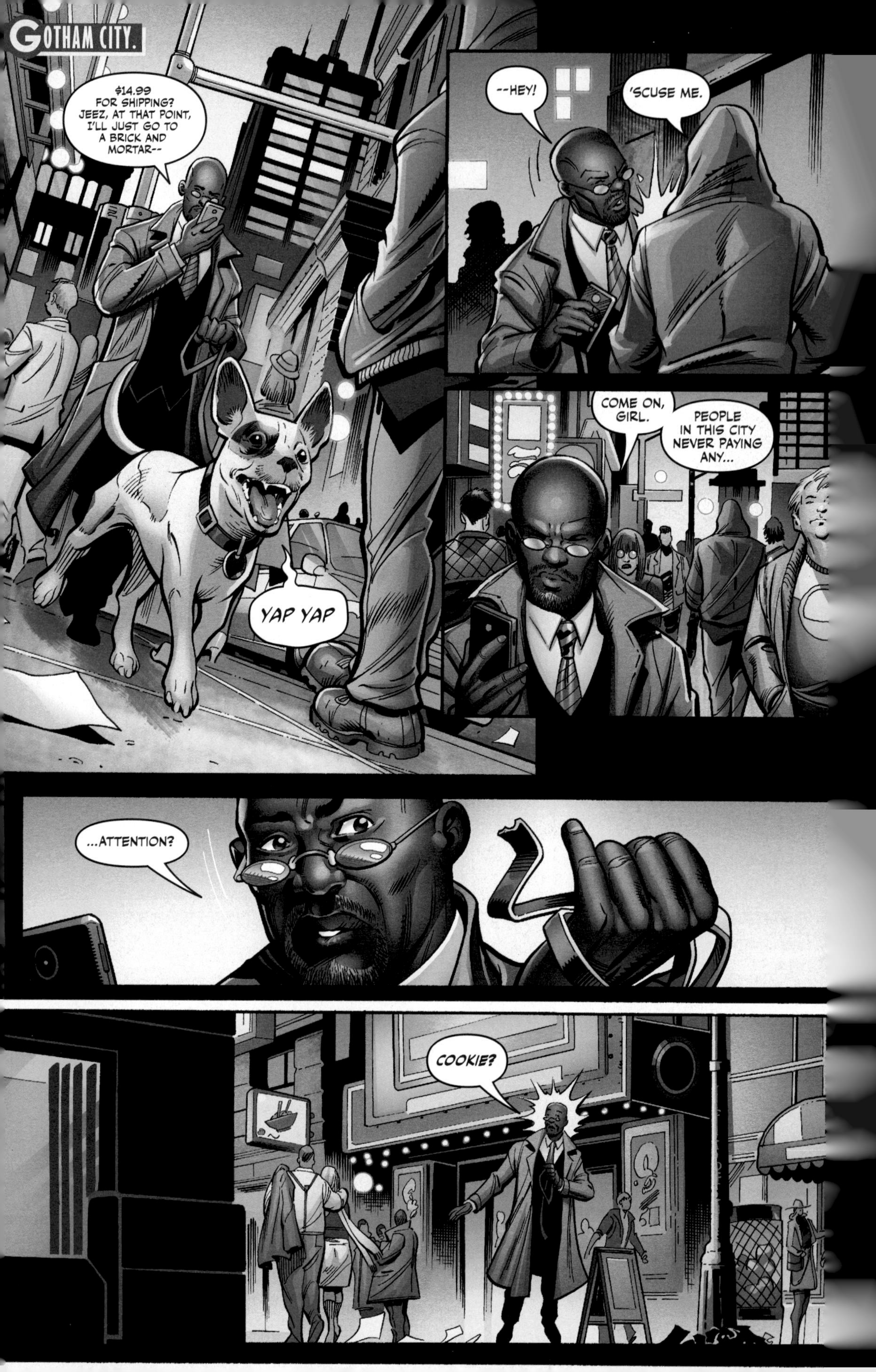
GOTHAM CITY.
$14.99 FOR SHIPPING? JEEZ, AT THAT POINT, I'LL JUST GO TO A BRICK AND MORTAR--
YAP YAP
--HEY!
'SCUSE ME.
COME ON, GIRL.
PEOPLE IN THIS CITY NEVER PAYING ANY...
...ATTENTION?
COOKIE?

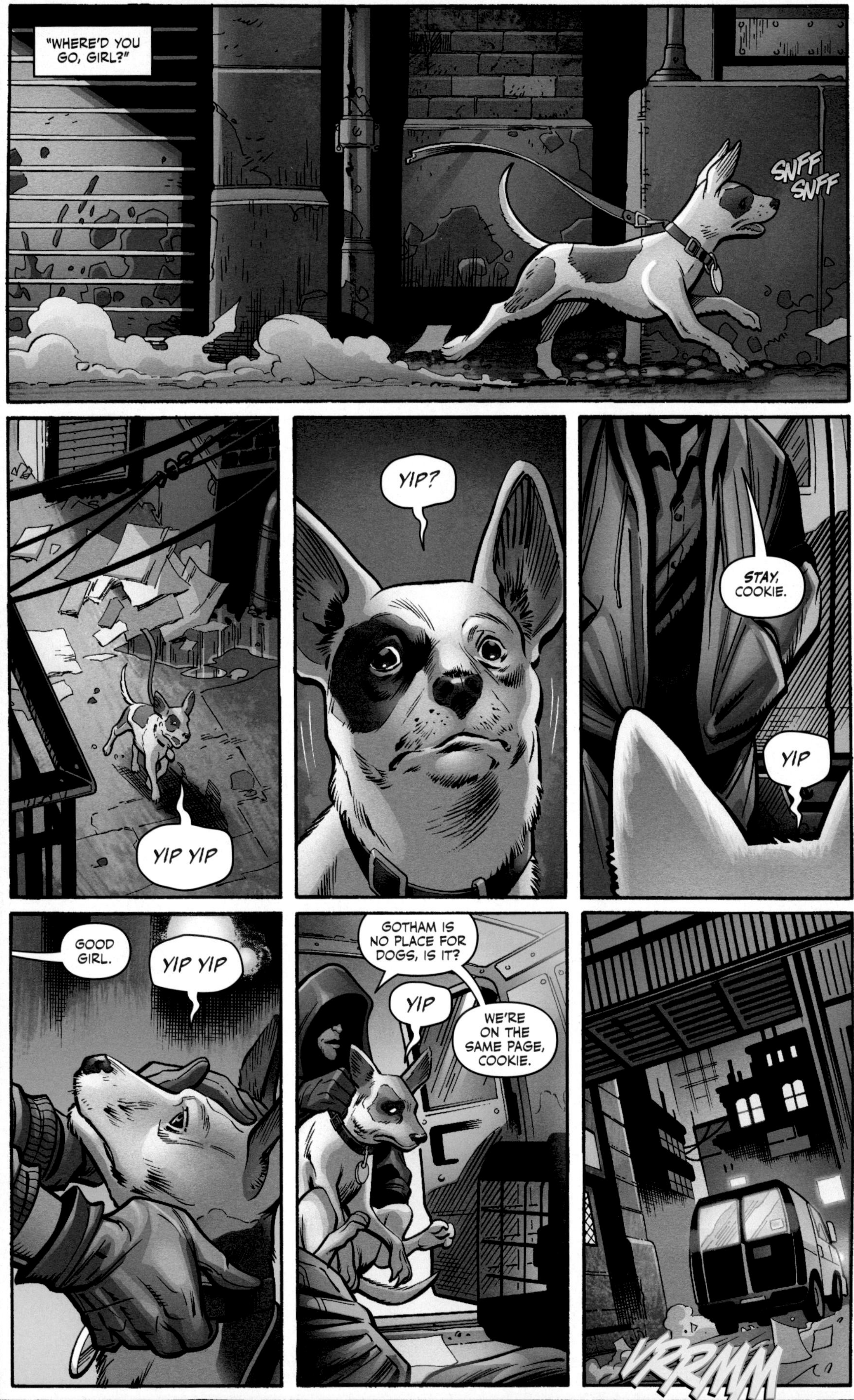
"WHERE'D YOU GO, GIRL?"
SNFF SNFF
YIP YIP
YIP?
STAY, COOKIE.
YIP
GOOD GIRL.
YIP YIP
GOTHAM IS NO PLACE FOR DOGS, IS IT?
YIP
WE'RE ON THE SAME PAGE, COOKIE.
VRRMM

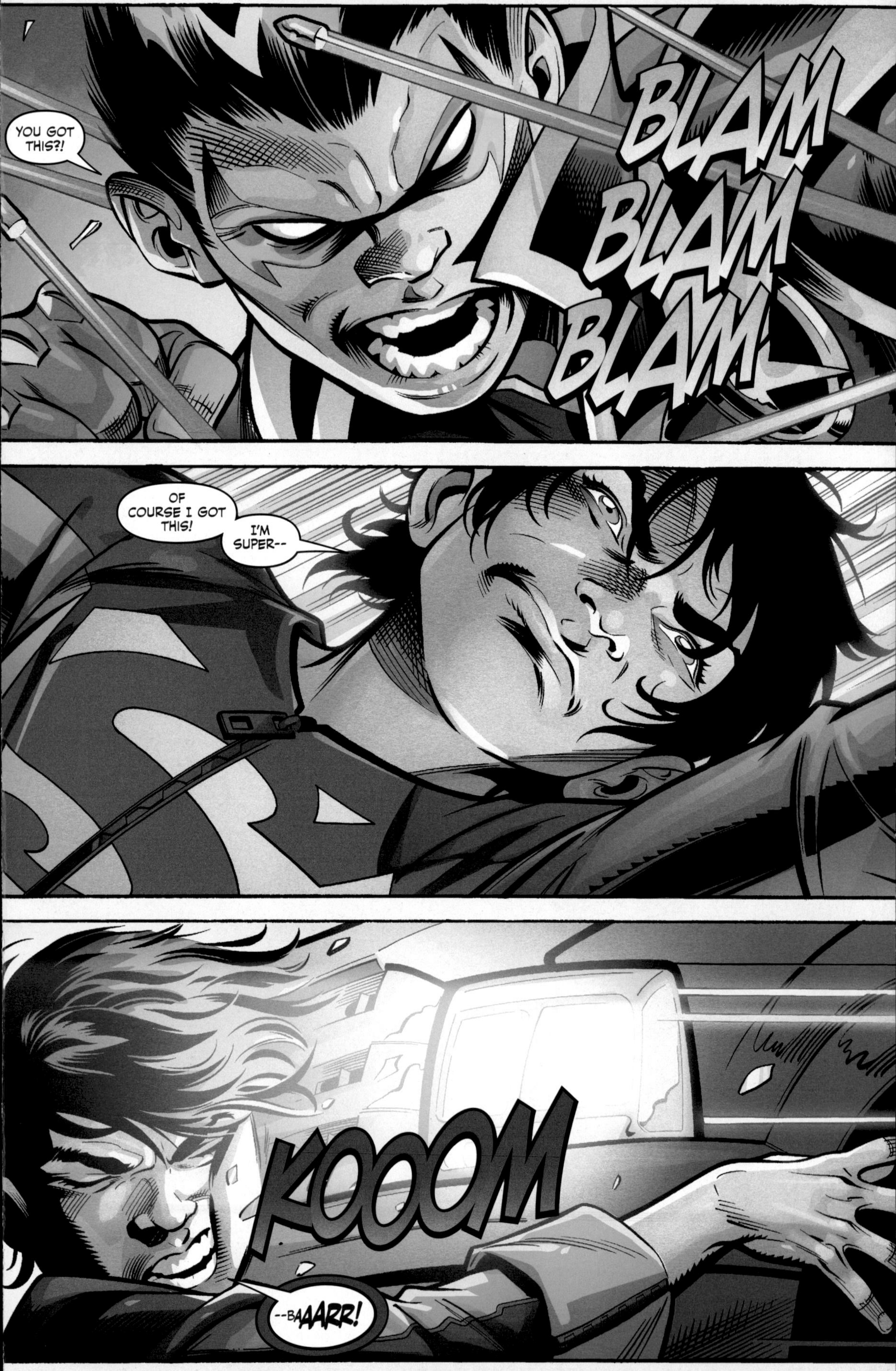
YOU GOT THIS?!
BLAM
BLAM
BLAM
OF COURSE I GOT THIS!
I'M SUPER--
KOOOM
--BAAARR!

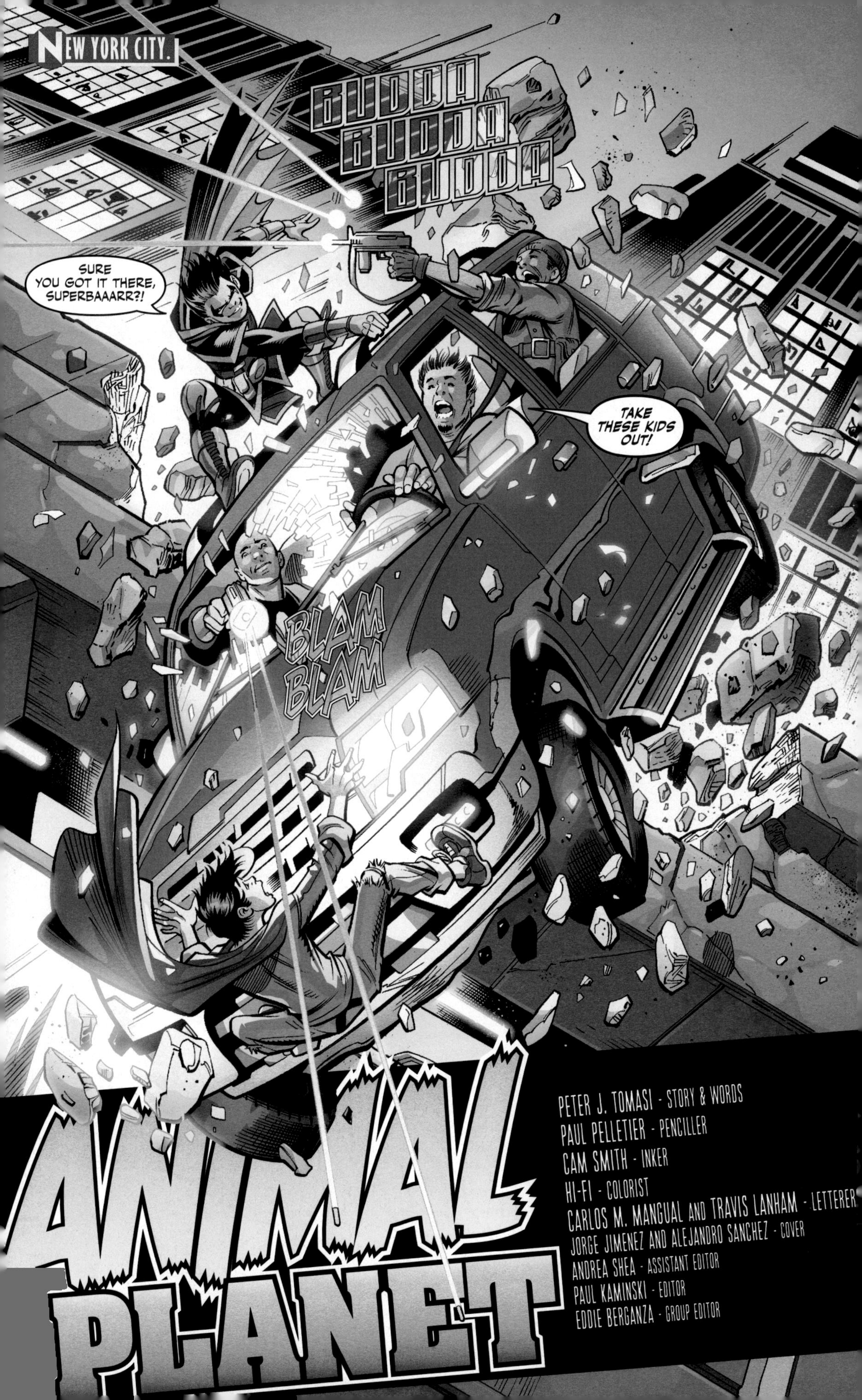
NEW YORK CITY.
BUDDA BUDDA BUDDA
SURE YOU GOT IT THERE, SUPERBAAARR?!
TAKE THESE KIDS OUT!
BLAM BLAM
ANIMAL PLANET
PETER J. TOMASI - STORY & WORDS
PAUL PELLETIER - PENCILLER
CAM SMITH - INKER
HI-FI - COLORIST
CARLOS M. MANGUAL AND TRAVIS LANHAM - LETTERER
JORGE JIMENEZ AND ALEJANDRO SANCHEZ - COVER
ANDREA SHEA - ASSISTANT EDITOR
PAUL KAMINSKI - EDITOR
EDDIE BERGANZA - GROUP EDITOR

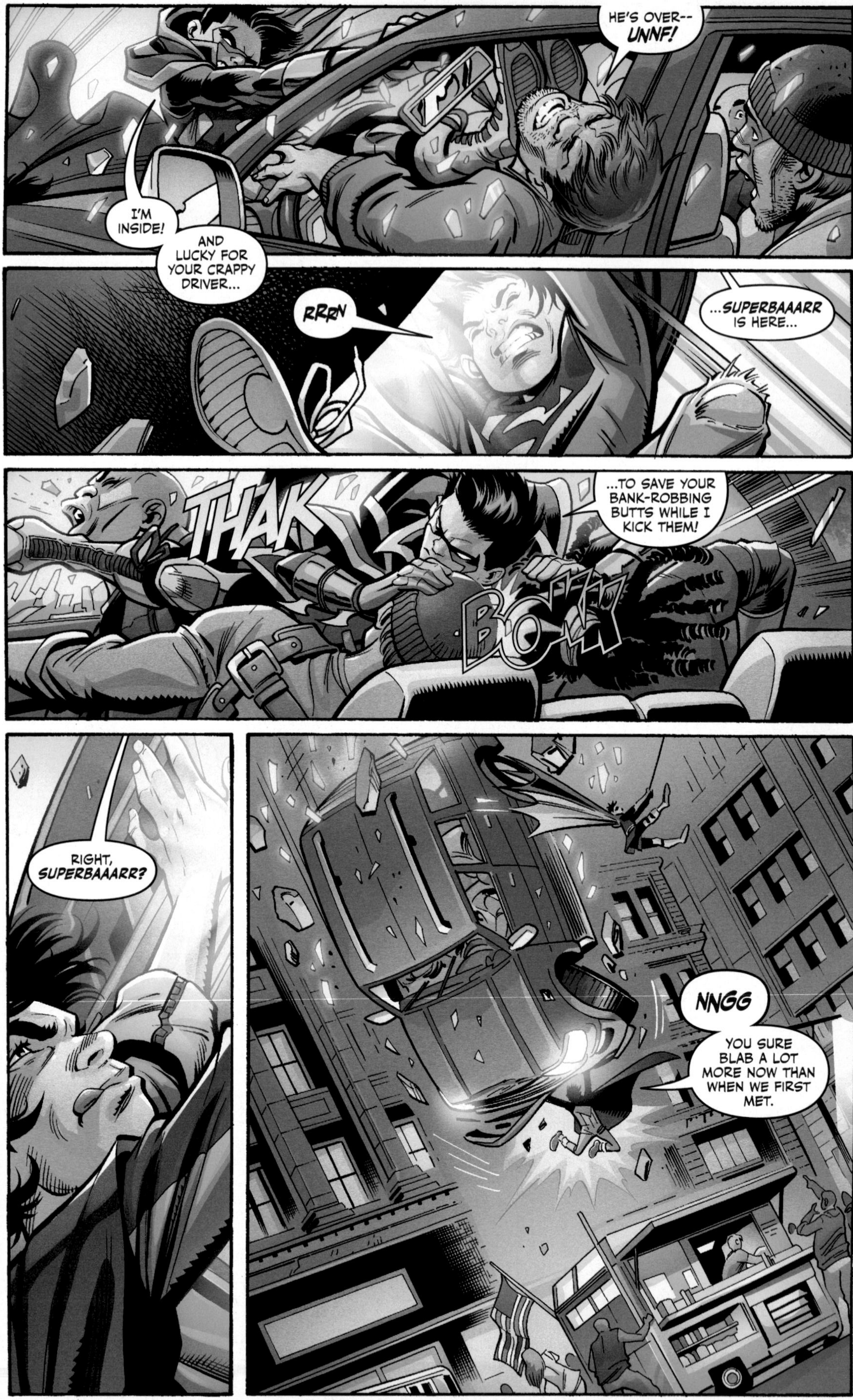
HE'S OVER-- UNNF!
I'M INSIDE!
AND LUCKY FOR YOUR CRAPPY DRIVER...
RRRN
...SUPERBAAARR IS HERE...
THAK
...TO SAVE YOUR BANK-ROBBING BUTTS WHILE I KICK THEM!
RIGHT, SUPERBAAARR?
NNGG
YOU SURE BLAB A LOT MORE NOW THAN WHEN WE FIRST MET.

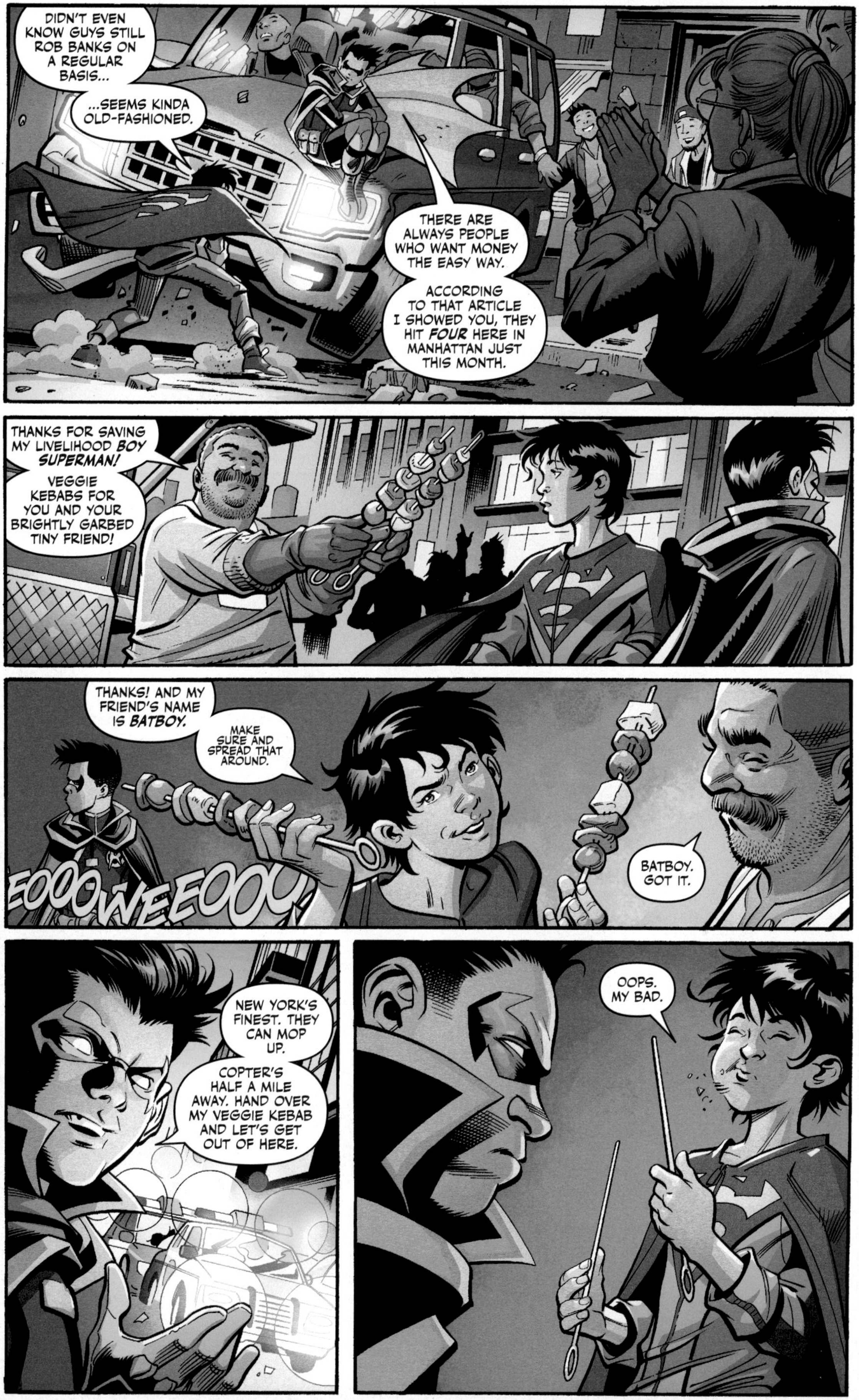
DIDN'T EVEN KNOW GUYS STILL ROB BANKS ON A REGULAR BASIS...
...SEEMS KINDA OLD-FASHIONED.
THERE ARE ALWAYS PEOPLE WHO WANT MONEY THE EASY WAY.
ACCORDING TO THAT ARTICLE I SHOWED YOU, THEY HIT FOUR HERE IN MANHATTAN JUST THIS MONTH.
THANKS FOR SAVING MY LIVELIHOOD BOY SUPERMAN!
VEGGIE KEBABS FOR YOU AND YOUR BRIGHTLY GARBED TINY FRIEND!
THANKS! AND MY FRIEND'S NAME IS BATBOY.
MAKE SURE AND SPREAD THAT AROUND.
EOOOWEEOOU
BATBOY. GOT IT.
NEW YORK'S FINEST. THEY CAN MOP UP.
COPTER'S HALF A MILE AWAY. HAND OVER MY VEGGIE KEBAB AND LET'S GET OUT OF HERE.
OOPS. MY BAD.

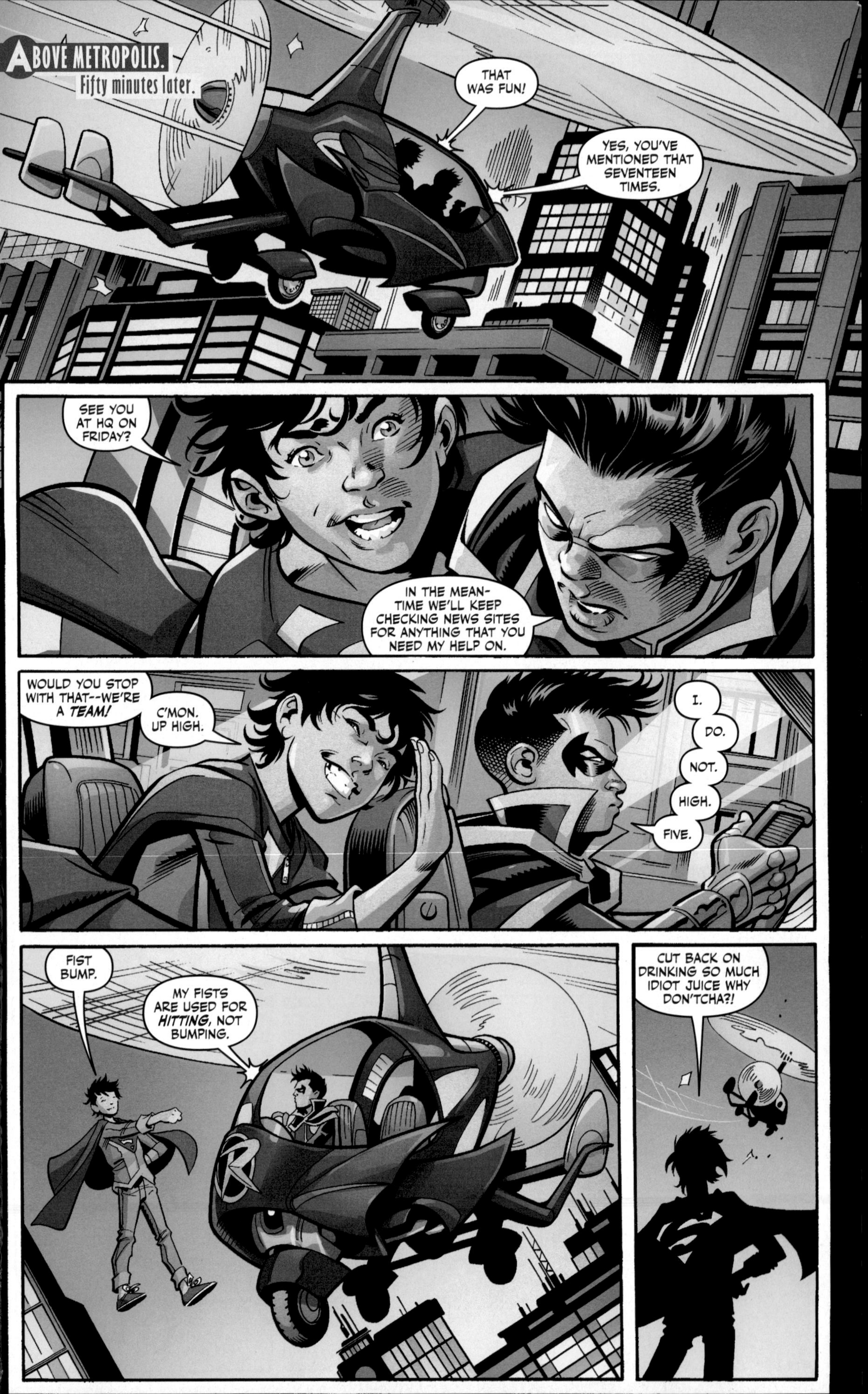
ABOVE METROPOLIS.
Fifty minutes later.
THAT WAS FUN!
YES, YOU'VE MENTIONED THAT SEVENTEEN TIMES.
SEE YOU AT HQ ON FRIDAY?
IN THE MEAN-TIME WE'LL KEEP CHECKING NEWS SITES FOR ANYTHING THAT YOU NEED MY HELP ON.
WOULD YOU STOP WITH THAT--WE'RE A TEAM!
C'MON. UP HIGH.
I.
DO.
NOT.
HIGH.
FIVE.
FIST BUMP.
MY FISTS ARE USED FOR HITTING, NOT BUMPING.
CUT BACK ON DRINKING SO MUCH IDIOT JUICE WHY DON'TCHA?!

HEY, KRYPTO!

MOM AND DAD NOT BACK FROM THEIR DATE NIGHT YET, *HUH?*

RRF

SOMEBODY'S IN A GOOD MOOD. YA MISS ME?

I WAS ONLY GONE A COUPLE OF HOURS.

SLURP!

SO...

...THAT'S ONE MORE DOWN. TOMORROW I'LL TACKLE THE MISSING ANIMALS.

DO A LITTLE GOOD EACH DAY. THAT'S MY MOTTO.

JEWEL HEIST!

Thie... local bank... all five boro...

DOG GONE GOTHAM

Rash of dog-nappings hound tri-state area!

GOT THAT, BOY...≥YAWN≤ A LITTLE...GOOD... ≥YAWN≤

...ZZZZZ...

GRRR

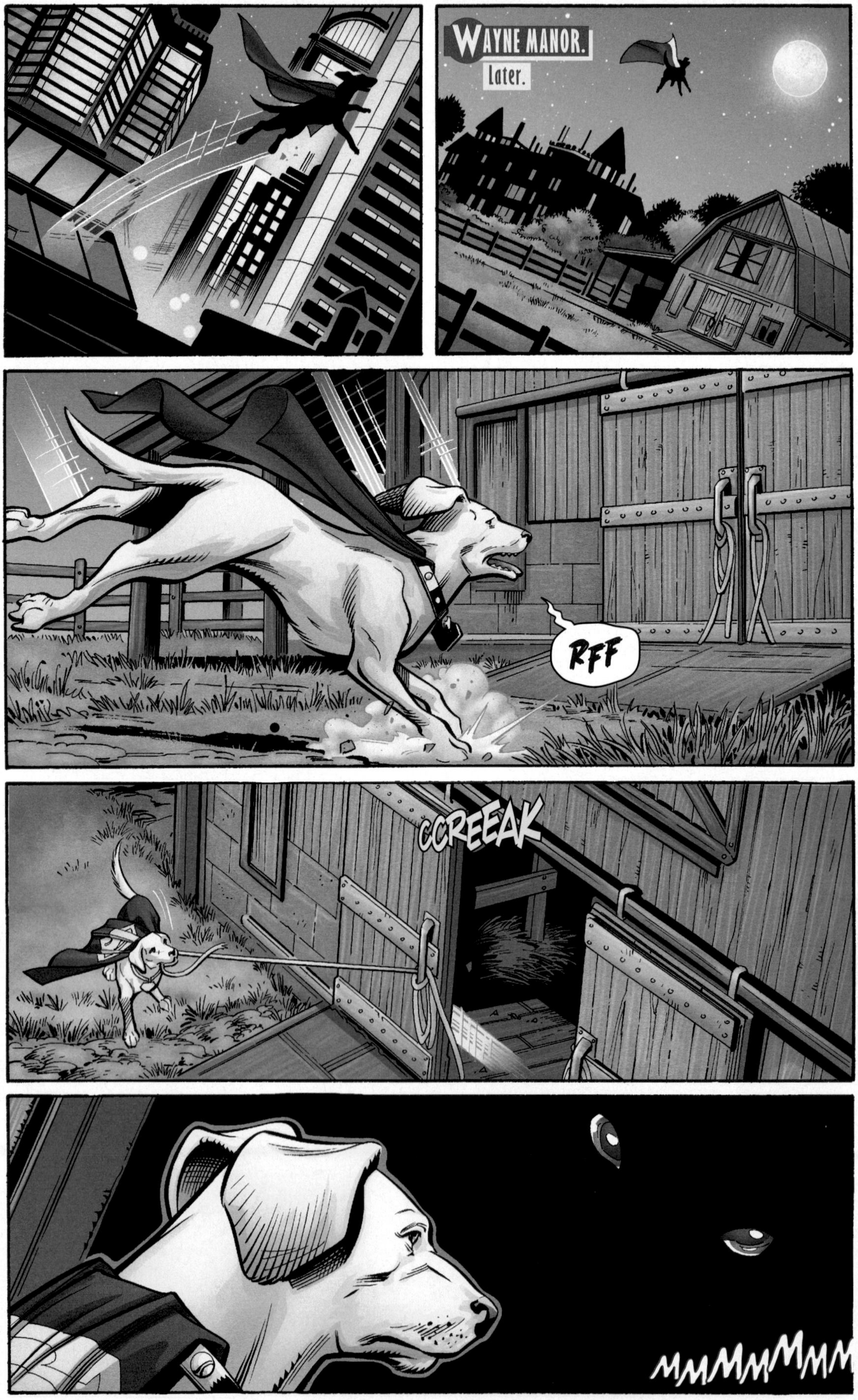
WAYNE MANOR.
Later.
RFF
CCREEAK
MMMMMMMM

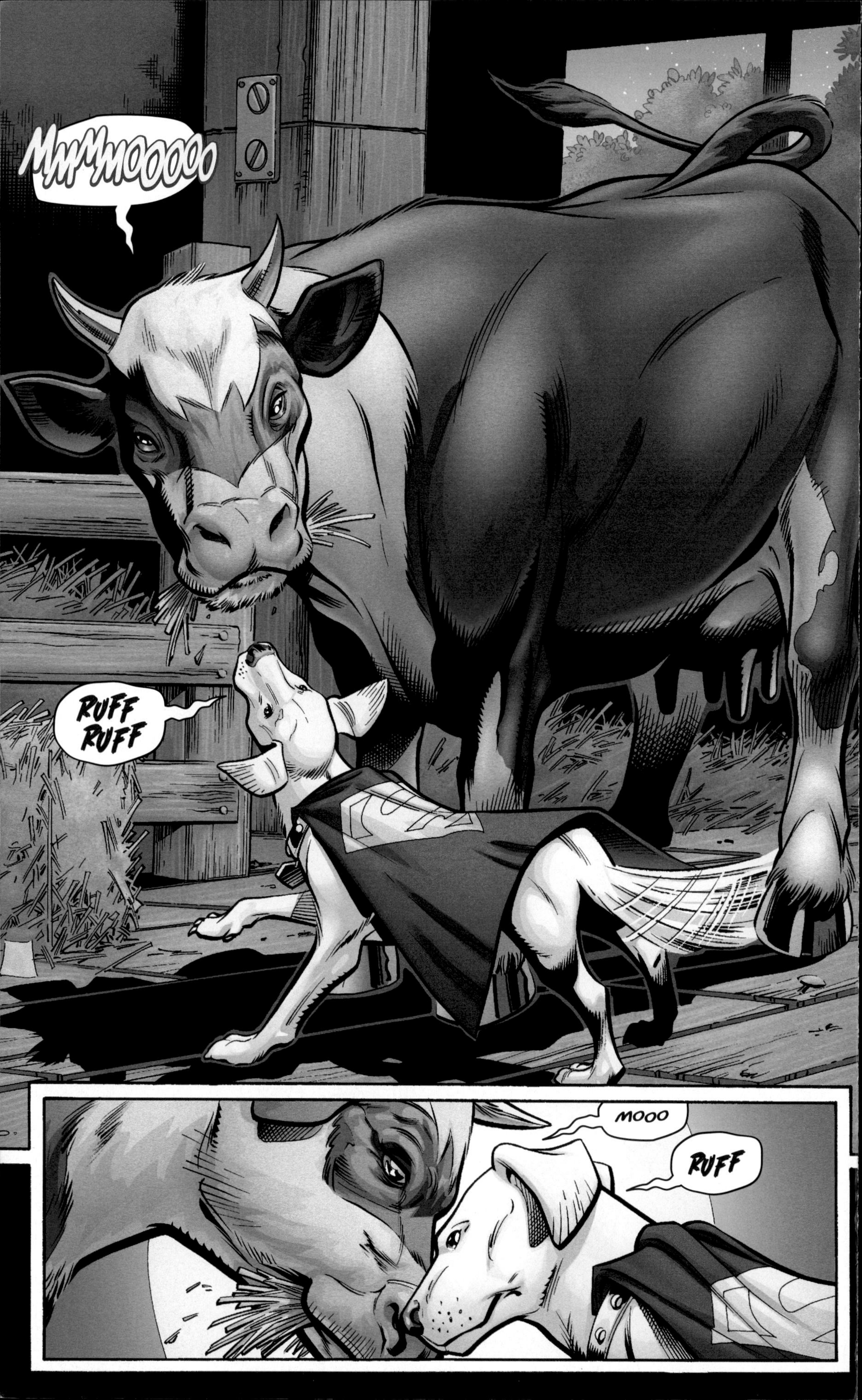
MMMMOOOOO
RUFF RUFF
MOOO
RUFF

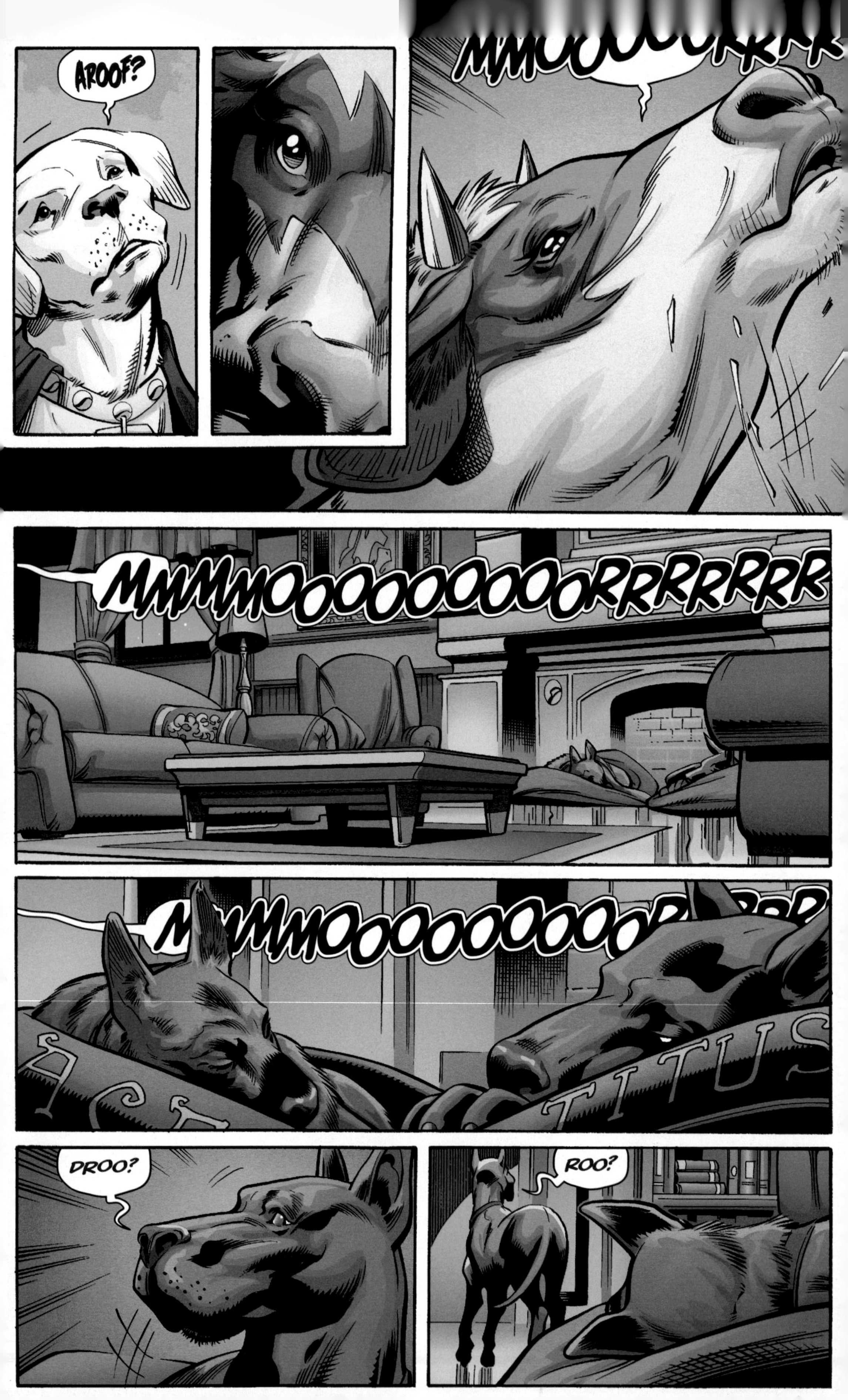

AROOF?
MMOOOOORRRR
MMMMOOOOOOOOOOORRRRRRR
MMMMOOOOOOOOOOOR
TITUS
DROO?
ROO?

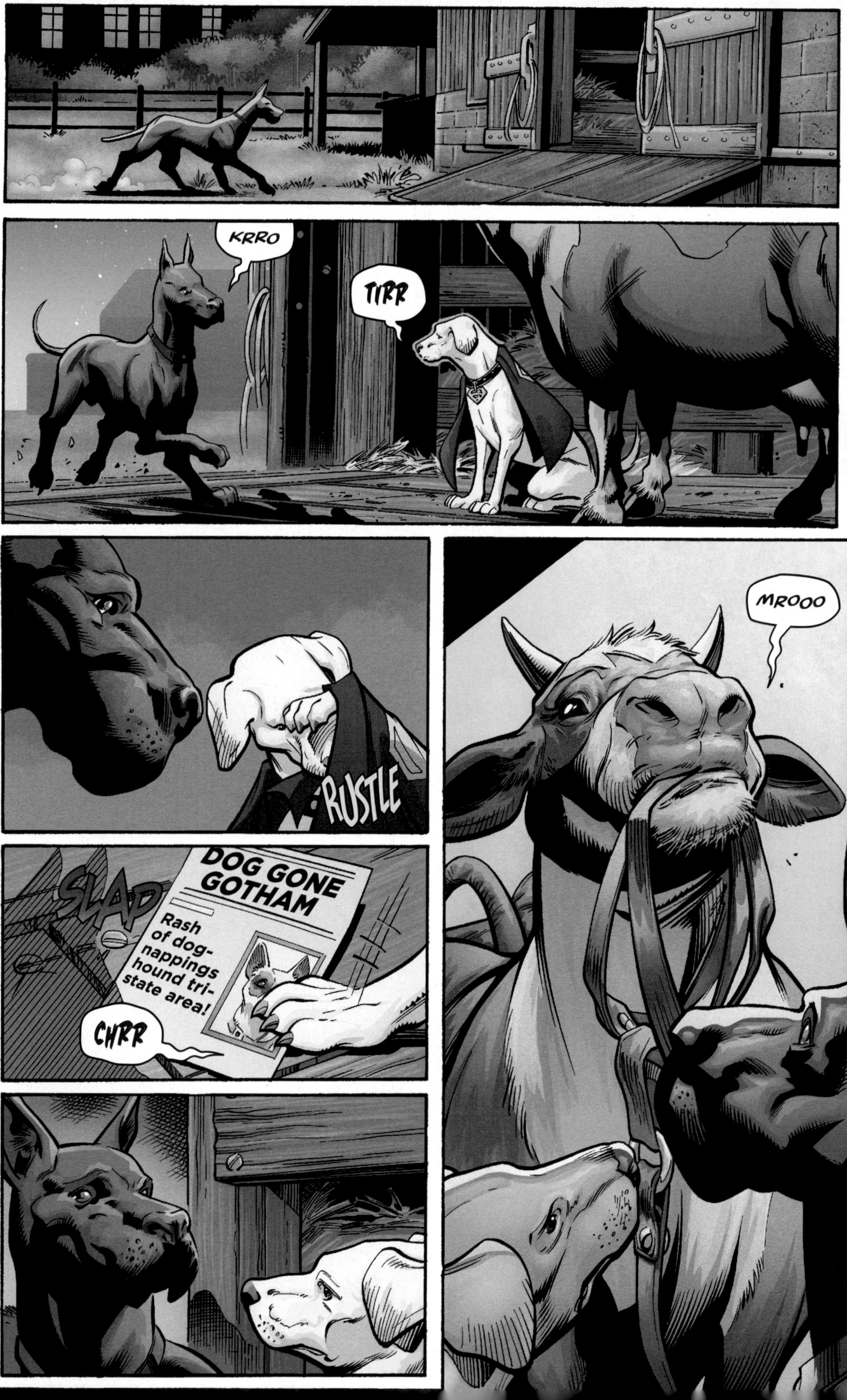
KRRO
TIRR
RUSTLE
MROOO
SLAP
DOG GONE GOTHAM
Rash of dog-nappings hound tri-state area!
CHRR

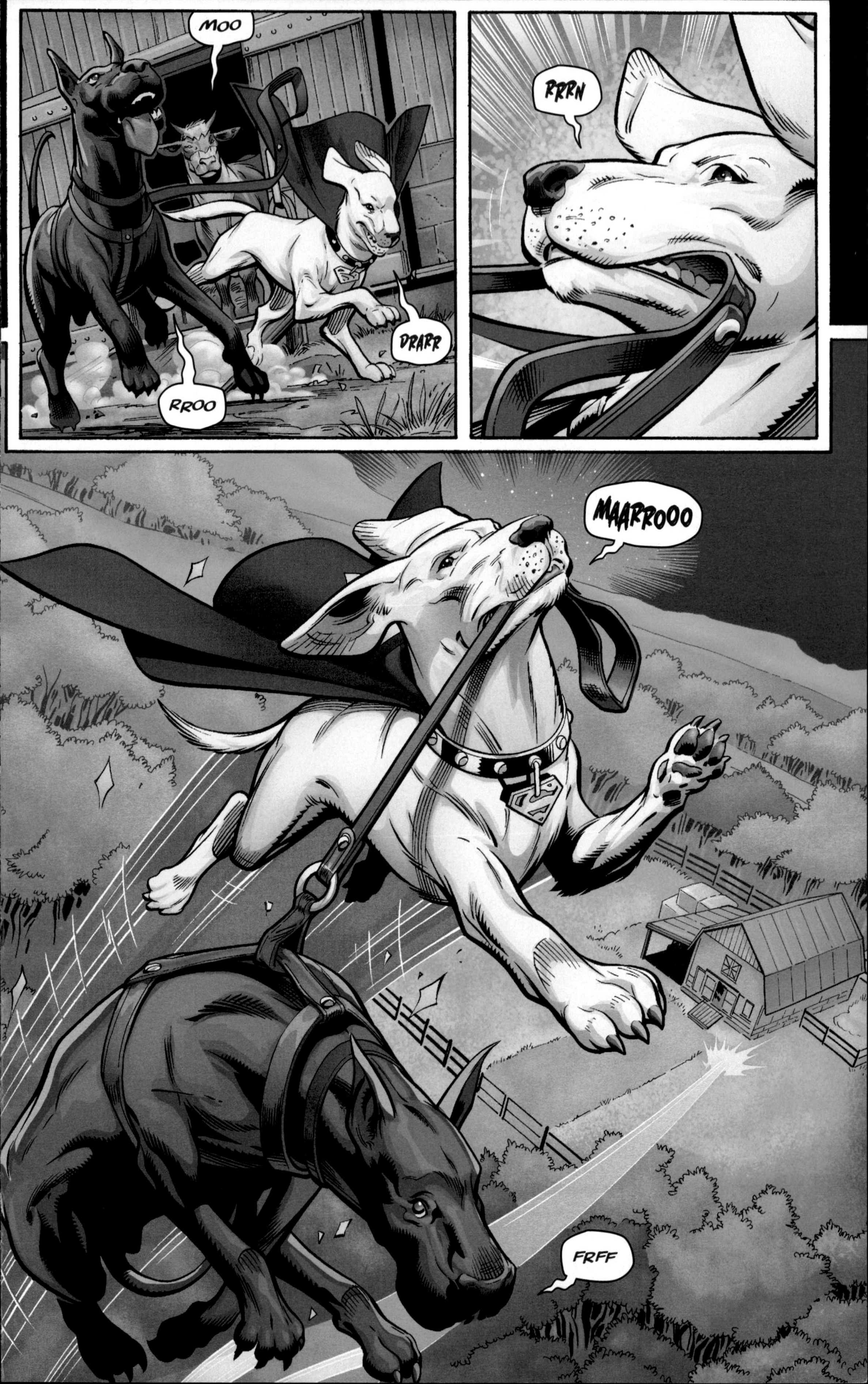
MOO
DRARR
RROO
RRRN
MAARROOO
FRFF

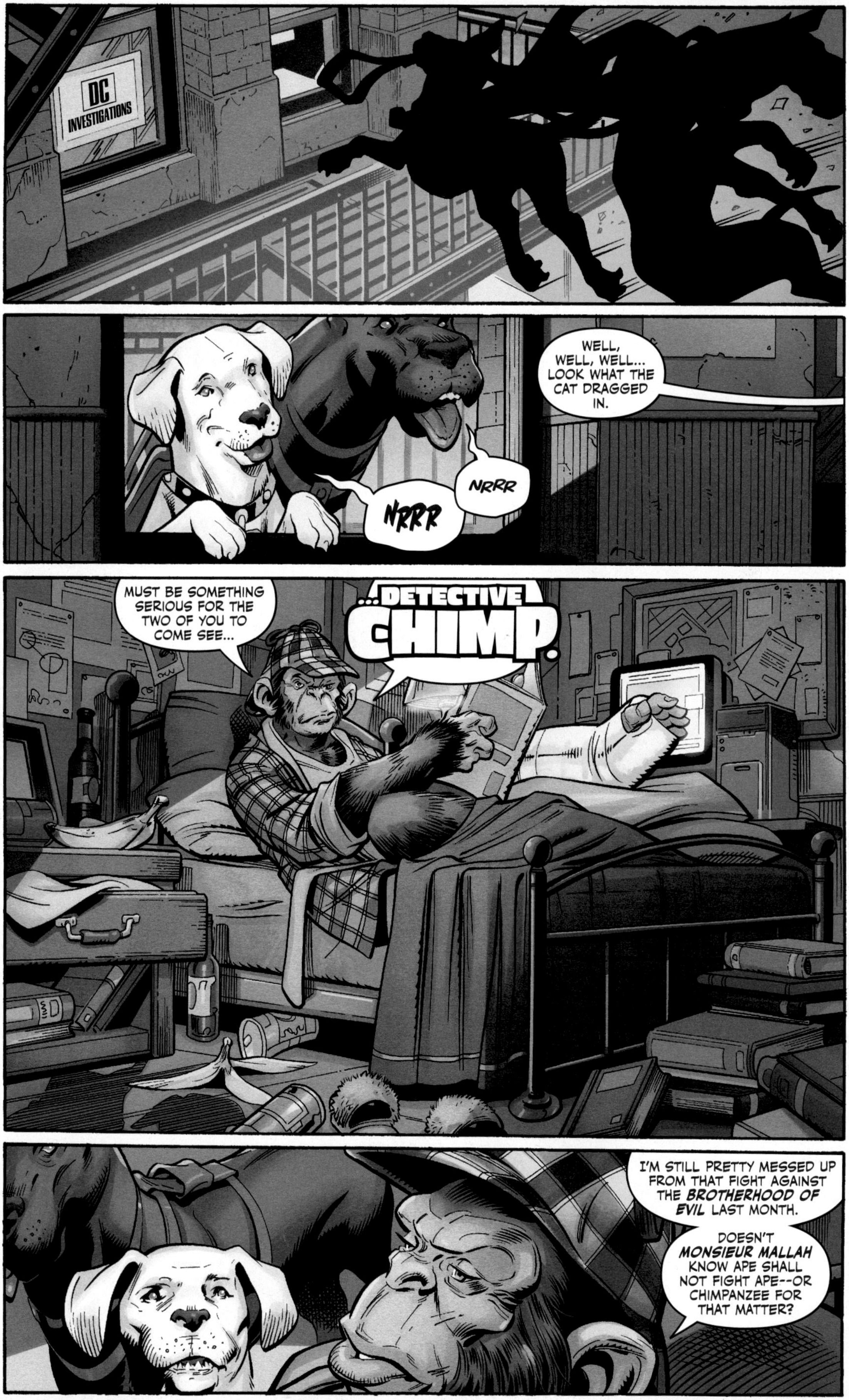
DC INVESTIGATIONS
WELL, WELL, WELL... LOOK WHAT THE CAT DRAGGED IN.
NRRR
NRRR
MUST BE SOMETHING SERIOUS FOR THE TWO OF YOU TO COME SEE...
...DETECTIVE CHIMP.
I'M STILL PRETTY MESSED UP FROM THAT FIGHT AGAINST THE *BROTHERHOOD OF EVIL* LAST MONTH.
DOESN'T *MONSIEUR MALLAH* KNOW APE SHALL NOT FIGHT APE--OR CHIMPANZEE FOR THAT MATTER?

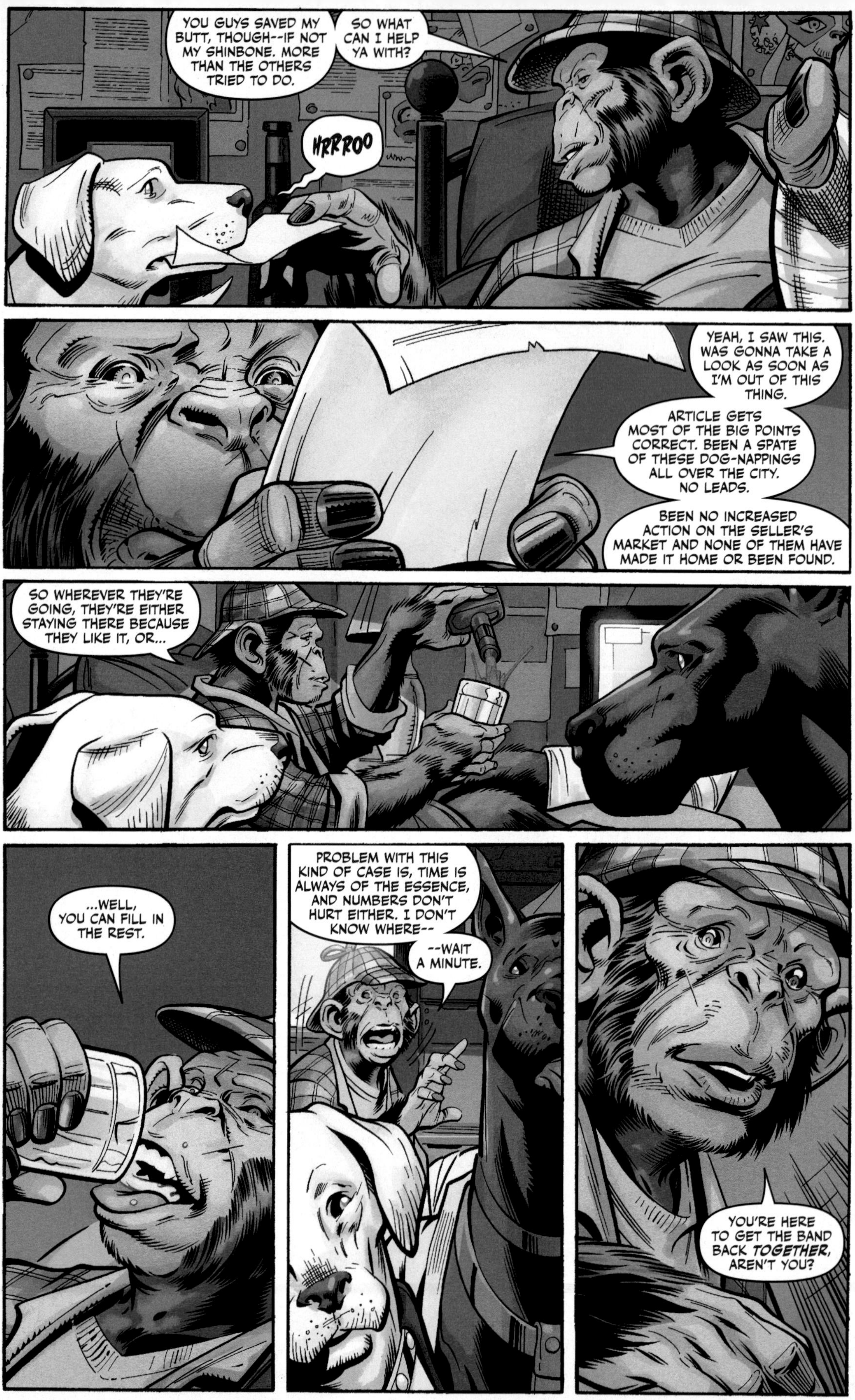
YOU GUYS SAVED MY BUTT, THOUGH--IF NOT MY SHINBONE. MORE THAN THE OTHERS TRIED TO DO.
SO WHAT CAN I HELP YA WITH?
HRRROO
YEAH, I SAW THIS. WAS GONNA TAKE A LOOK AS SOON AS I'M OUT OF THIS THING.
ARTICLE GETS MOST OF THE BIG POINTS CORRECT. BEEN A SPATE OF THESE DOG-NAPPINGS ALL OVER THE CITY. NO LEADS.
BEEN NO INCREASED ACTION ON THE SELLER'S MARKET AND NONE OF THEM HAVE MADE IT HOME OR BEEN FOUND.
SO WHEREVER THEY'RE GOING, THEY'RE EITHER STAYING THERE BECAUSE THEY LIKE IT, OR...
...WELL, YOU CAN FILL IN THE REST.
PROBLEM WITH THIS KIND OF CASE IS, TIME IS ALWAYS OF THE ESSENCE, AND NUMBERS DON'T HURT EITHER. I DON'T KNOW WHERE--
--WAIT A MINUTE.
YOU'RE HERE TO GET THE BAND BACK *TOGETHER*, AREN'T YOU?

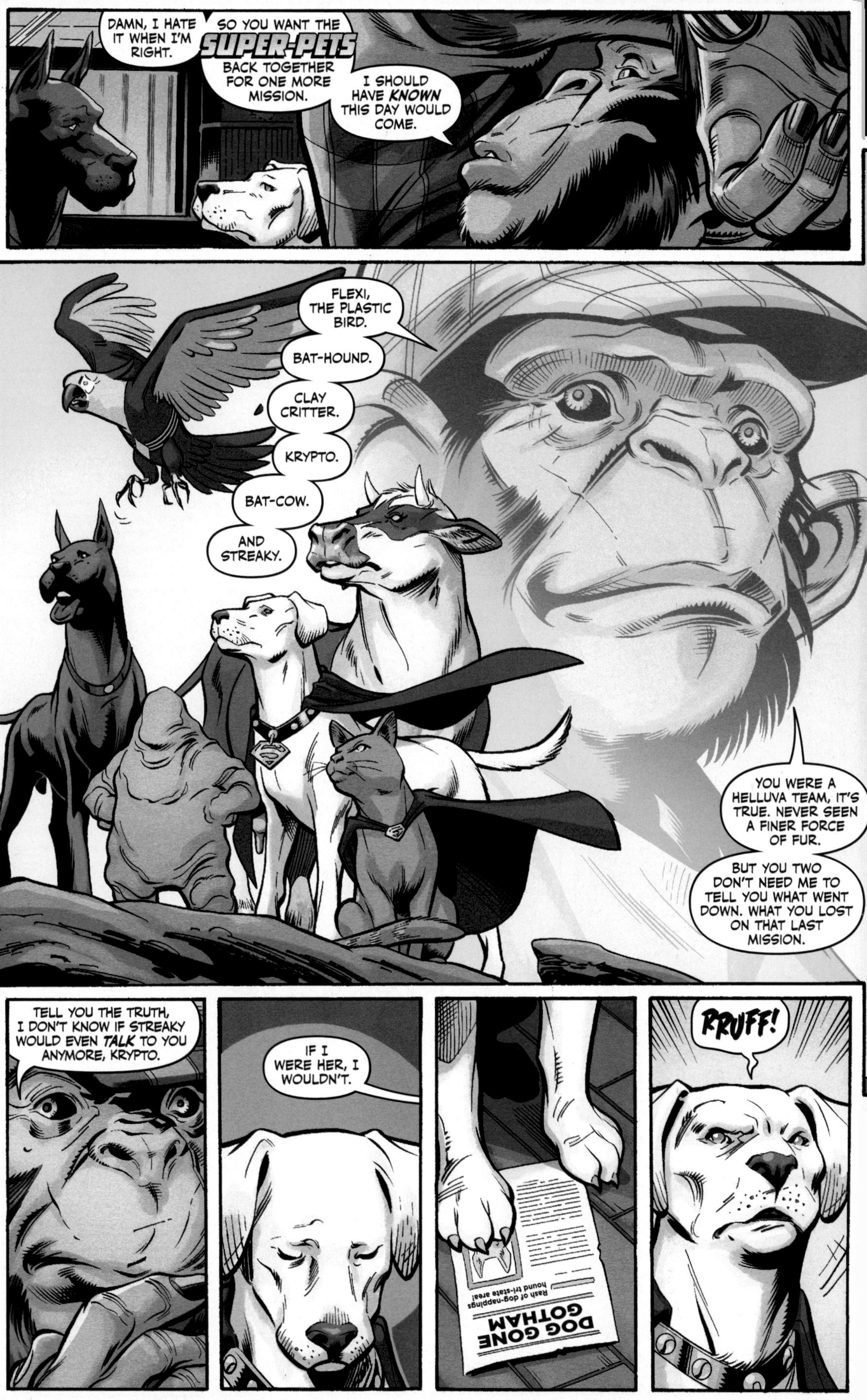
DAMN, I HATE IT WHEN I'M RIGHT.
SO YOU WANT THE SUPER-PETS BACK TOGETHER FOR ONE MORE MISSION.
I SHOULD HAVE *KNOWN* THIS DAY WOULD COME.
FLEXI, THE PLASTIC BIRD.
BAT-HOUND.
CLAY CRITTER.
KRYPTO.
BAT-COW.
AND STREAKY.
YOU WERE A HELLUVA TEAM, IT'S TRUE. NEVER SEEN A FINER FORCE OF FUR.
BUT YOU TWO DON'T NEED ME TO TELL YOU WHAT WENT DOWN. WHAT YOU LOST ON THAT LAST MISSION.
TELL YOU THE TRUTH, I DON'T KNOW IF STREAKY WOULD EVEN *TALK* TO YOU ANYMORE, KRYPTO.
IF I WERE HER, I WOULDN'T.
DOG GONE GOTHAM
Rash of dog-nappings hound tri-state area!
RRUFF!

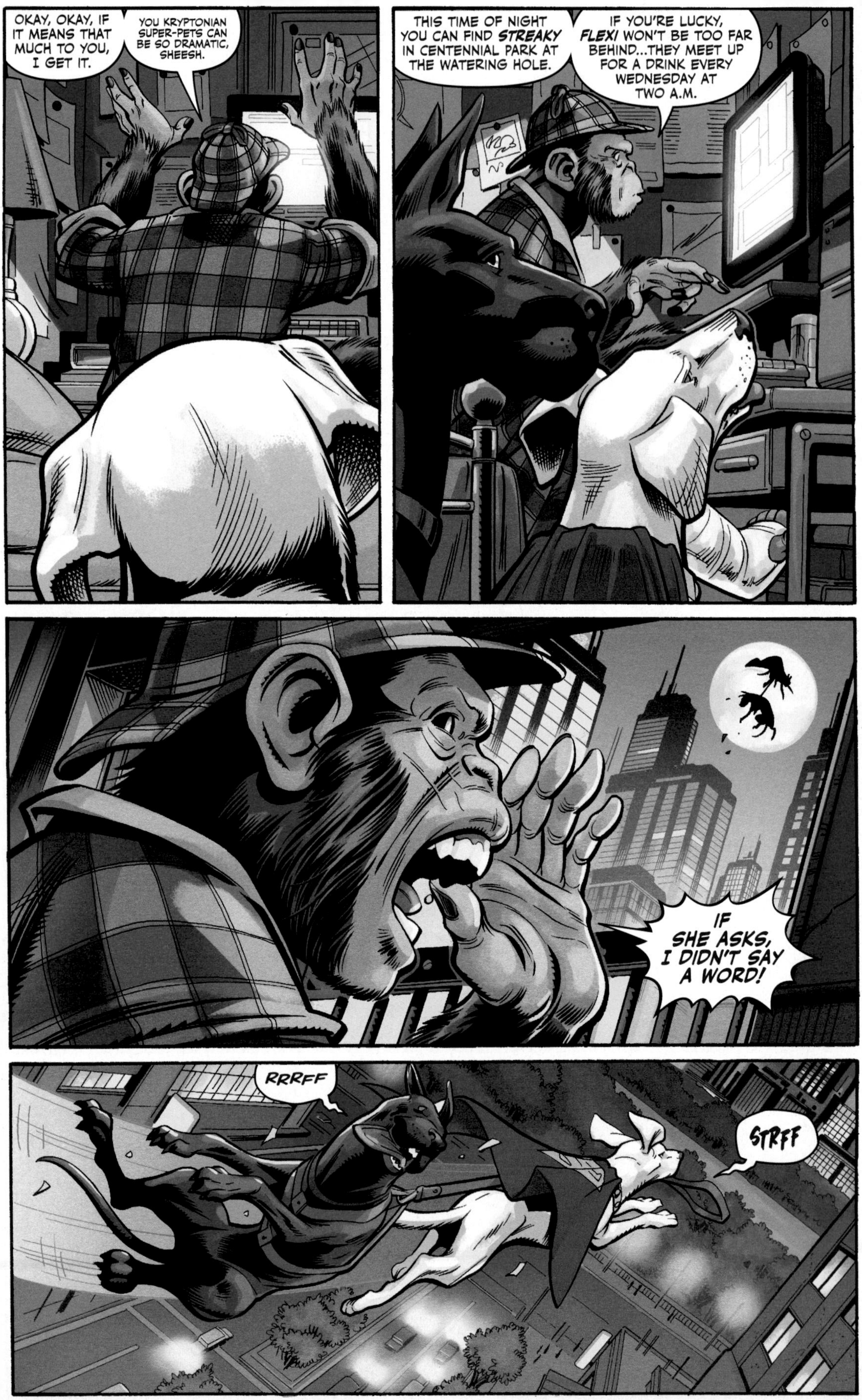
OKAY, OKAY, IF IT MEANS THAT MUCH TO YOU, I GET IT.
YOU KRYPTONIAN SUPER-PETS CAN BE SO DRAMATIC, SHEESH.
THIS TIME OF NIGHT YOU CAN FIND STREAKY IN CENTENNIAL PARK AT THE WATERING HOLE.
IF YOU'RE LUCKY, FLEXI WON'T BE TOO FAR BEHIND...THEY MEET UP FOR A DRINK EVERY WEDNESDAY AT TWO A.M.
IF SHE ASKS, I DIDN'T SAY A WORD!
RRRFF
STRFF

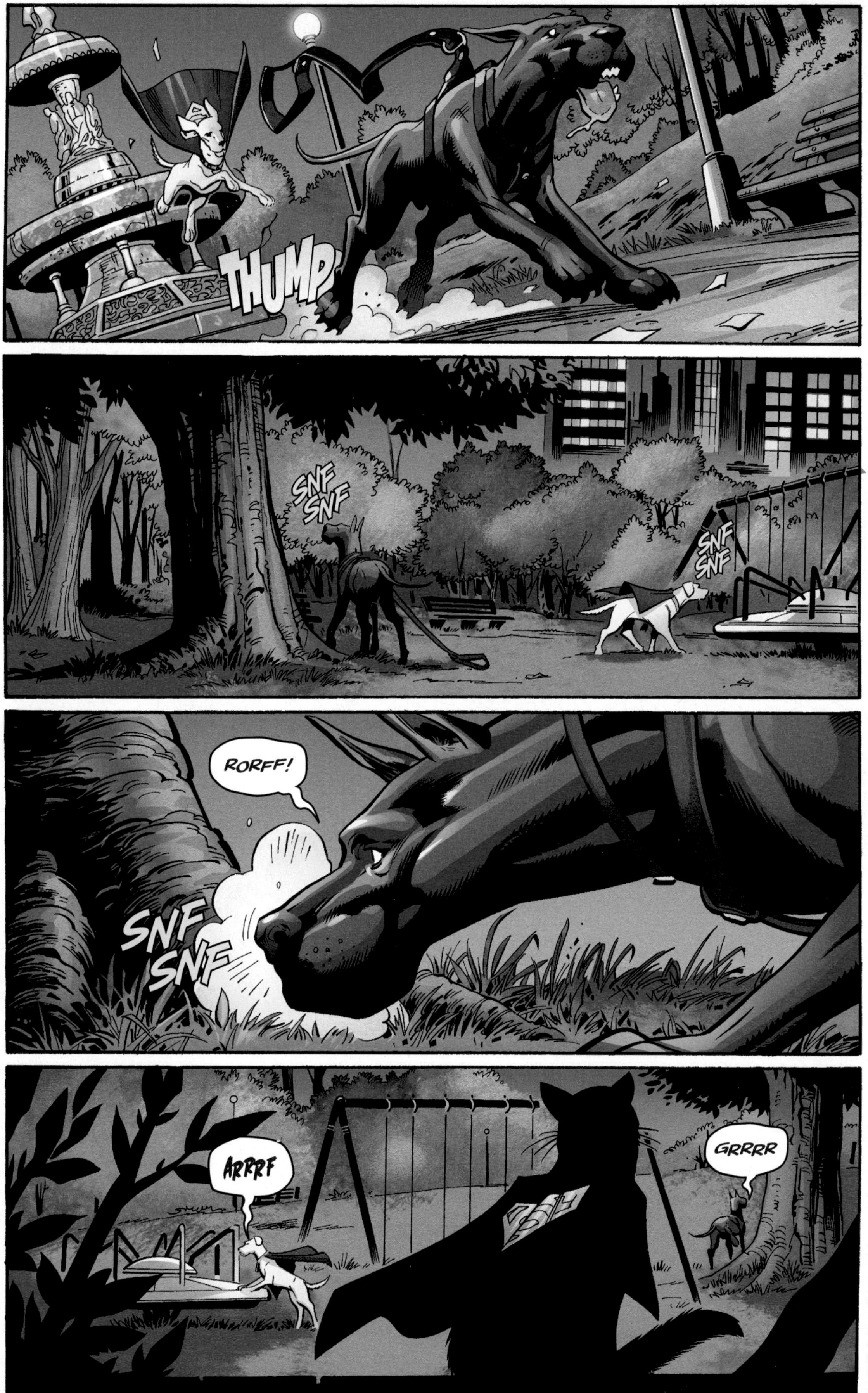
THUMP
SNF SNF
SNF SNF
RORFF!
SNF SNF
ARRRF
GRRRR

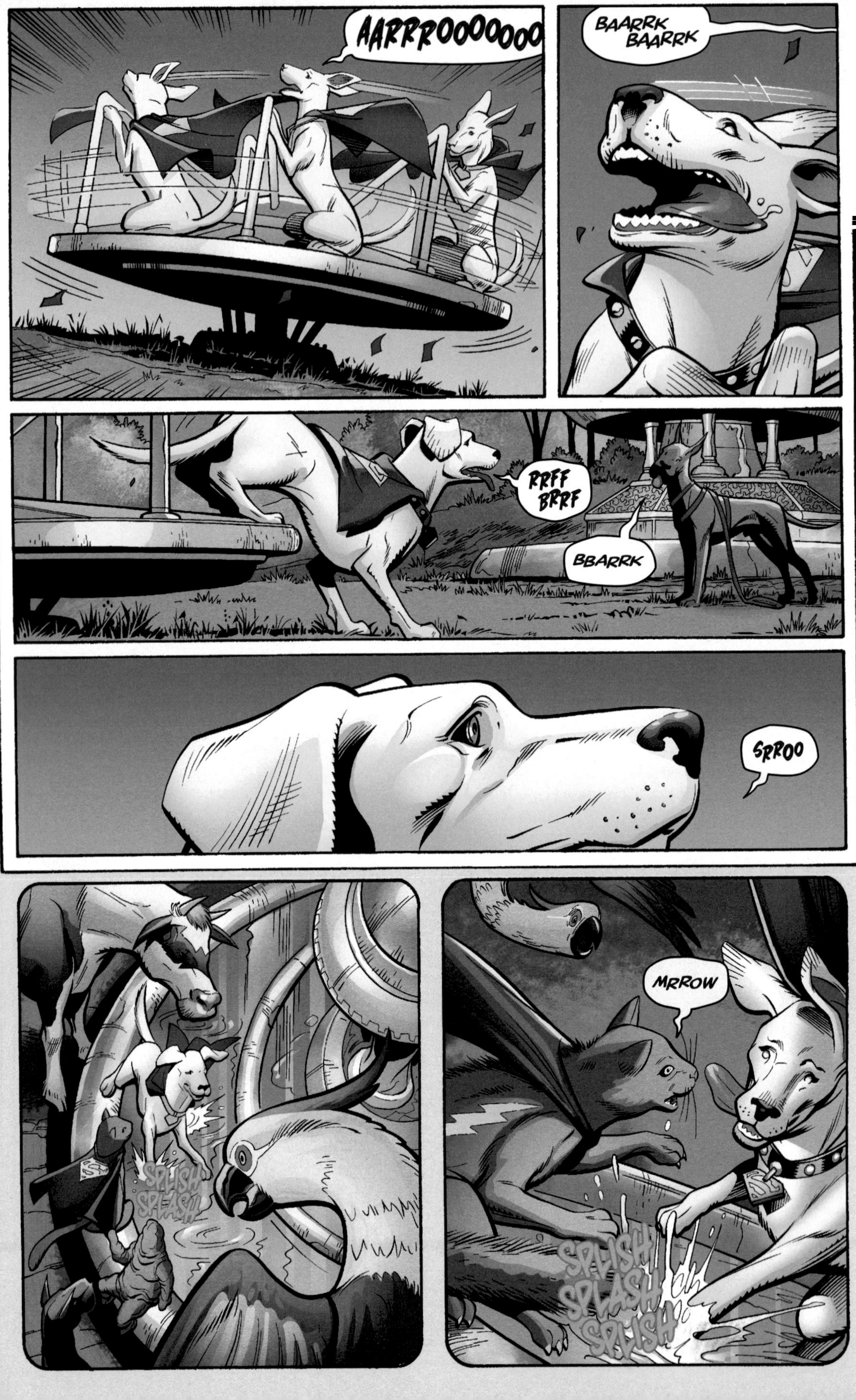
AARRROOOOOOO
BAARRK BAARRK
RRFF BRRF
BBARRK
SPROO
SPLISH SPLASH
MRROW
SPLISH SPLASH SPLISH

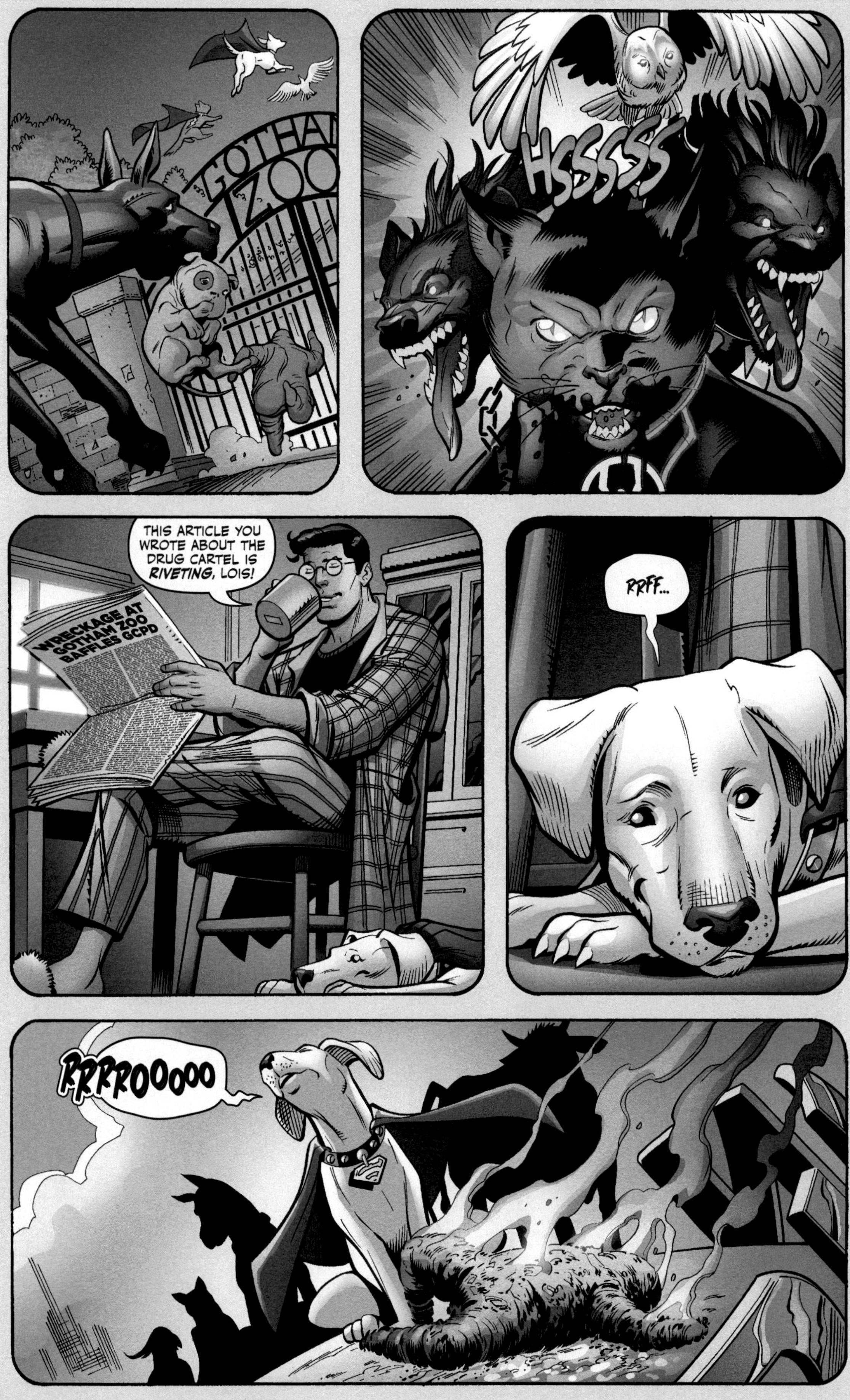

GOTHAM ZOO
HSSSSS
THIS ARTICLE YOU WROTE ABOUT THE DRUG CARTEL IS *RIVETING*, LOIS!
WRECKAGE AT GOTHAM ZOO BAFFLES GCPD
RRFF...
RRRROOOOOO

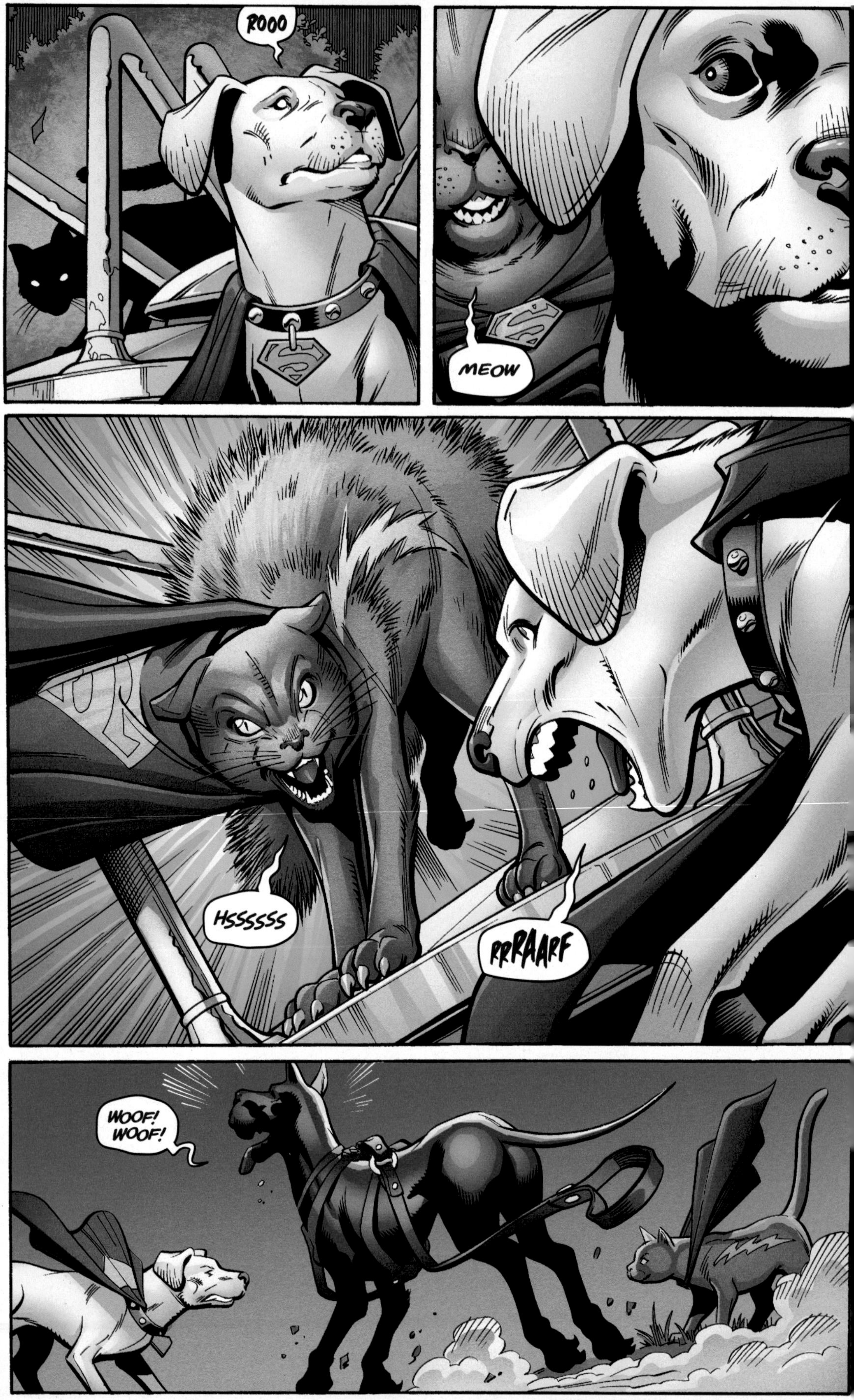
ROOO
MEOW
HSSSSSS
RRRAARF
WOOF!
WOOF!

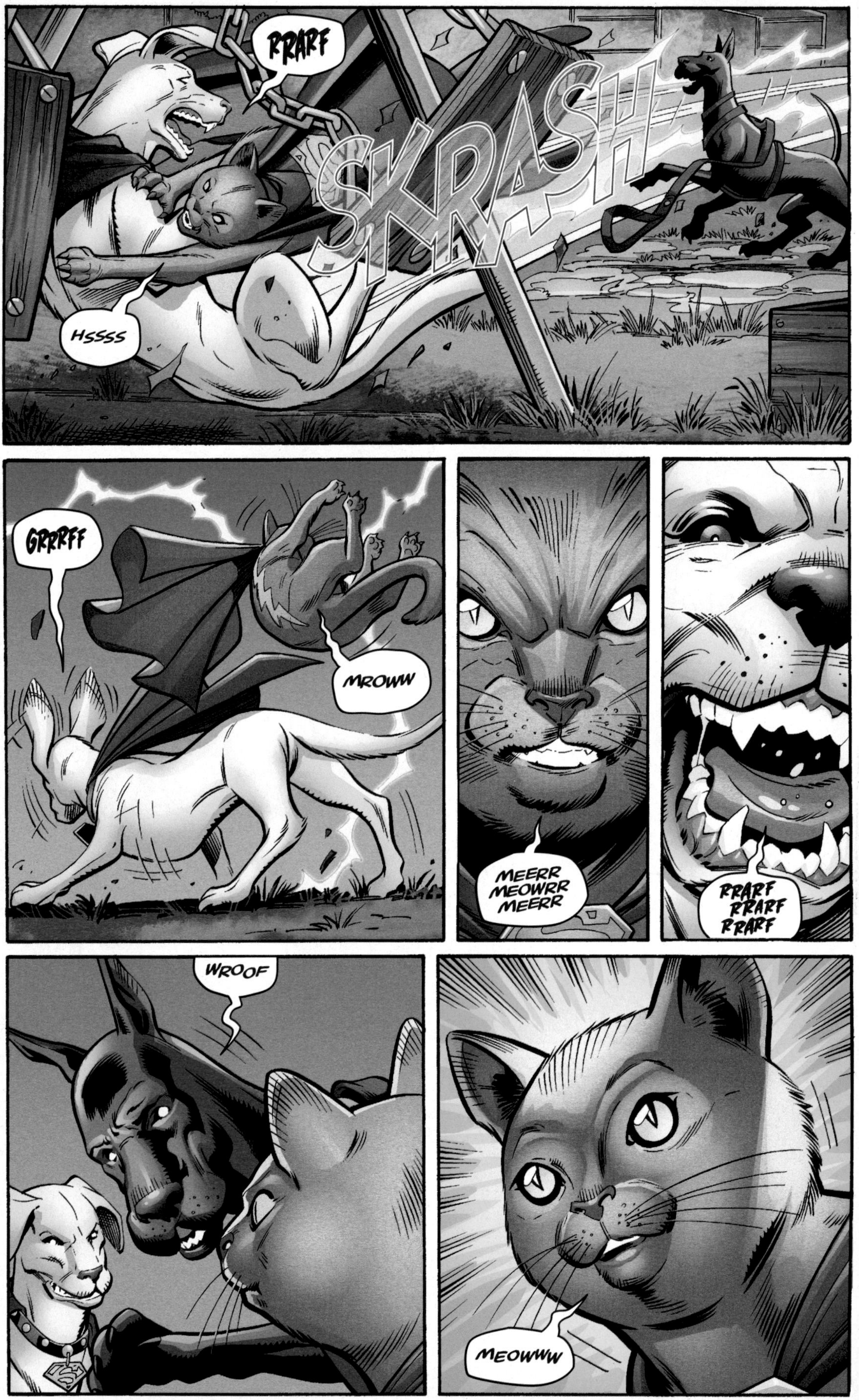
RRARF
SKRASH
HSSSS
GRRRFF
MROWW
MEERR MEOWRR MEERR
RRARF RRARF RRARF
WROOF
MEOWWW

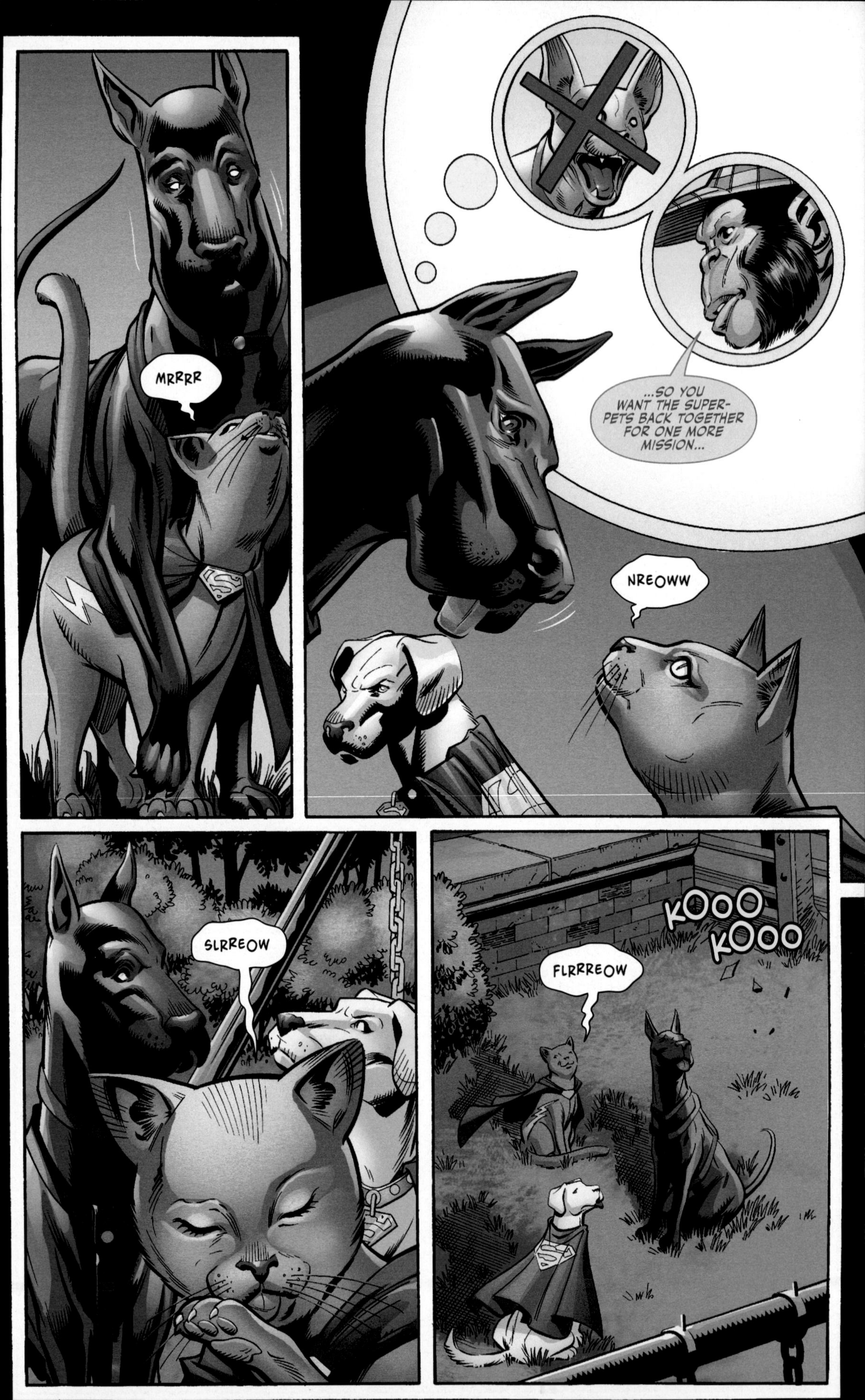
MRRRR
...SO YOU WANT THE SUPER-PETS BACK TOGETHER FOR ONE MORE MISSION...
NREOWW
SLRREOW
KOOO KOOO
FLRRREOW

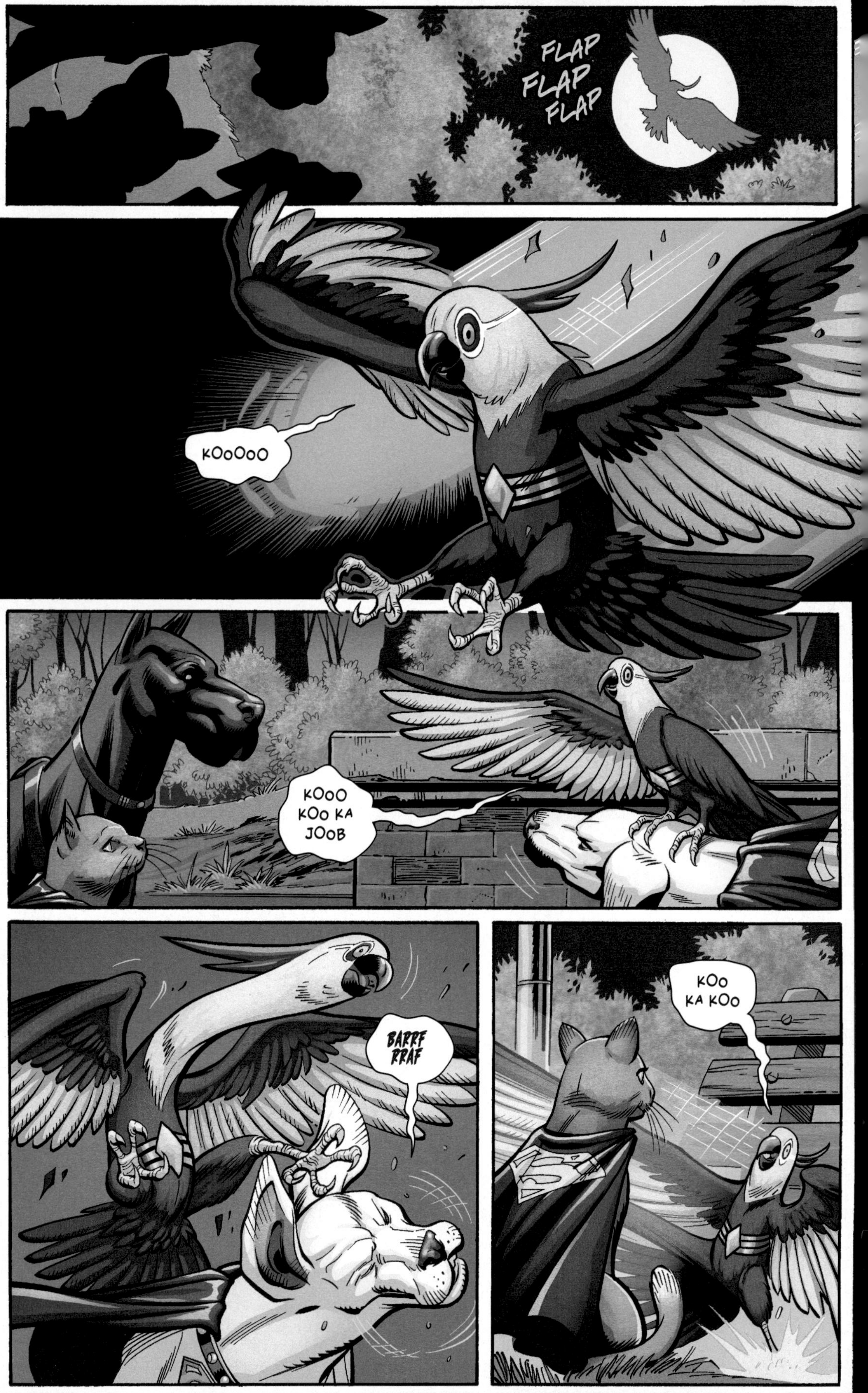
FLAP FLAP FLAP
KOOOOO
KOOO KOO KA JOOB
BARRF RRAF
KOO KA KOO

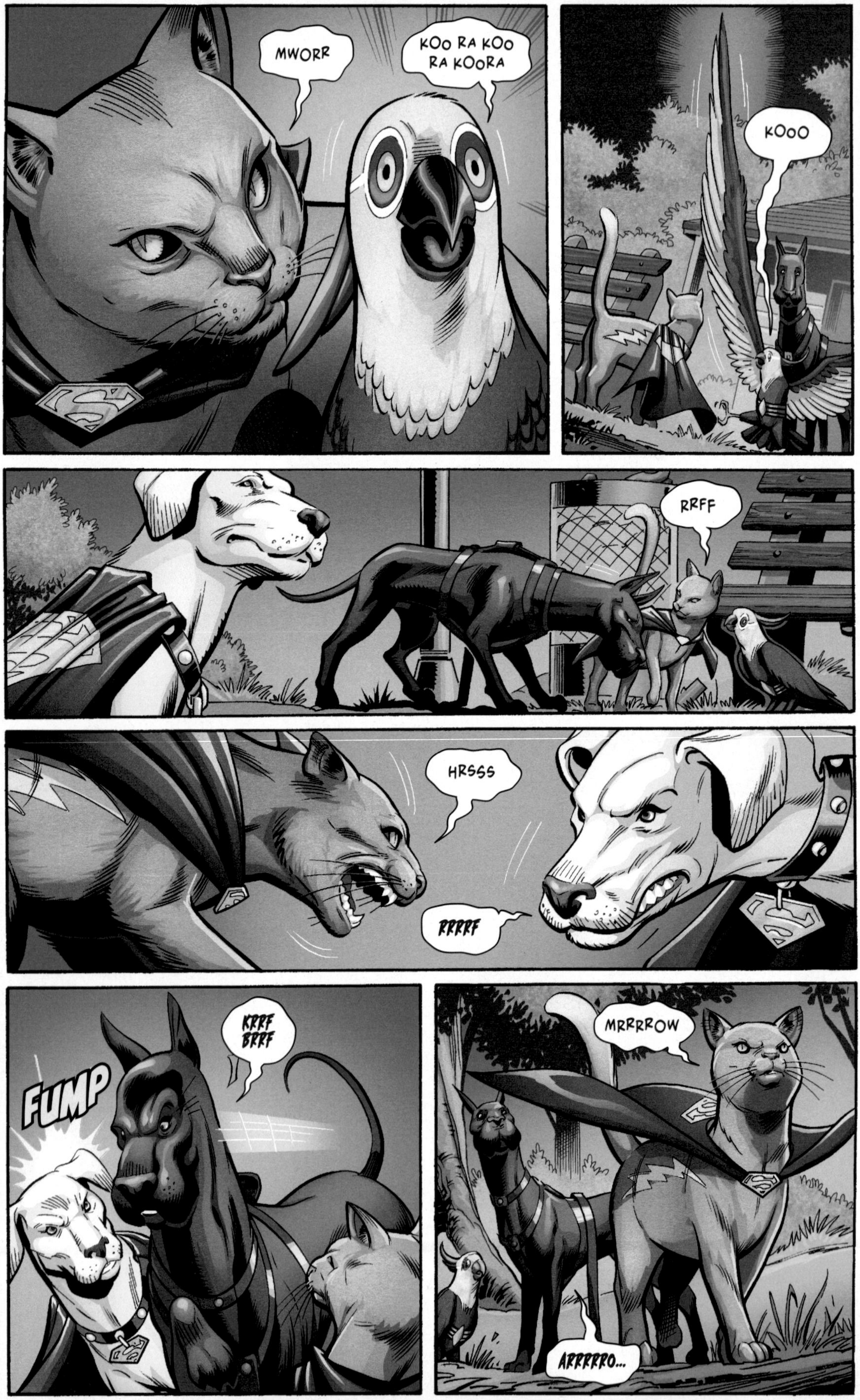
MWORR
KOO RA KOO RA KOORA
KOOO
RRFF
HRSSS
RRRRF
FUMP
KRRF BRRF
MRRRROW
ARRRRRO...

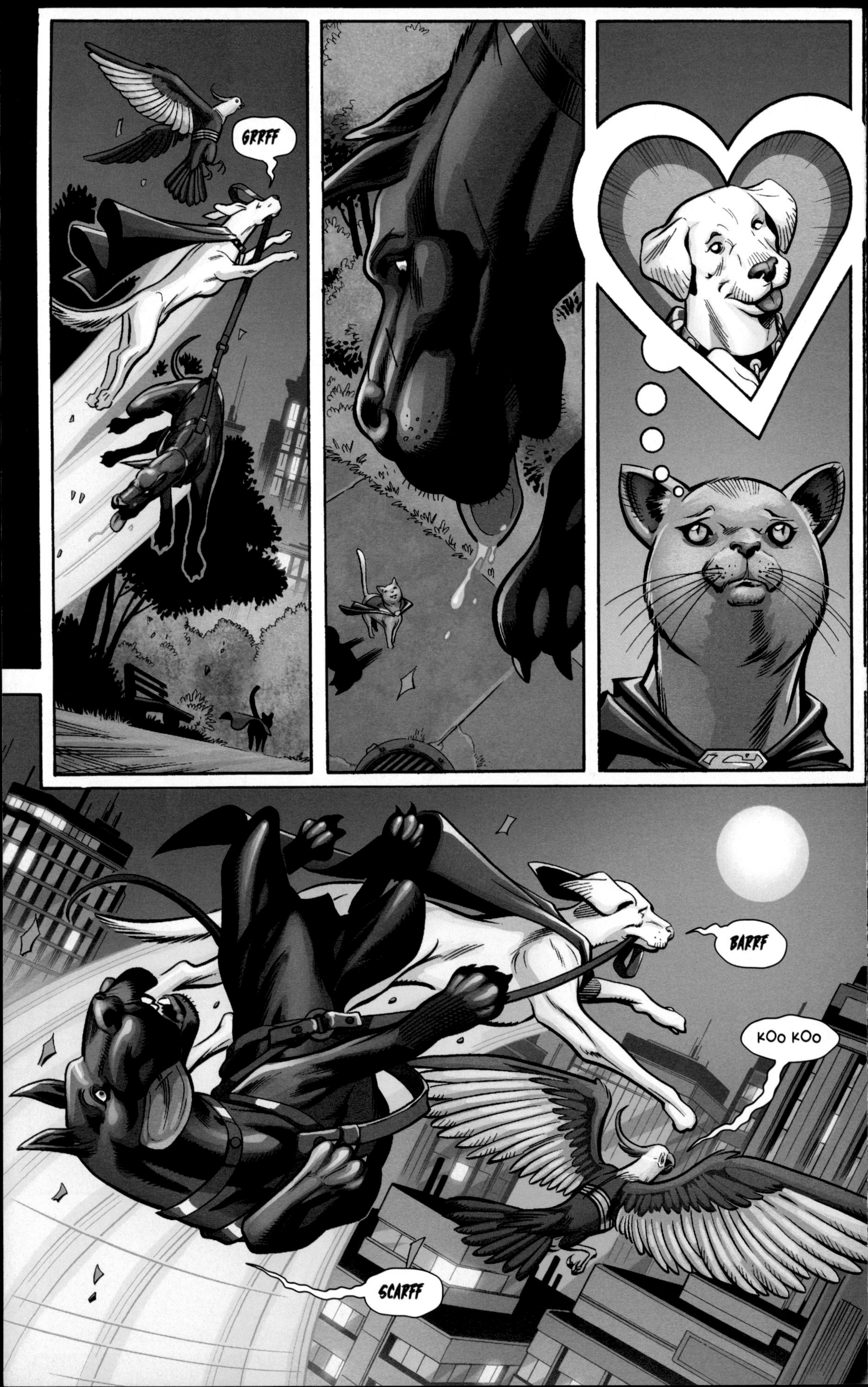
GRRFF
BARRF
KOO KOO
SCARFF

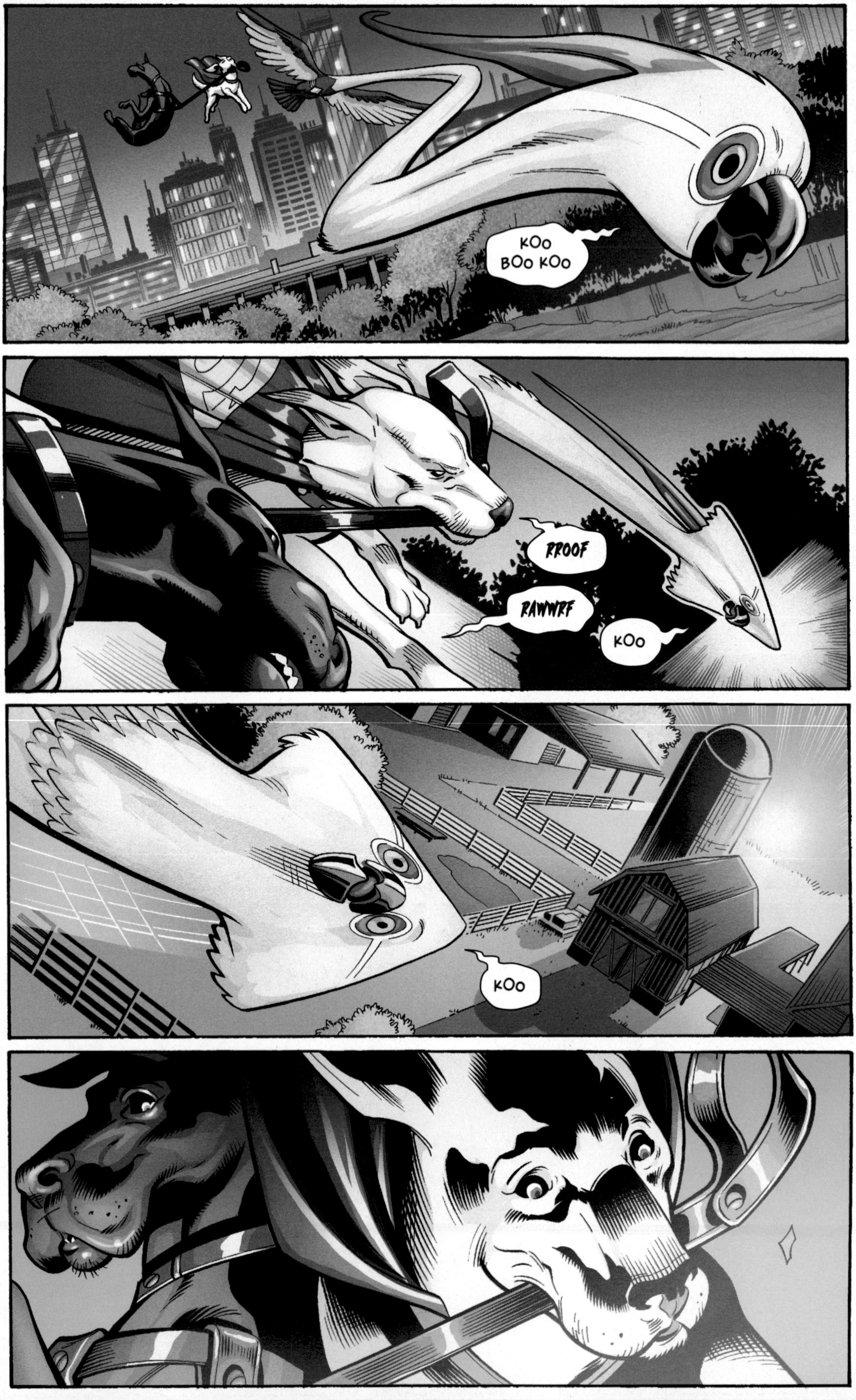
KOO
BOO KOO
RROOF
RAWWRF
KOO
KOO

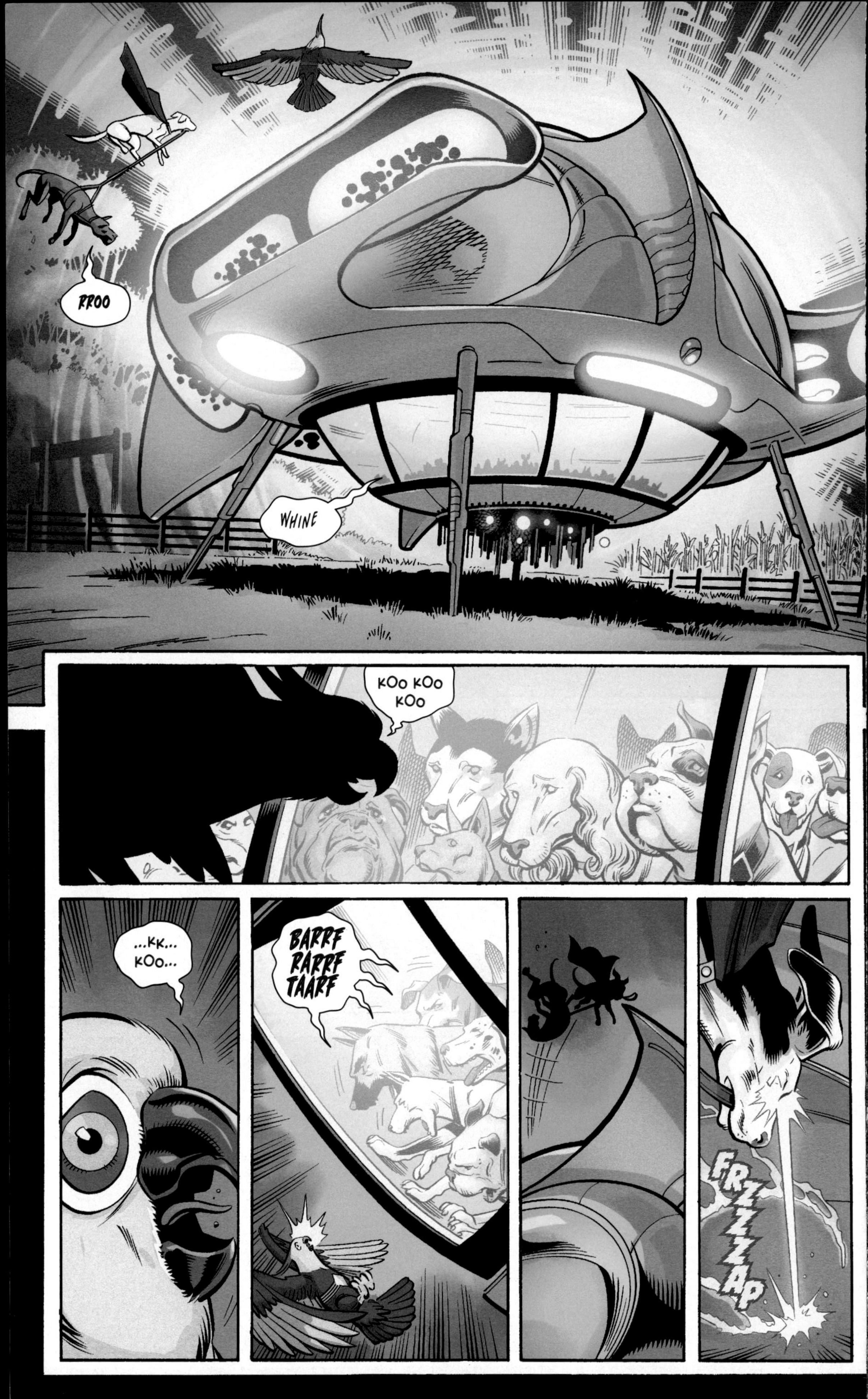
RROO
WHINE
KOO KOO KOO
...KK... KOO...
BARRF RARRF TAARF
FRZZZZAP

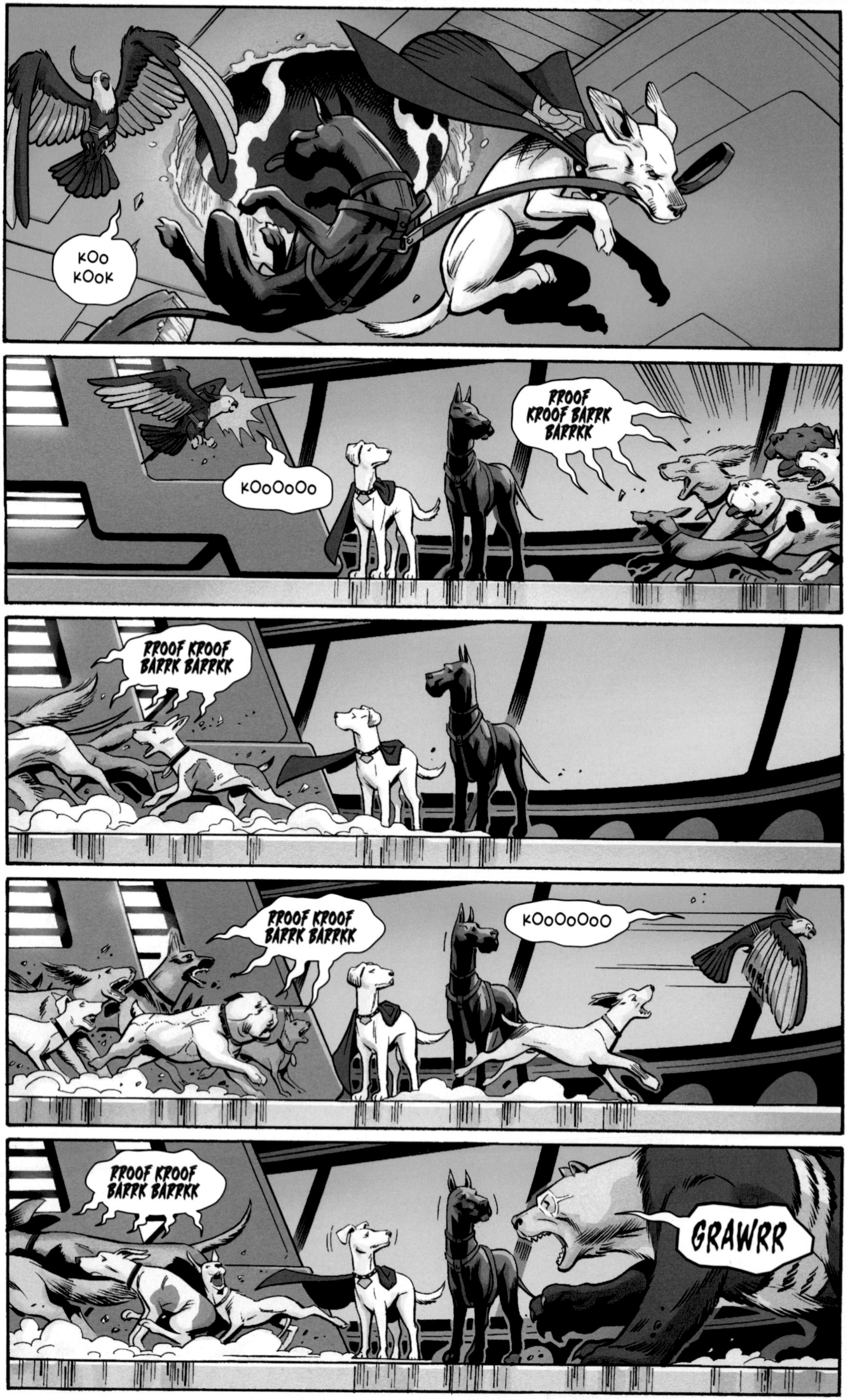
KOO KOOK
KOOOOOO
RROOF KROOF BARRK BARRKK
RROOF KROOF BARRK BARRKK
RROOF KROOF BARRK BARRKK
KOOOOOOO
RROOF KROOF BARRK BARRKK
GRAWRR

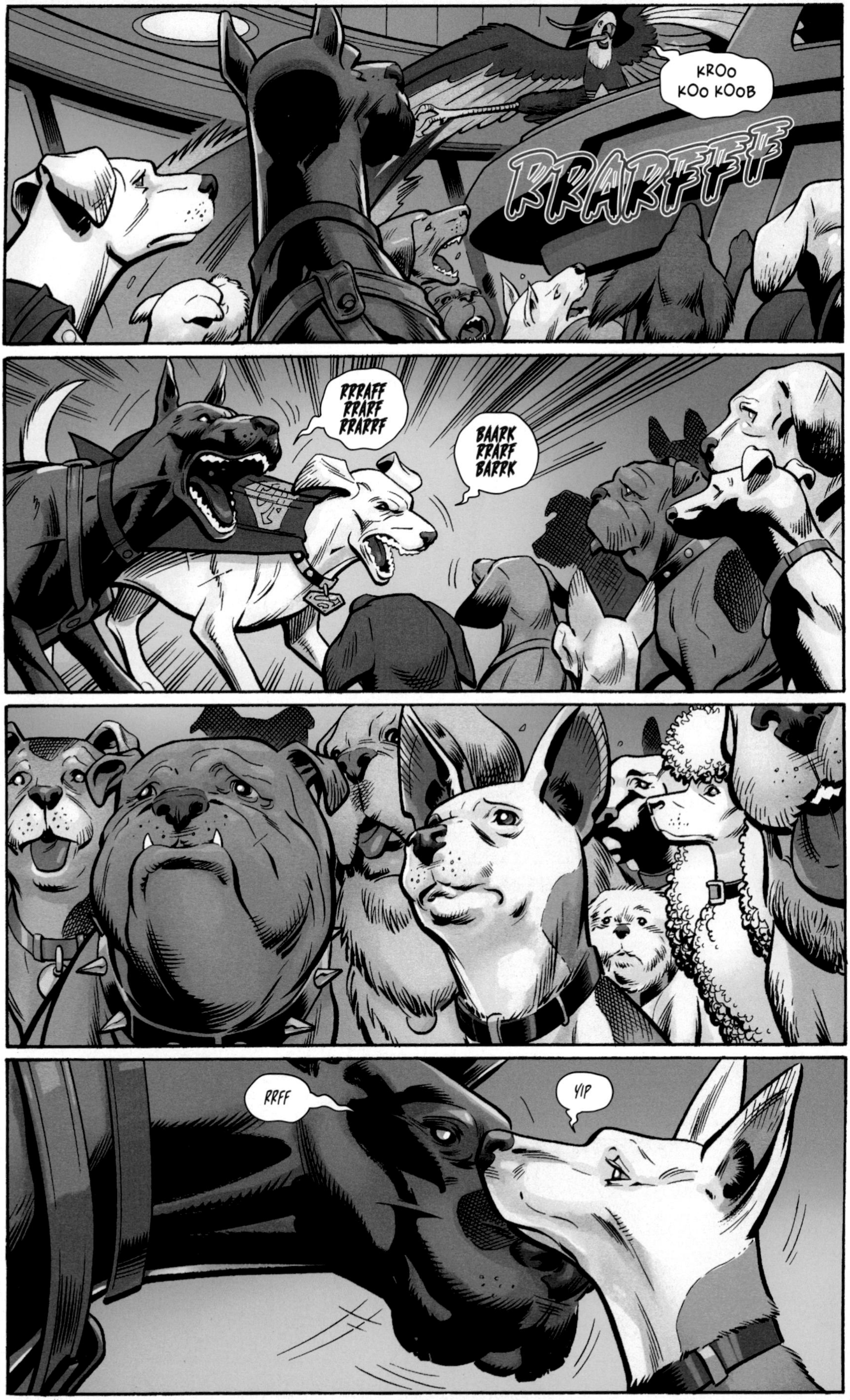
KROO
KOO KOOB
BRARFFF
RRRAFF
RRARF
RRARRF
BAARK
RRARF
BARRK
RRFF
YIP

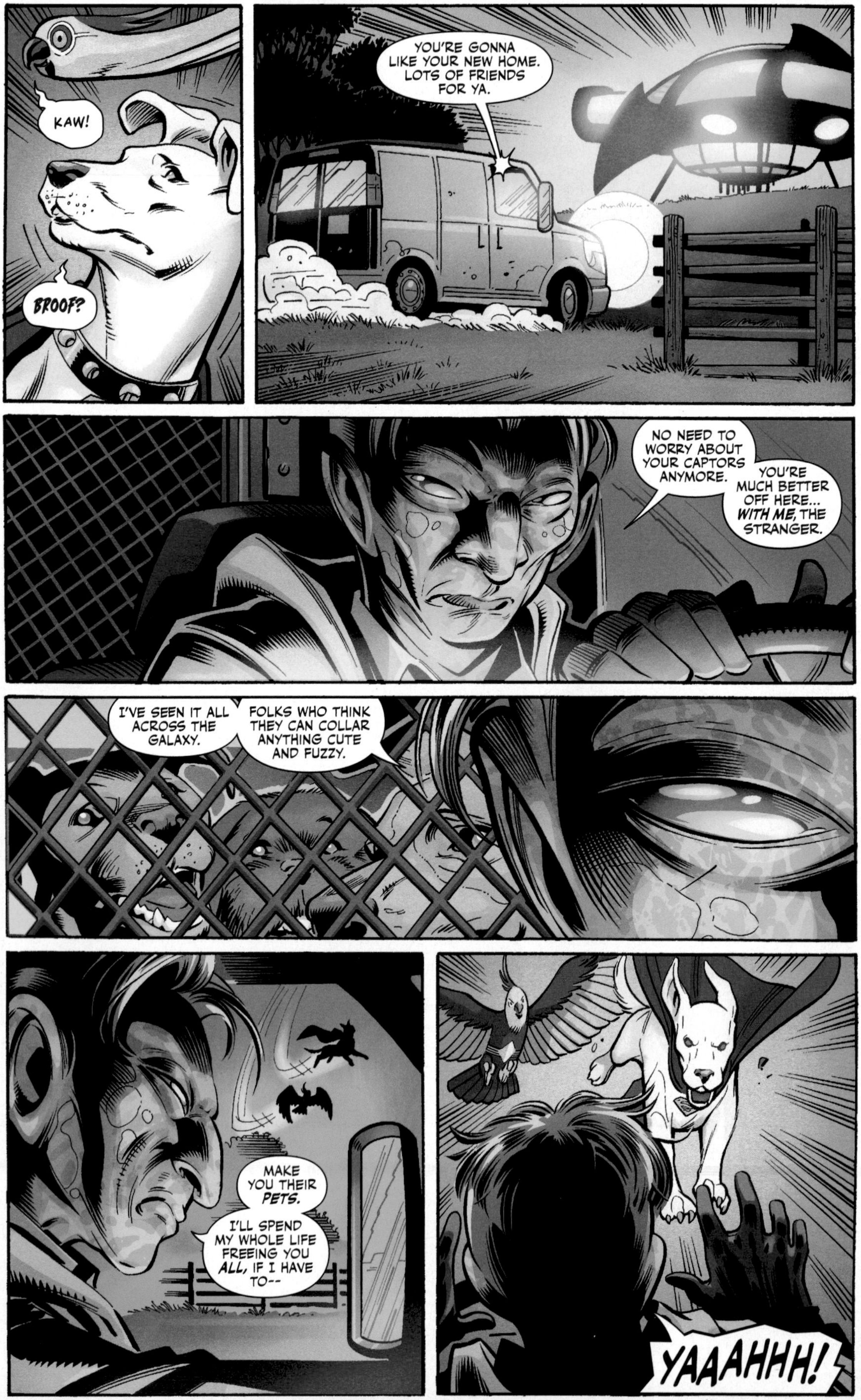
KAW!
BROOF?
YOU'RE GONNA LIKE YOUR NEW HOME. LOTS OF FRIENDS FOR YA.
NO NEED TO WORRY ABOUT YOUR CAPTORS ANYMORE.
YOU'RE MUCH BETTER OFF HERE... WITH ME, THE STRANGER.
I'VE SEEN IT ALL ACROSS THE GALAXY.
FOLKS WHO THINK THEY CAN COLLAR ANYTHING CUTE AND FUZZY.
MAKE YOU THEIR PETS.
I'LL SPEND MY WHOLE LIFE FREEING YOU ALL, IF I HAVE TO--
YAAAHHH!

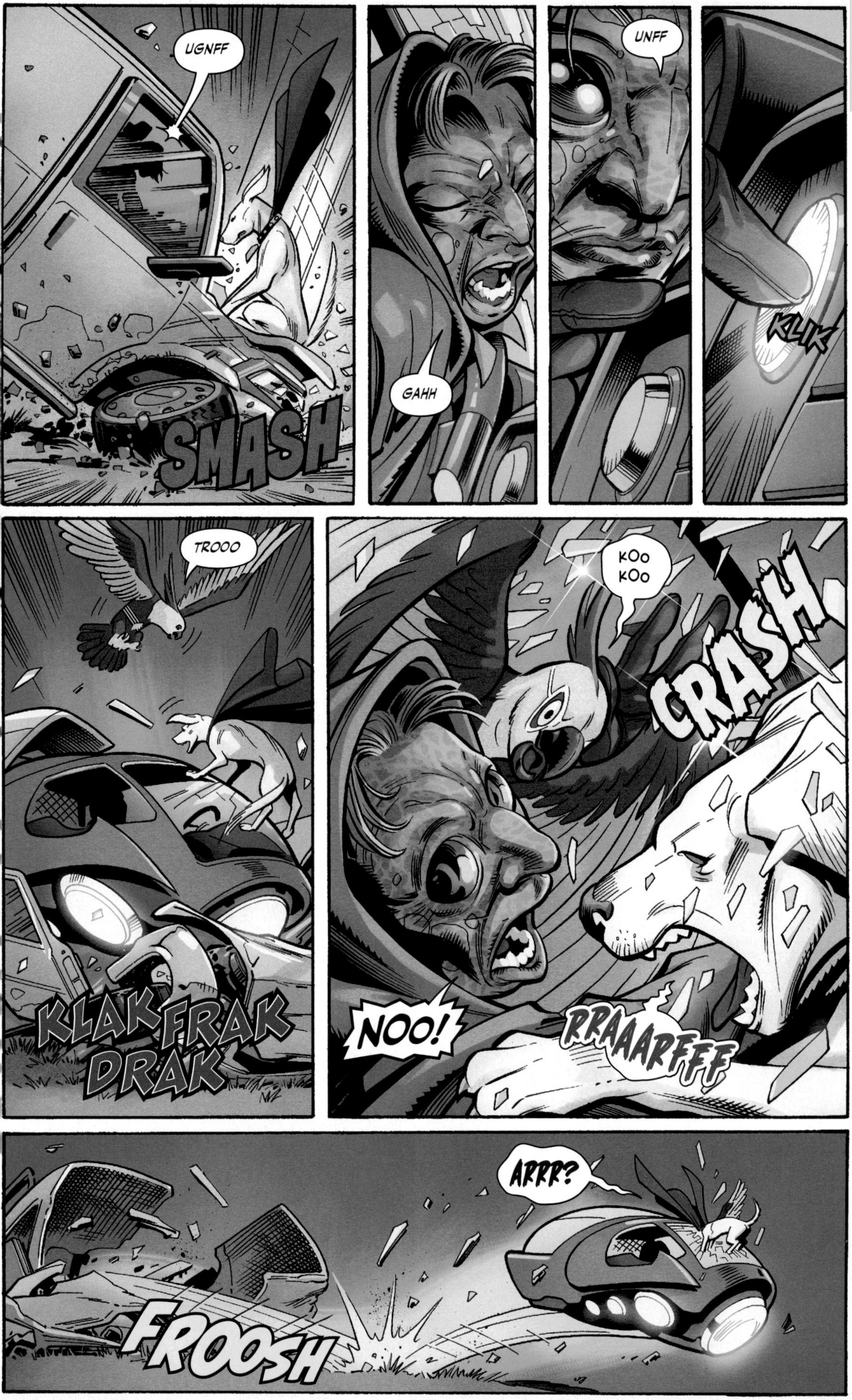
UGNFF
SMASH
GAHH
UNFF
KLIK
TROOO
KLAK FRAK DRAK
KOO KOO
CRASH
NOO!
RRAAARFFF
ARRR?
FROOSH

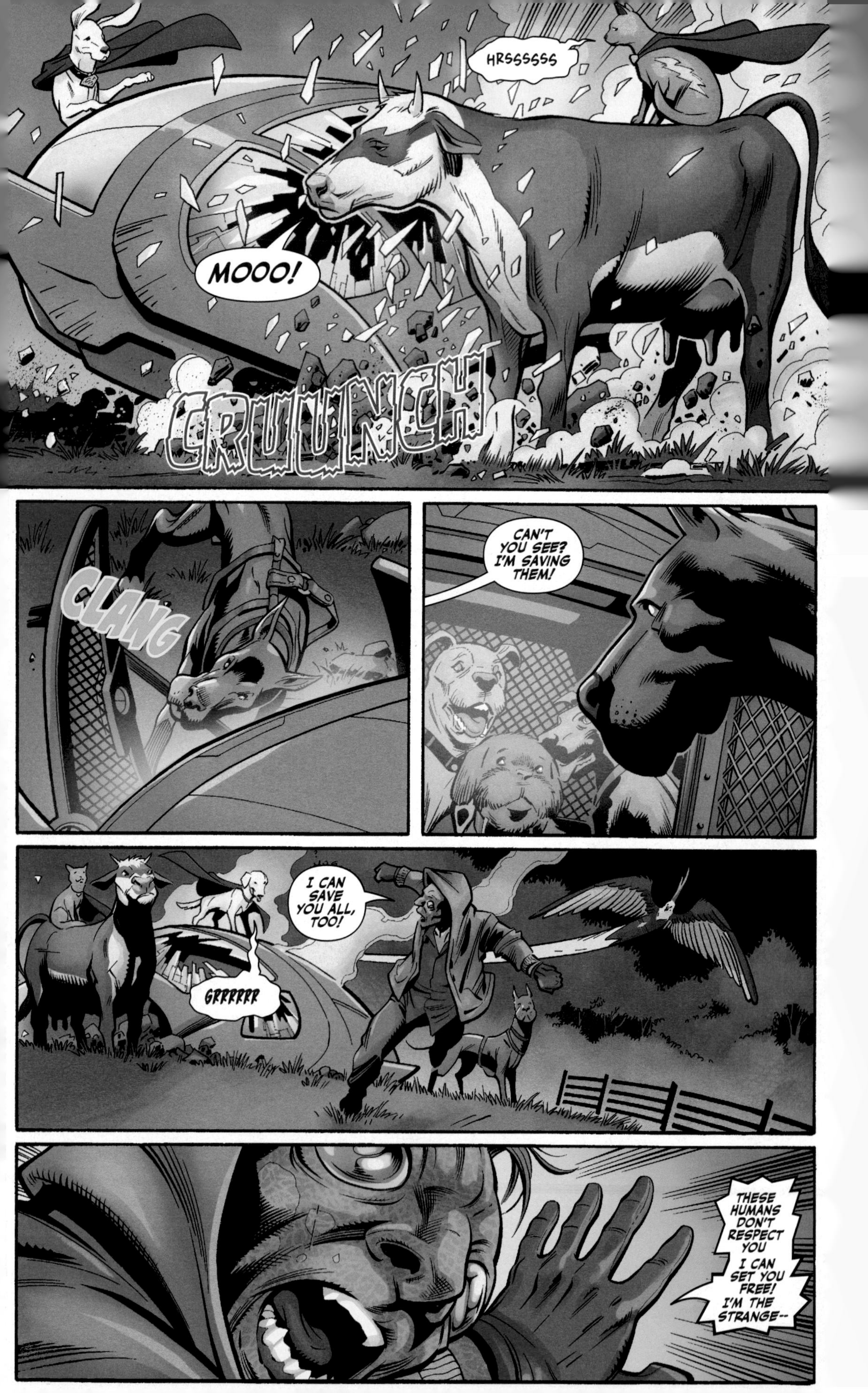
HRSSSSSS
MOOO!
CRUUNCH
CLANG
CAN'T YOU SEE? I'M SAVING THEM!
I CAN SAVE YOU ALL, TOO!
GRRRRRR
THESE HUMANS DON'T RESPECT YOU
I CAN SET YOU FREE! I'M THE STRANGE--

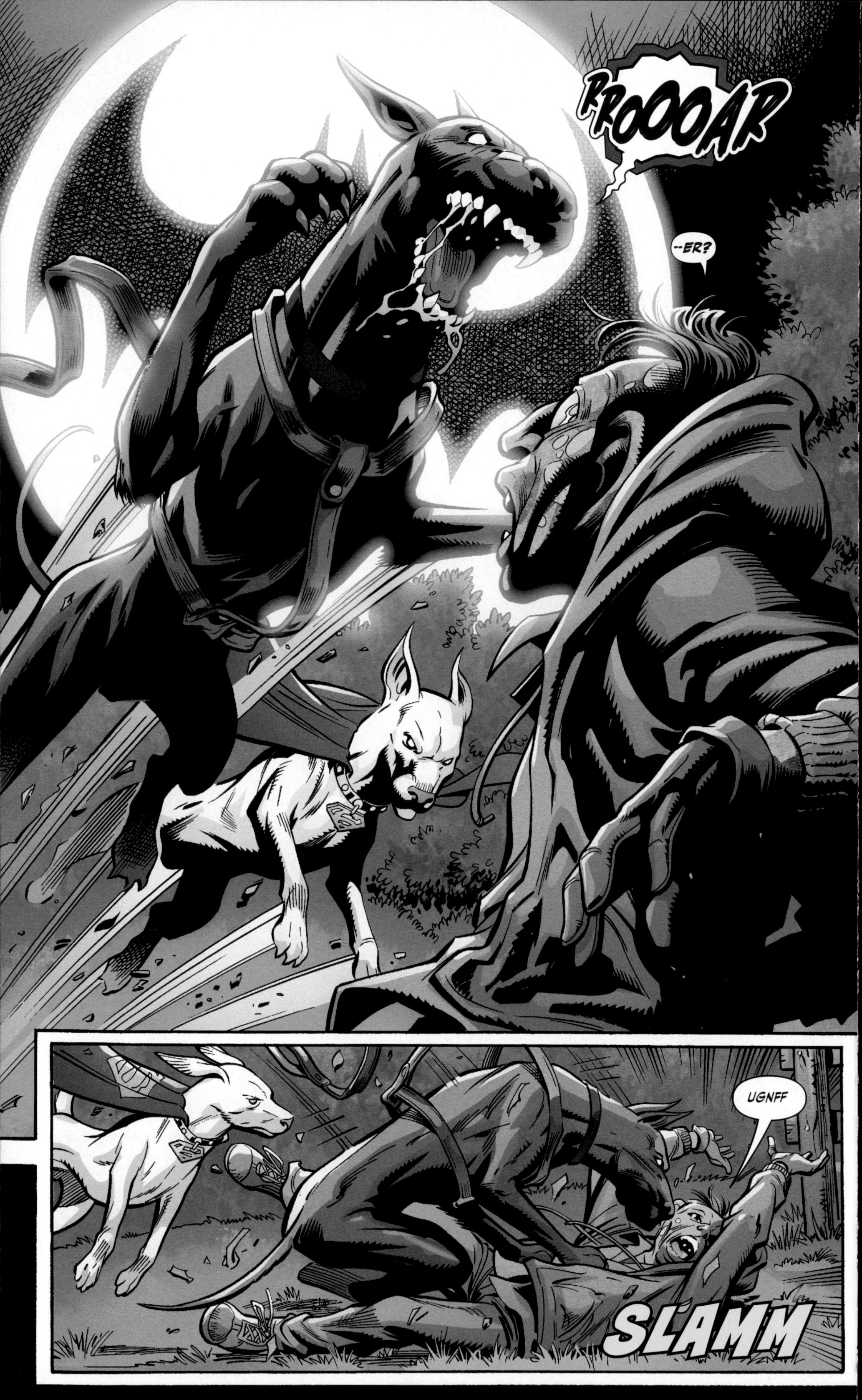
RROOOAR
--ER?
UGNFF
SLAMM

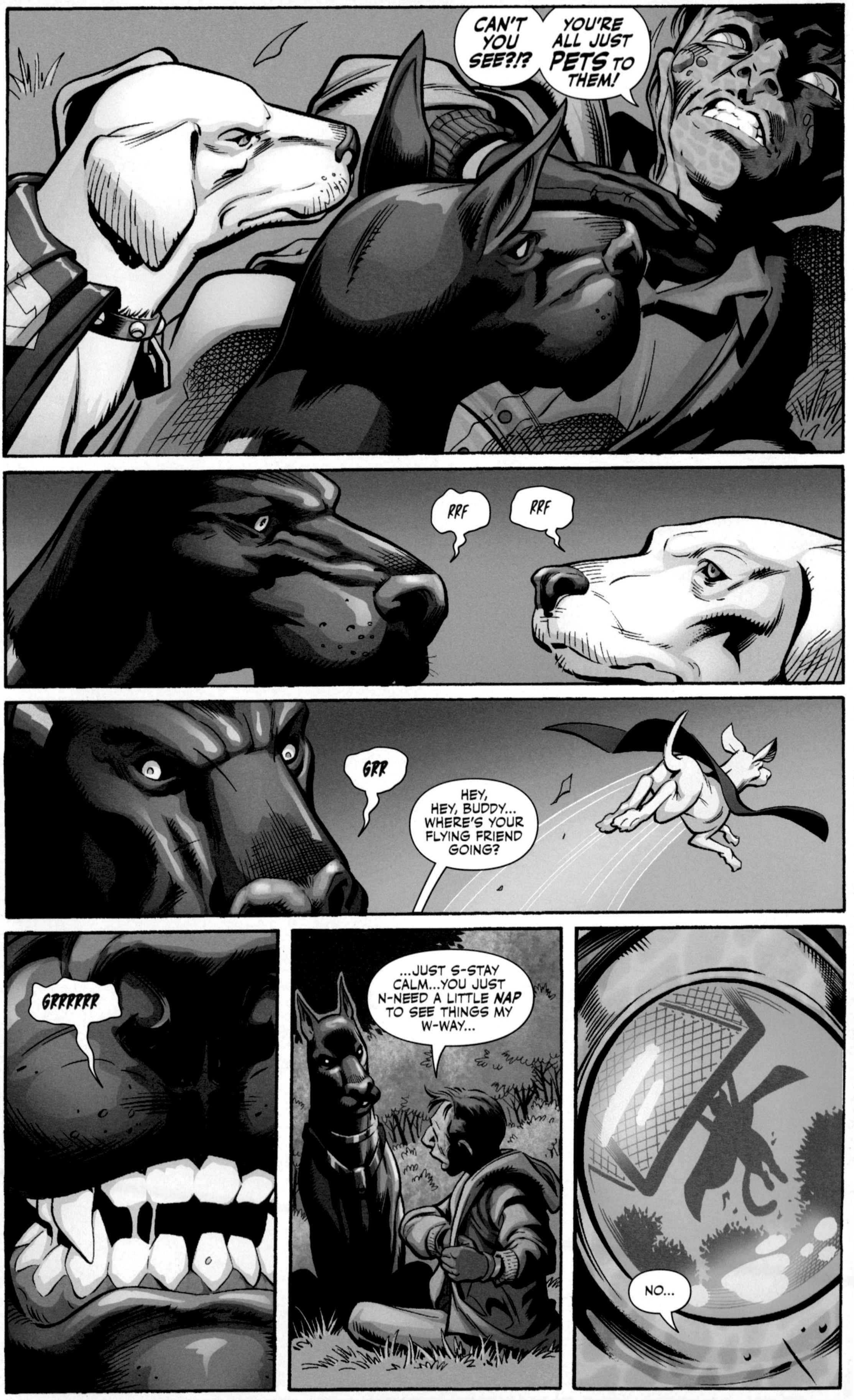
CAN'T YOU SEE?!?
YOU'RE ALL JUST PETS TO THEM!
RRF
RRF
GRR
HEY, HEY, BUDDY... WHERE'S YOUR FLYING FRIEND GOING?
GRRRRRR
...JUST S-STAY CALM...YOU JUST N-NEED A LITTLE NAP TO SEE THINGS MY W-WAY...
NO...

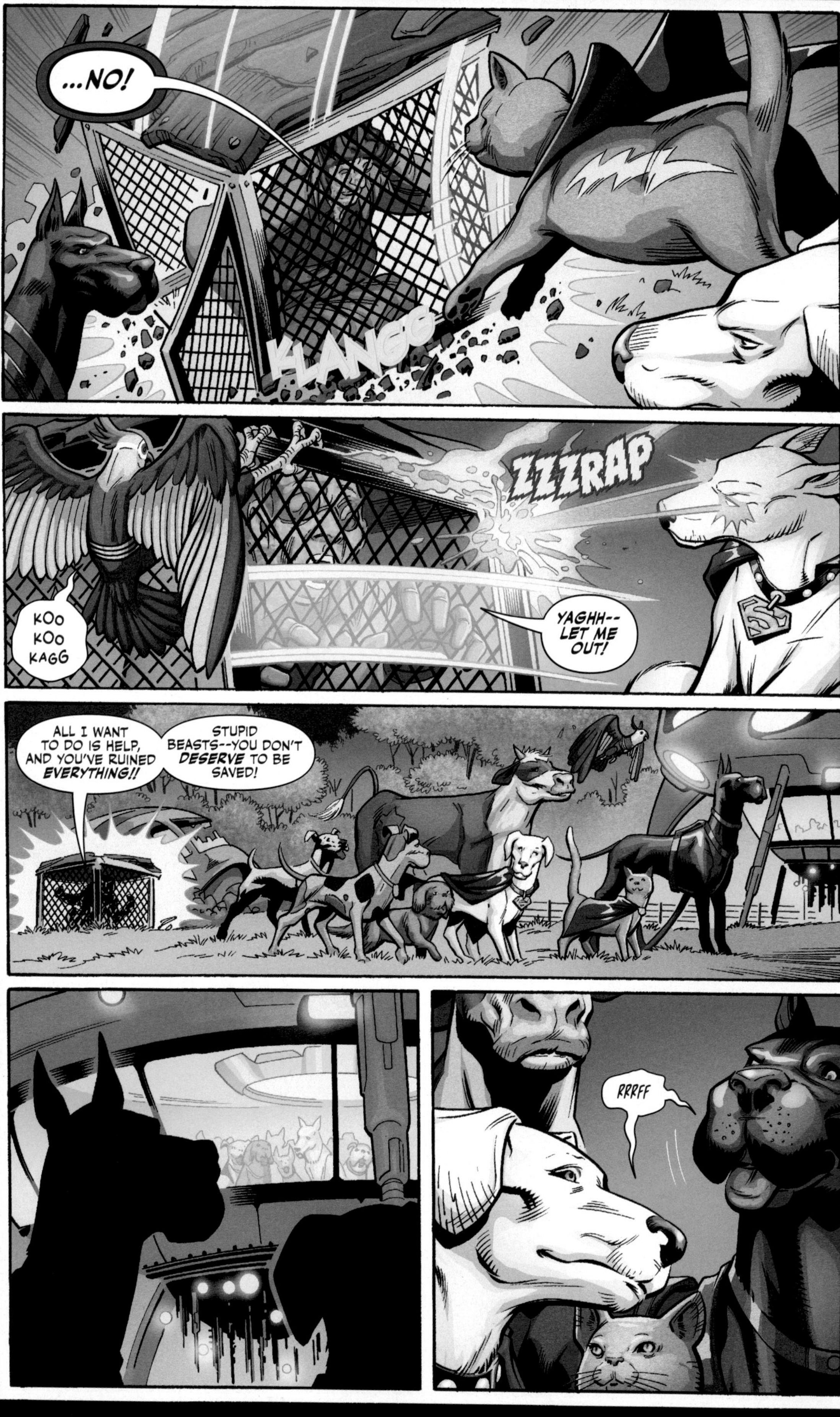
...NO!
KLANGG
ZZZRAP
KOO KOO KAGG
YAGHH-- LET ME OUT!
ALL I WANT TO DO IS HELP, AND YOU'VE RUINED EVERYTHING!!
STUPID BEASTS--YOU DON'T DESERVE TO BE SAVED!
RRRFF

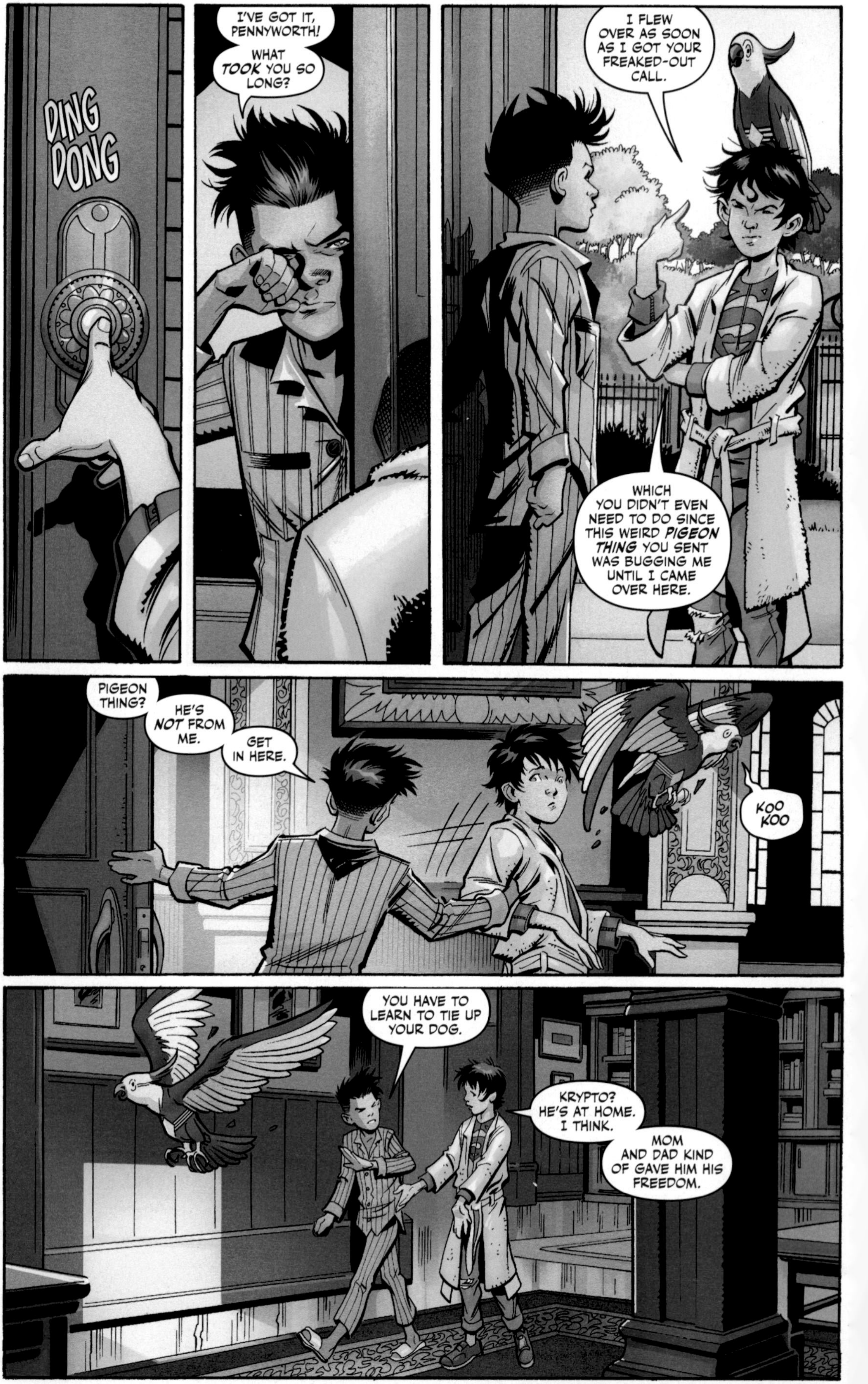
DING DONG
I'VE GOT IT, PENNYWORTH!
WHAT *TOOK* YOU SO LONG?
I FLEW OVER AS SOON AS I GOT YOUR FREAKED-OUT CALL.
WHICH YOU DIDN'T EVEN NEED TO DO SINCE THIS WEIRD *PIGEON THING* YOU SENT WAS BUGGING ME UNTIL I CAME OVER HERE.
PIGEON THING?
HE'S *NOT* FROM ME.
GET IN HERE.
KOO KOO
YOU HAVE TO LEARN TO TIE UP YOUR DOG.
KRYPTO? HE'S AT HOME. I THINK.
MOM AND DAD KIND OF GAVE HIM HIS FREEDOM.

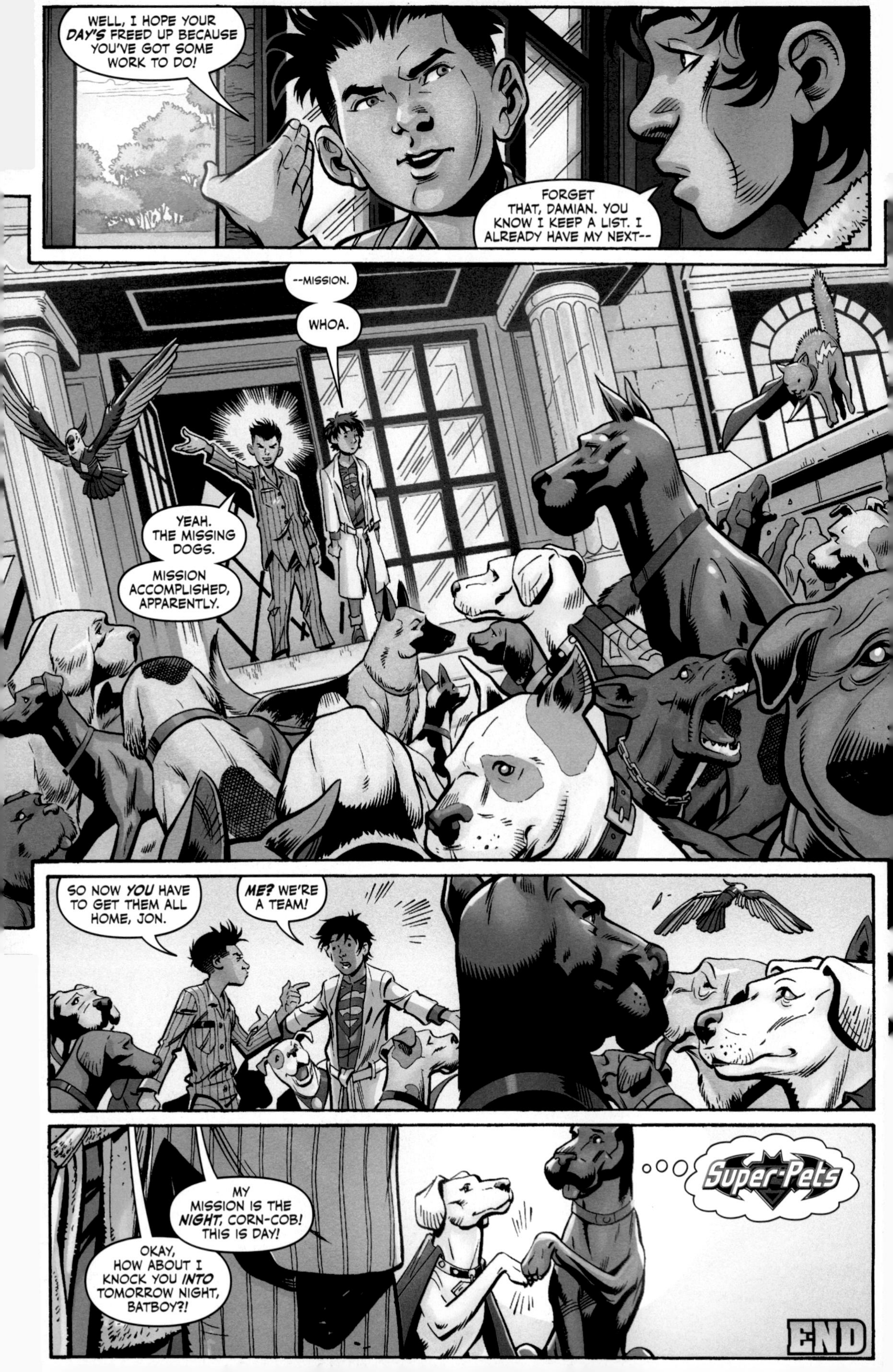
WELL, I HOPE YOUR *DAY'S* FREED UP BECAUSE YOU'VE GOT SOME WORK TO DO!
FORGET THAT, DAMIAN. YOU KNOW I KEEP A LIST. I ALREADY HAVE MY NEXT--
--MISSION.
WHOA.
YEAH. THE MISSING DOGS.
MISSION ACCOMPLISHED, APPARENTLY.
SO NOW *YOU* HAVE TO GET THEM ALL HOME, JON.
ME? WE'RE A TEAM!
MY MISSION IS THE *NIGHT,* CORN-COB! THIS IS DAY!
OKAY, HOW ABOUT I KNOCK YOU *INTO* TOMORROW NIGHT, BATBOY?!
Super-Pets
END

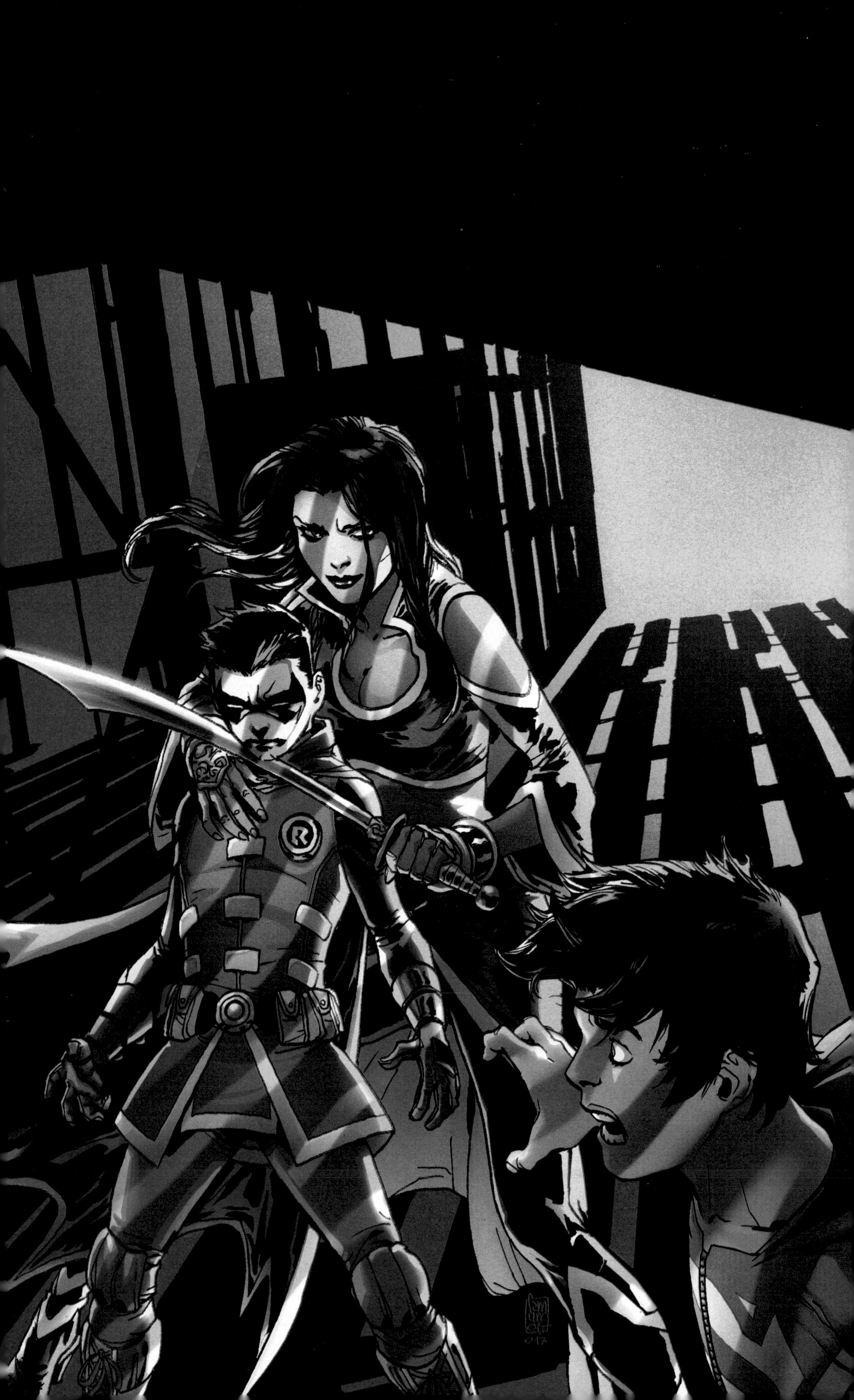

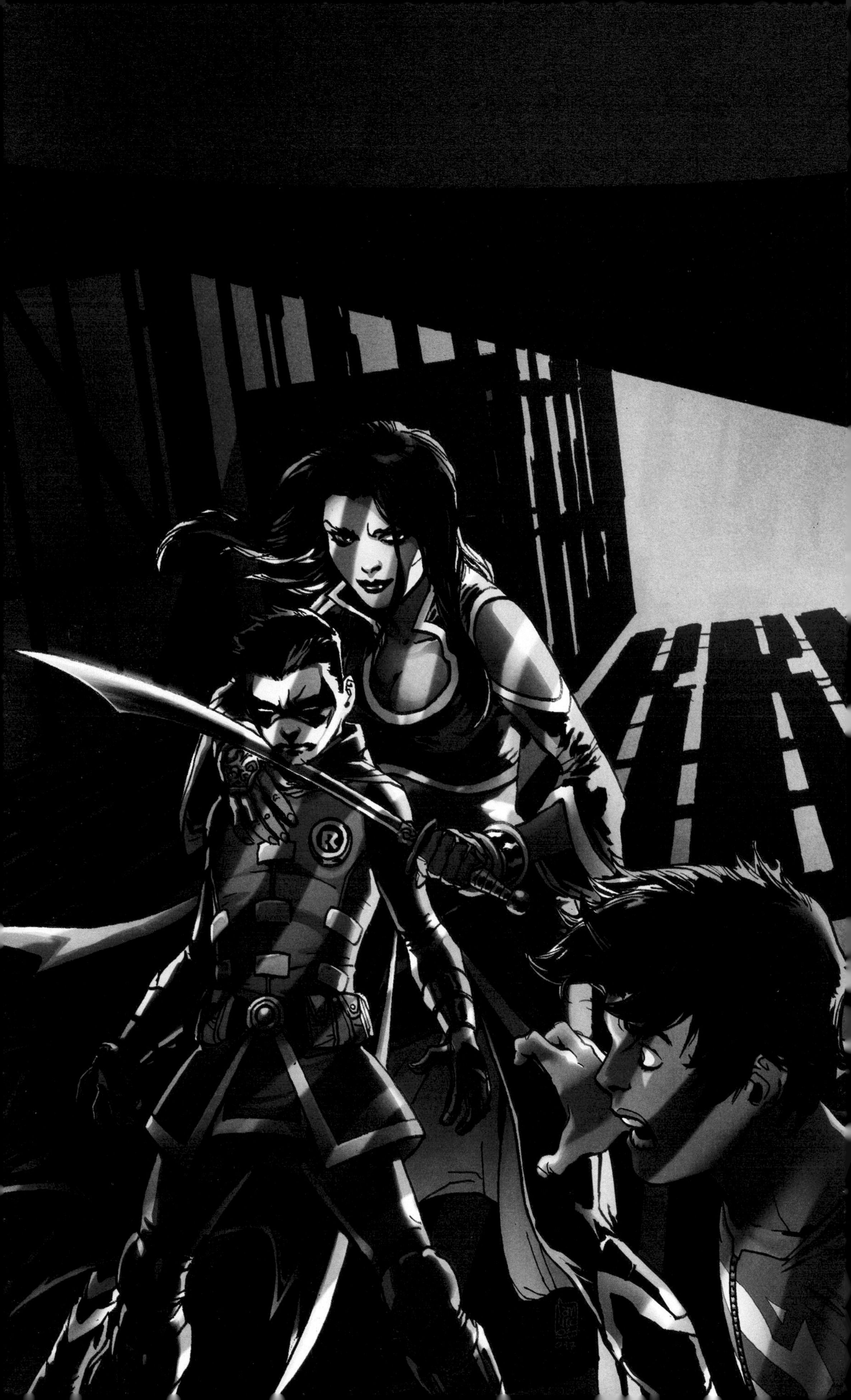

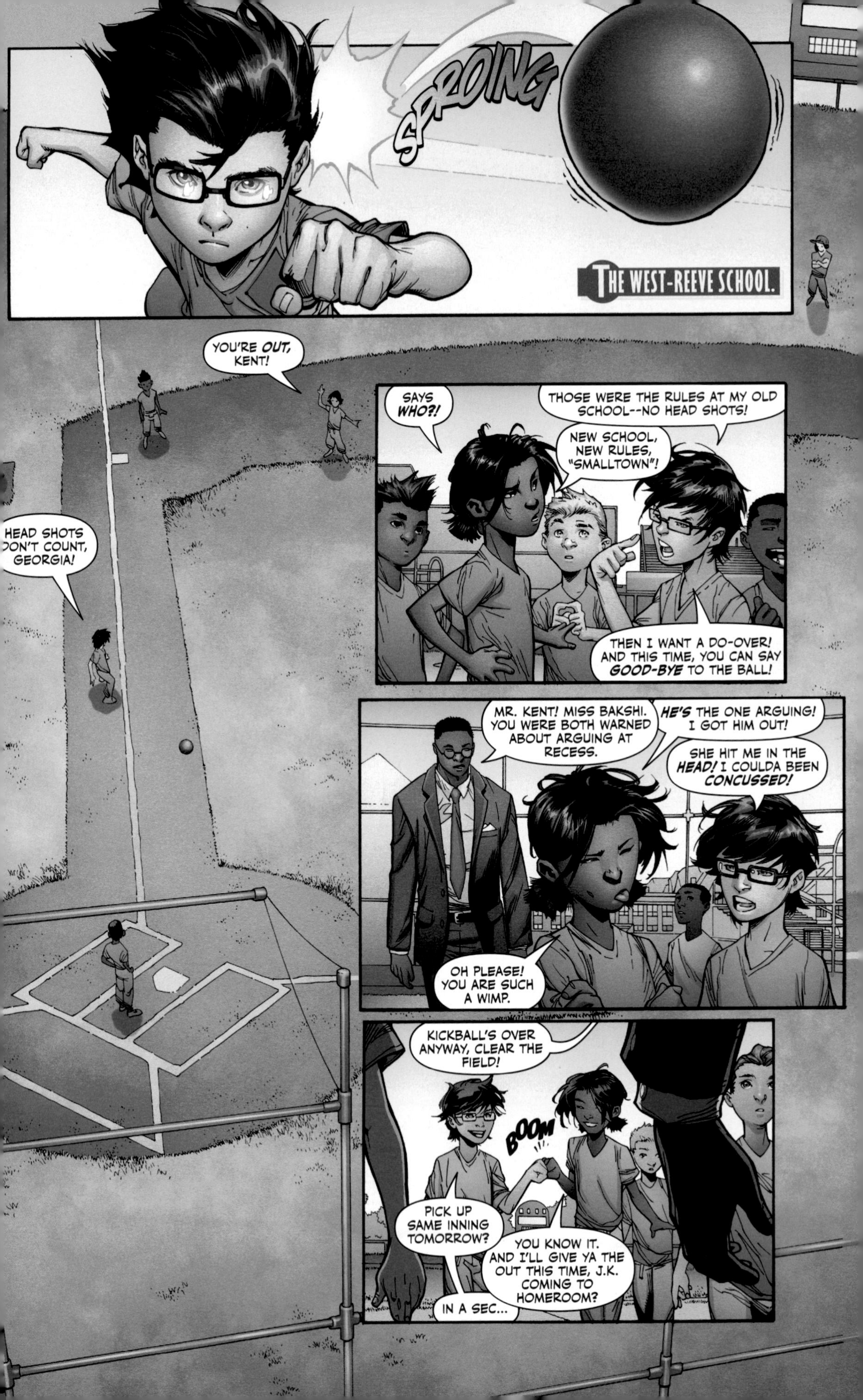
SPROING
THE WEST-REEVE SCHOOL.
YOU'RE OUT, KENT!
HEAD SHOTS DON'T COUNT, GEORGIA!
SAYS WHO?!
THOSE WERE THE RULES AT MY OLD SCHOOL--NO HEAD SHOTS!
NEW SCHOOL, NEW RULES, "SMALLTOWN"!
THEN I WANT A DO-OVER! AND THIS TIME, YOU CAN SAY GOOD-BYE TO THE BALL!
MR. KENT! MISS BAKSHI. YOU WERE BOTH WARNED ABOUT ARGUING AT RECESS.
HE'S THE ONE ARGUING! I GOT HIM OUT!
SHE HIT ME IN THE HEAD! I COULDA BEEN CONCUSSED!
OH PLEASE! YOU ARE SUCH A WIMP.
KICKBALL'S OVER ANYWAY, CLEAR THE FIELD!
BOOM
PICK UP SAME INNING TOMORROW?
YOU KNOW IT. AND I'LL GIVE YA THE OUT THIS TIME, J.K. COMING TO HOMEROOM?
IN A SEC...

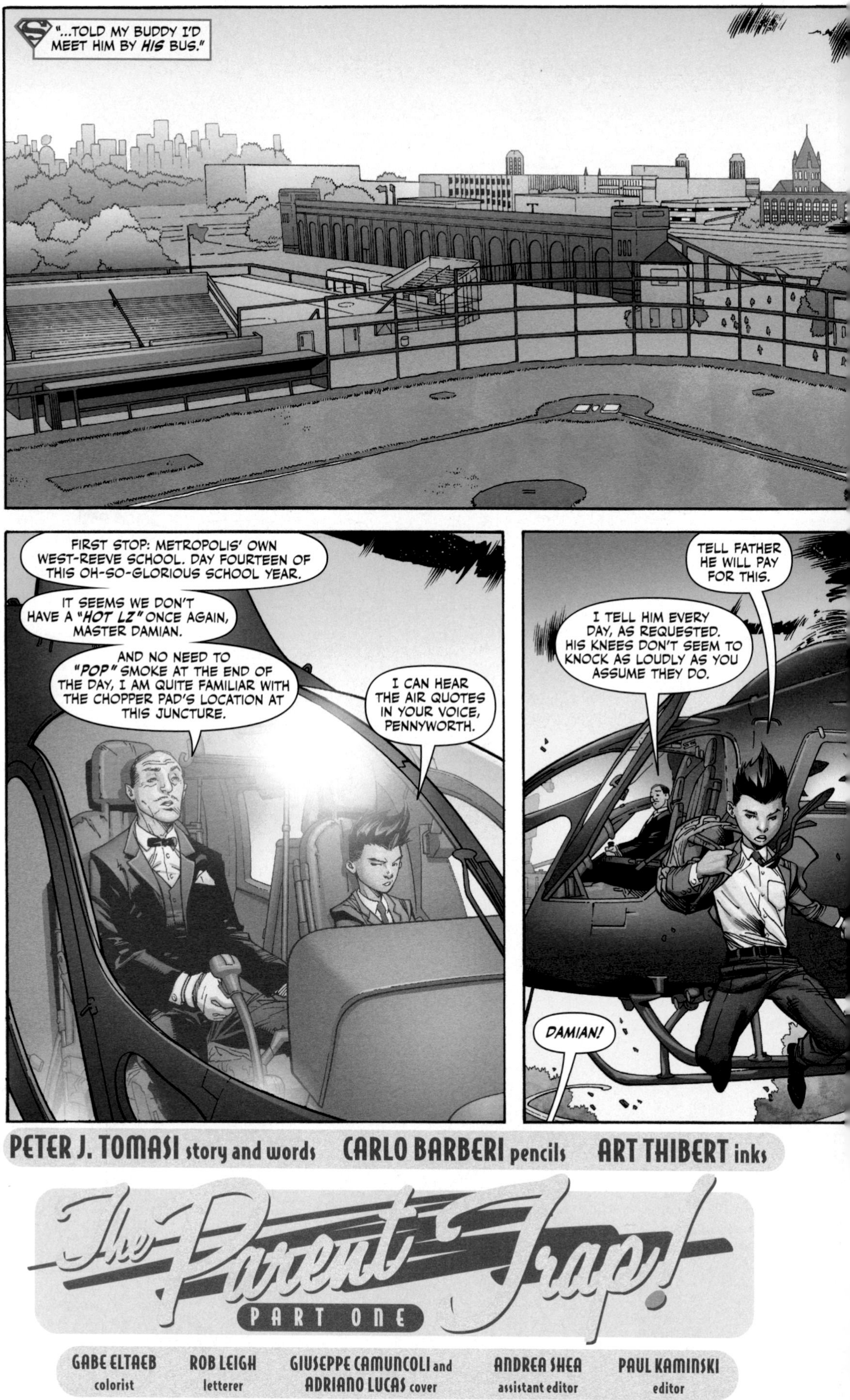
"...TOLD MY BUDDY I'D MEET HIM BY *HIS* BUS."
FIRST STOP: METROPOLIS' OWN WEST-REEVE SCHOOL. DAY FOURTEEN OF THIS OH-SO-GLORIOUS SCHOOL YEAR.
IT SEEMS WE DON'T HAVE A *"HOT LZ"* ONCE AGAIN, MASTER DAMIAN.
AND NO NEED TO *"POP"* SMOKE AT THE END OF THE DAY, I AM QUITE FAMILIAR WITH THE CHOPPER PAD'S LOCATION AT THIS JUNCTURE.
I CAN HEAR THE AIR QUOTES IN YOUR VOICE, PENNYWORTH.
TELL FATHER HE WILL PAY FOR THIS.
I TELL HIM EVERY DAY, AS REQUESTED. HIS KNEES DON'T SEEM TO KNOCK AS LOUDLY AS YOU ASSUME THEY DO.
DAMIAN!

PETER J. TOMASI story and words **CARLO BARBERI** pencils **ART THIBERT** inks

The Parent Trap!

PART ONE

GABE ELTAEB colorist **ROB LEIGH** letterer **GIUSEPPE CAMUNCOLI** and **ADRIANO LUCAS** cover **ANDREA SHEA** assistant editor **PAUL KAMINSKI** editor

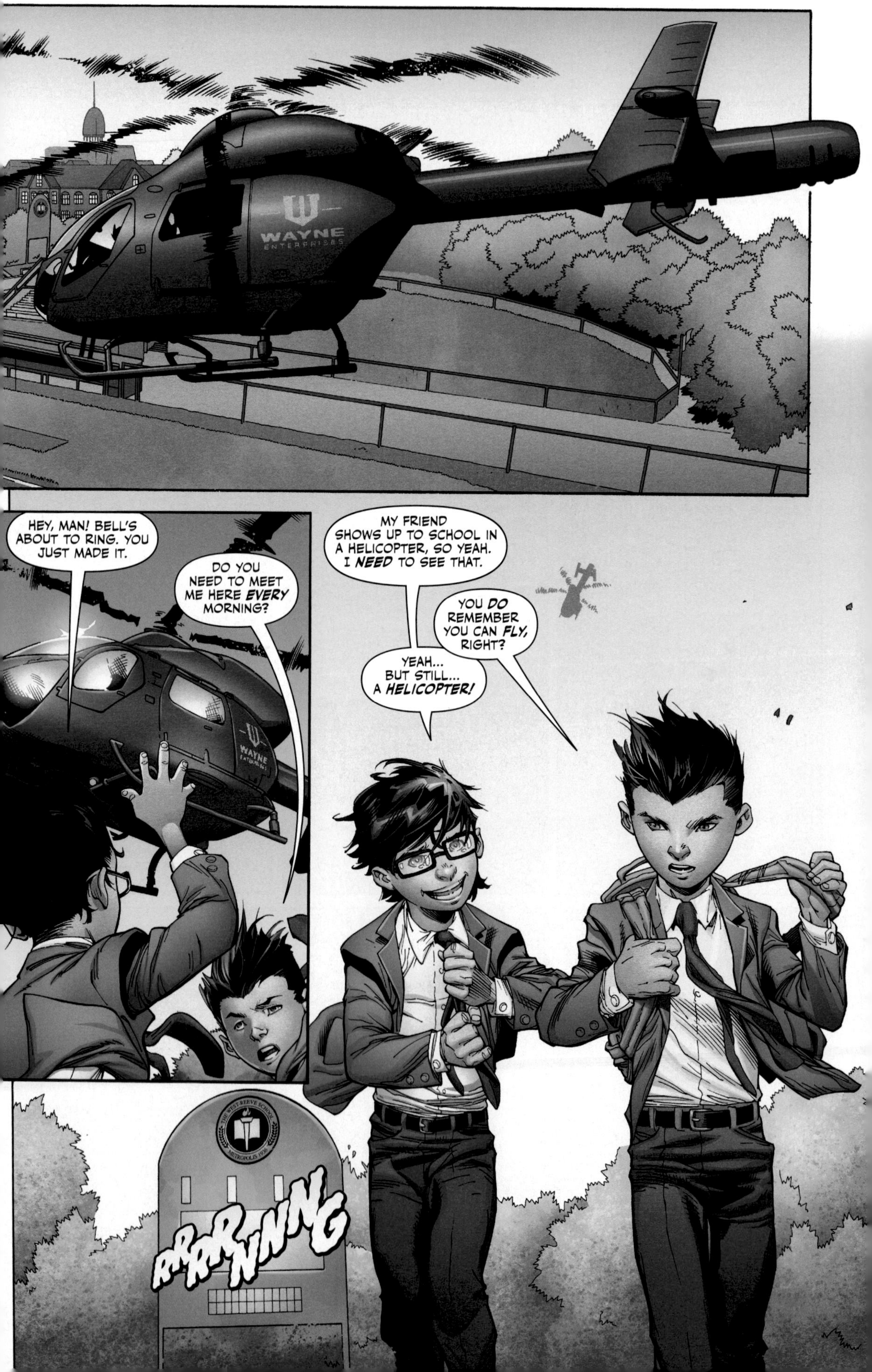
HEY, MAN! BELL'S ABOUT TO RING. YOU JUST MADE IT.
DO YOU NEED TO MEET ME HERE *EVERY* MORNING?
MY FRIEND SHOWS UP TO SCHOOL IN A HELICOPTER, SO YEAH. I *NEED* TO SEE THAT.
YOU *DO* REMEMBER YOU CAN *FLY*, RIGHT?
YEAH... BUT STILL... A *HELICOPTER!*
RRRRNNNG

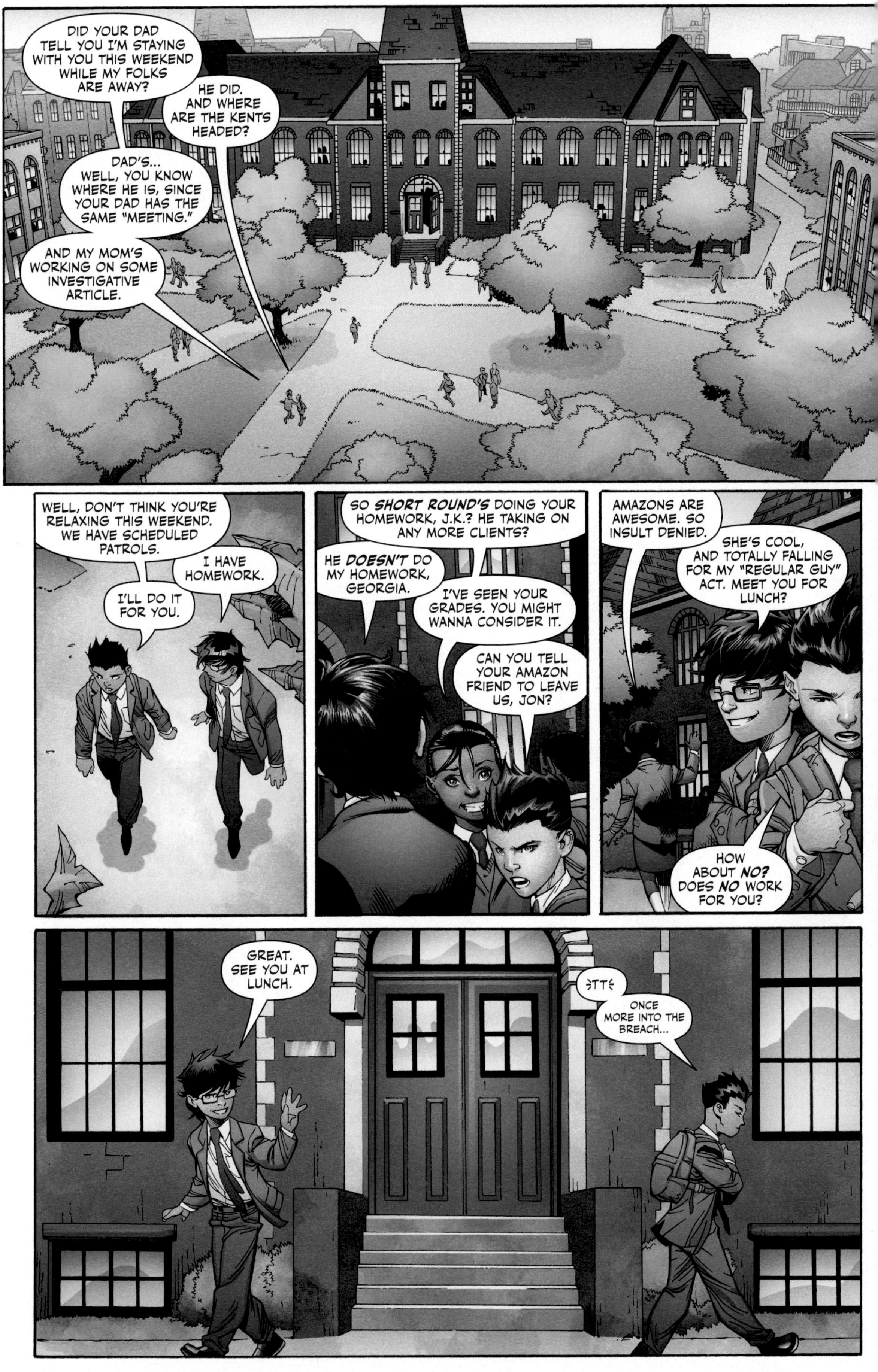

DID YOUR DAD TELL YOU I'M STAYING WITH YOU THIS WEEKEND WHILE MY FOLKS ARE AWAY?
HE DID. AND WHERE ARE THE KENTS HEADED?
DAD'S... WELL, YOU KNOW WHERE HE IS, SINCE YOUR DAD HAS THE SAME "MEETING."
AND MY MOM'S WORKING ON SOME INVESTIGATIVE ARTICLE.
WELL, DON'T THINK YOU'RE RELAXING THIS WEEKEND. WE HAVE SCHEDULED PATROLS.
I HAVE HOMEWORK.
I'LL DO IT FOR YOU.
SO *SHORT ROUND'S* DOING YOUR HOMEWORK, J.K.? HE TAKING ON ANY MORE CLIENTS?
HE *DOESN'T* DO MY HOMEWORK, GEORGIA.
I'VE SEEN YOUR GRADES. YOU MIGHT WANNA CONSIDER IT.
CAN YOU TELL YOUR AMAZON FRIEND TO LEAVE US, JON?
AMAZONS ARE AWESOME. SO INSULT DENIED.
SHE'S COOL, AND TOTALLY FALLING FOR MY "REGULAR GUY" ACT. MEET YOU FOR LUNCH?
HOW ABOUT *NO?* DOES *NO* WORK FOR YOU?
GREAT. SEE YOU AT LUNCH.
TT
ONCE MORE INTO THE BREACH...

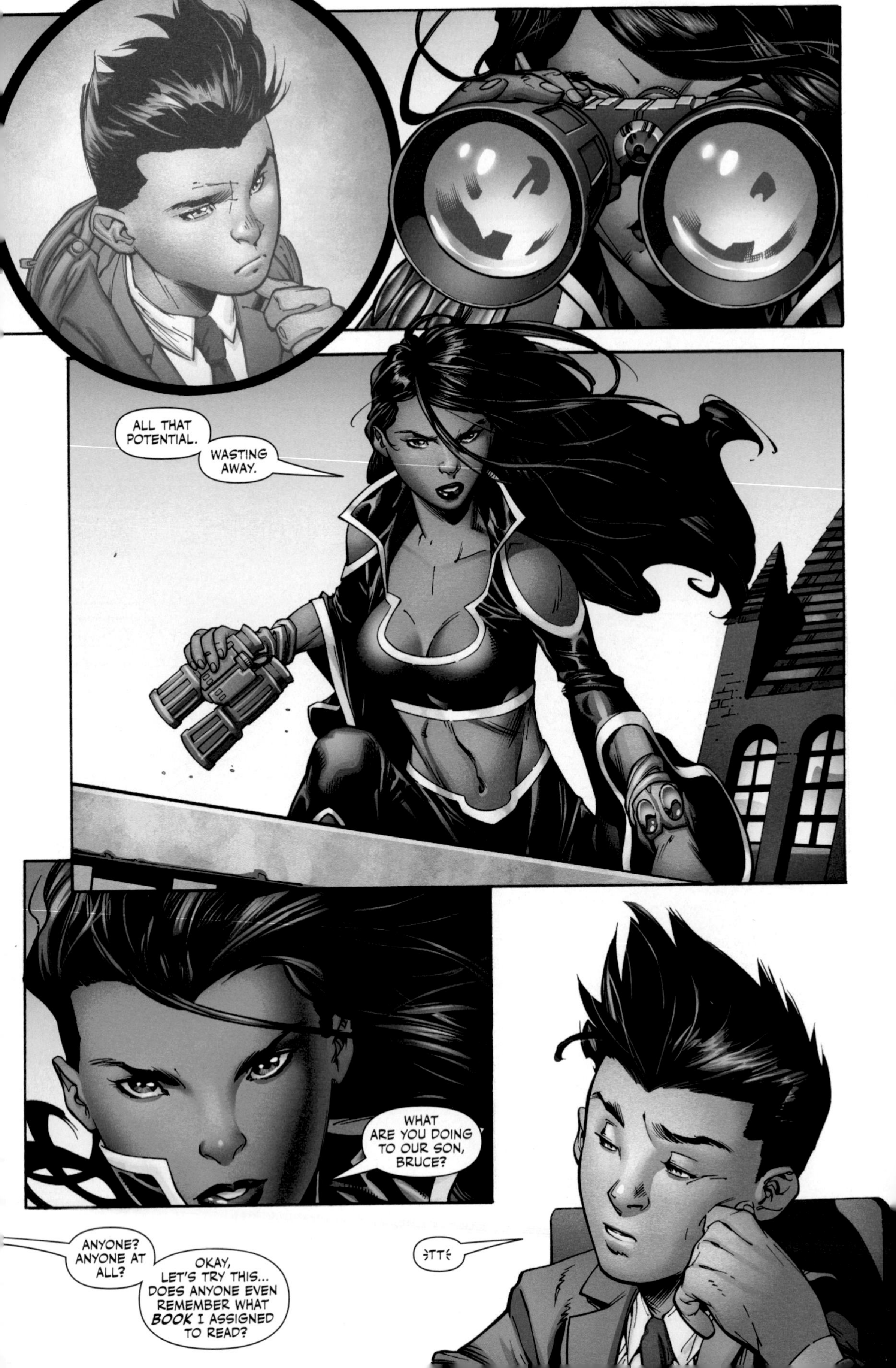
ALL THAT POTENTIAL.
WASTING AWAY.
WHAT ARE YOU DOING TO OUR SON, BRUCE?
ANYONE? ANYONE AT ALL?
OKAY, LET'S TRY THIS... DOES ANYONE EVEN REMEMBER WHAT *BOOK* I ASSIGNED TO READ?
ƎTTƐ

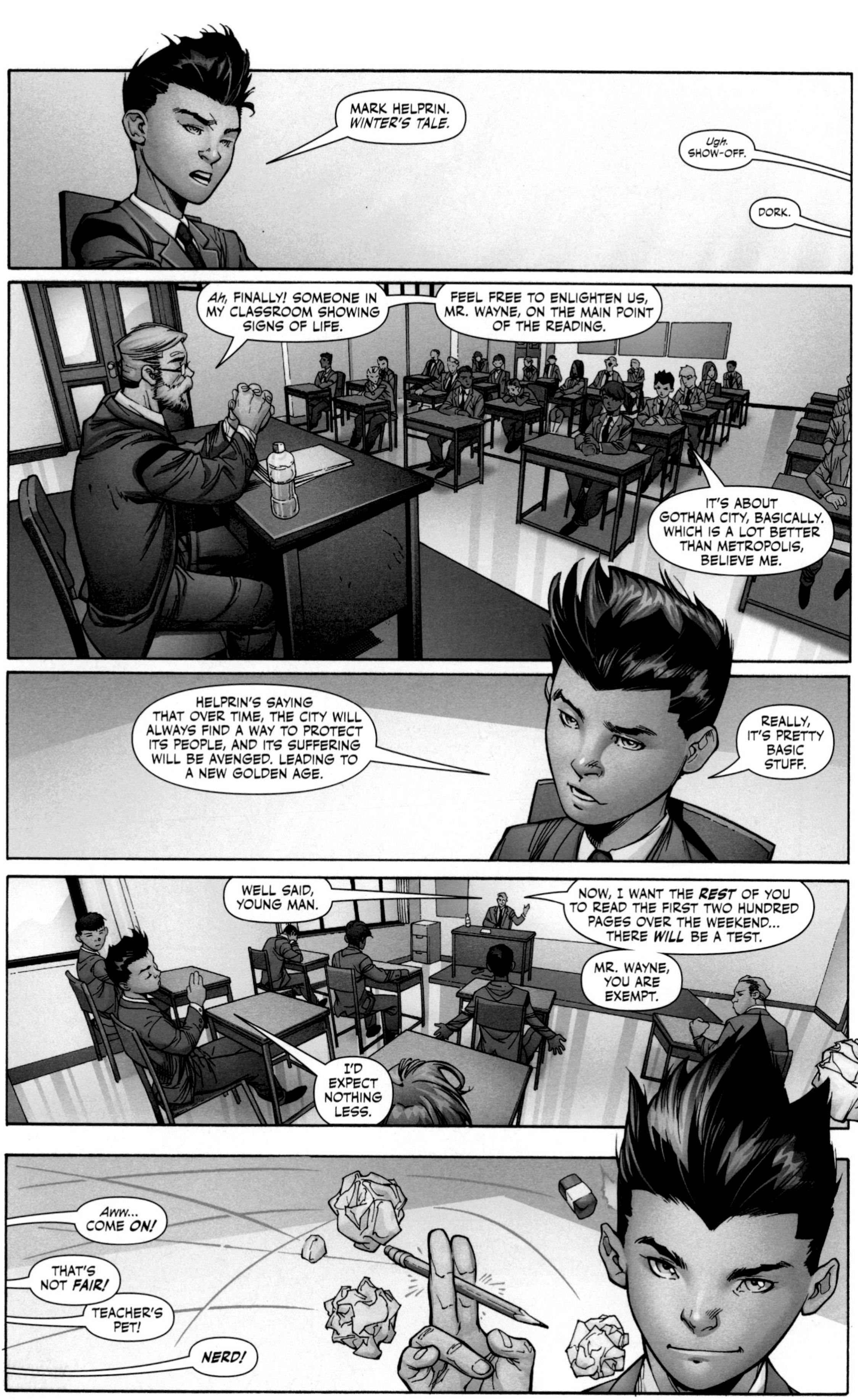
MARK HELPRIN. *WINTER'S TALE.*
Ugh. SHOW-OFF.
DORK.
Ah, FINALLY! SOMEONE IN MY CLASSROOM SHOWING SIGNS OF LIFE.
FEEL FREE TO ENLIGHTEN US, MR. WAYNE, ON THE MAIN POINT OF THE READING.
IT'S ABOUT GOTHAM CITY, BASICALLY. WHICH IS A LOT BETTER THAN METROPOLIS, BELIEVE ME.
HELPRIN'S SAYING THAT OVER TIME, THE CITY WILL ALWAYS FIND A WAY TO PROTECT ITS PEOPLE, AND ITS SUFFERING WILL BE AVENGED. LEADING TO A NEW GOLDEN AGE.
REALLY, IT'S PRETTY BASIC STUFF.
WELL SAID, YOUNG MAN.
NOW, I WANT THE ***REST*** OF YOU TO READ THE FIRST TWO HUNDRED PAGES OVER THE WEEKEND... THERE ***WILL*** BE A TEST.
MR. WAYNE, YOU ARE EXEMPT.
I'D EXPECT NOTHING LESS.
Aww... COME ***ON!***
THAT'S NOT ***FAIR!***
TEACHER'S PET!
NERD!

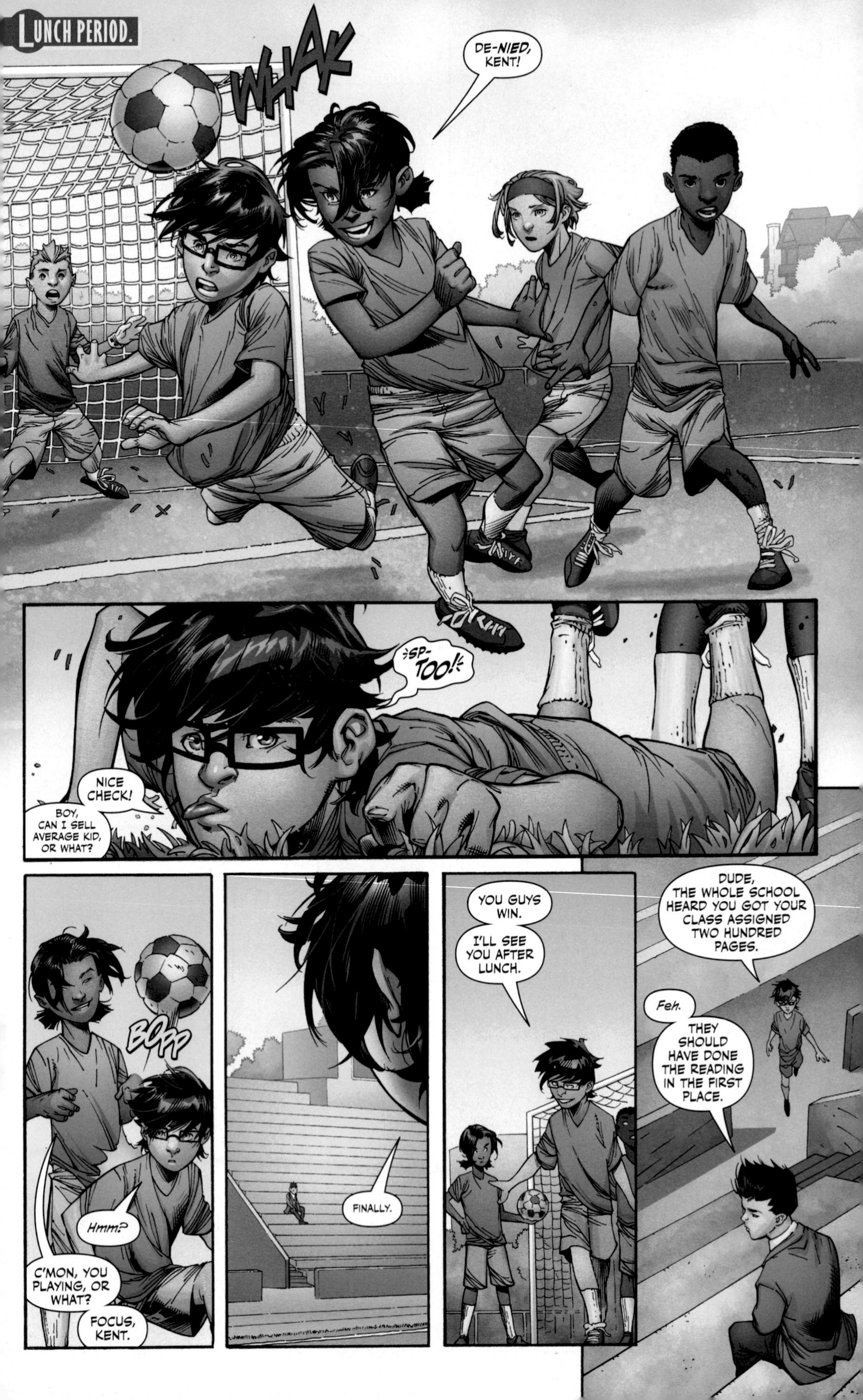
LUNCH PERIOD.
WHAK
DE-NIED, KENT!
SP-TOO!
NICE CHECK!
BOY, CAN I SELL AVERAGE KID, OR WHAT?
BOPP
Hmm?
C'MON, YOU PLAYING, OR WHAT?
FOCUS, KENT.
FINALLY.
YOU GUYS WIN.
I'LL SEE YOU AFTER LUNCH.
DUDE, THE WHOLE SCHOOL HEARD YOU GOT YOUR CLASS ASSIGNED TWO HUNDRED PAGES.
Feh.
THEY SHOULD HAVE DONE THE READING IN THE FIRST PLACE.

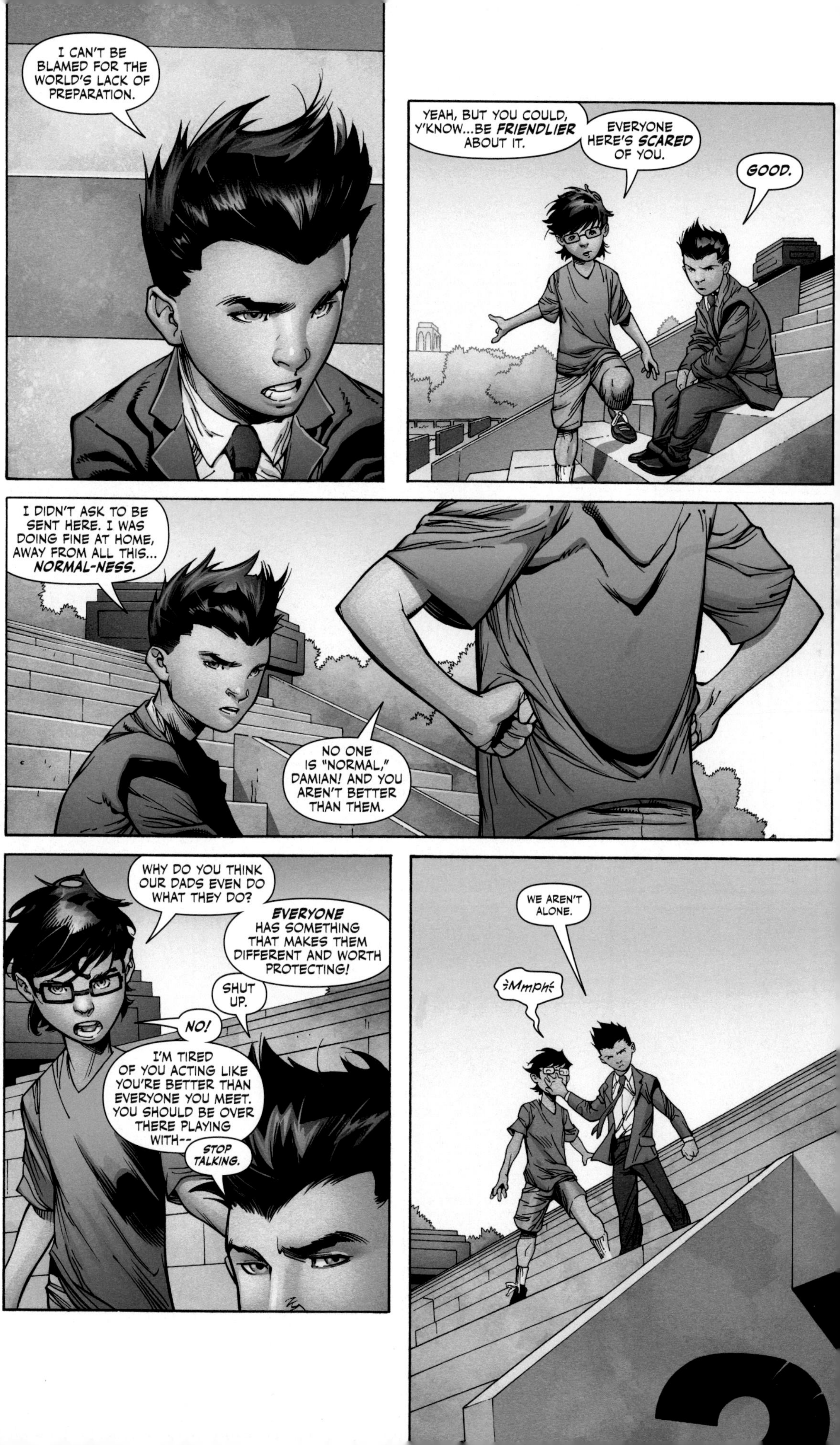
I CAN'T BE BLAMED FOR THE WORLD'S LACK OF PREPARATION.
YEAH, BUT YOU COULD, Y'KNOW...BE FRIENDLIER ABOUT IT.
EVERYONE HERE'S SCARED OF YOU.
GOOD.
I DIDN'T ASK TO BE SENT HERE. I WAS DOING FINE AT HOME, AWAY FROM ALL THIS... NORMAL-NESS.
NO ONE IS "NORMAL," DAMIAN! AND YOU AREN'T BETTER THAN THEM.
WHY DO YOU THINK OUR DADS EVEN DO WHAT THEY DO?
EVERYONE HAS SOMETHING THAT MAKES THEM DIFFERENT AND WORTH PROTECTING!
SHUT UP.
NO!
I'M TIRED OF YOU ACTING LIKE YOU'RE BETTER THAN EVERYONE YOU MEET. YOU SHOULD BE OVER THERE PLAYING WITH--
STOP TALKING.
WE AREN'T ALONE.
Mmph

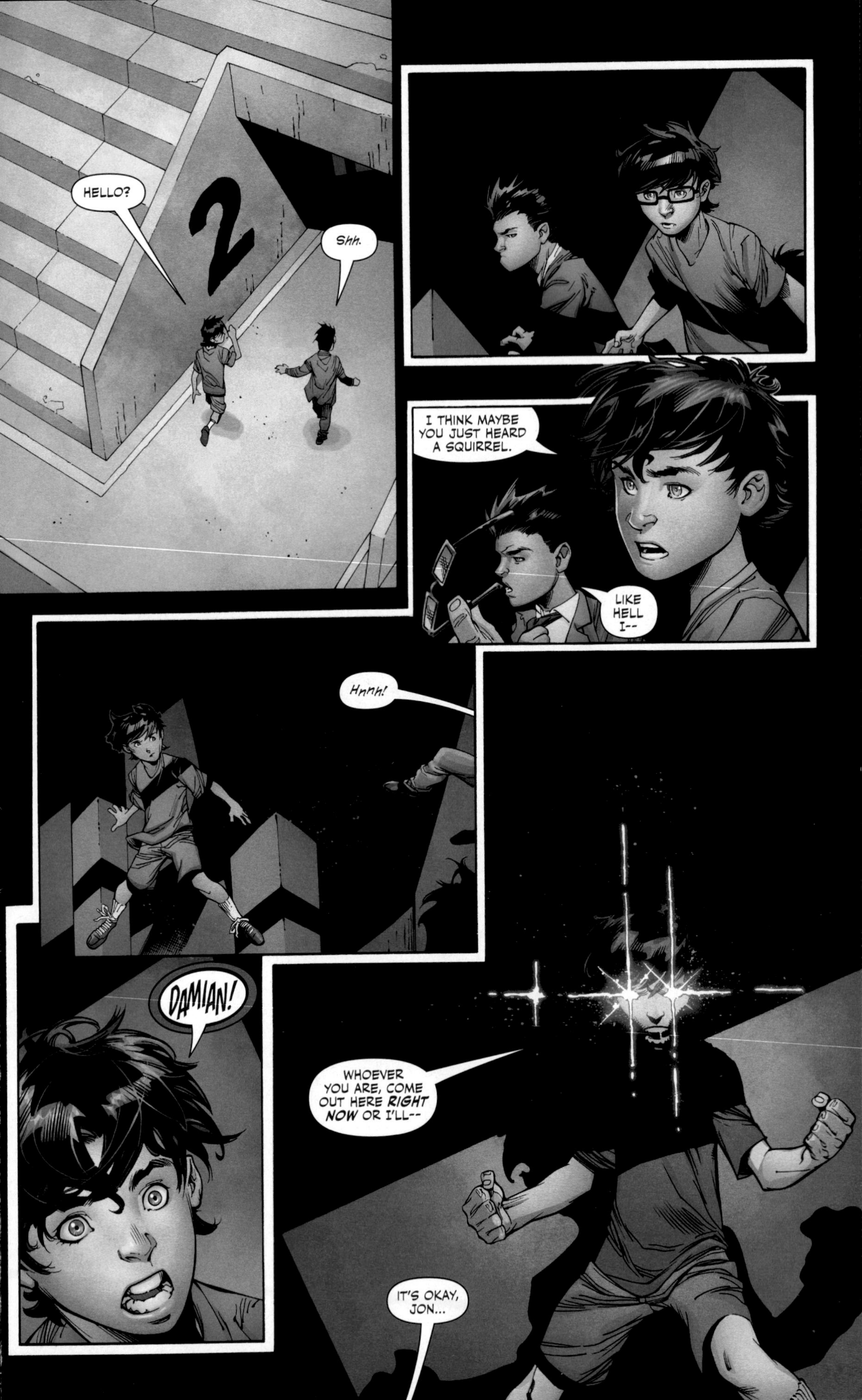
HELLO?
Shh.
I THINK MAYBE YOU JUST HEARD A SQUIRREL.
LIKE HELL I--
Hnnh!
DAMIAN!
WHOEVER YOU ARE, COME OUT HERE RIGHT NOW OR I'LL--
IT'S OKAY, JON...

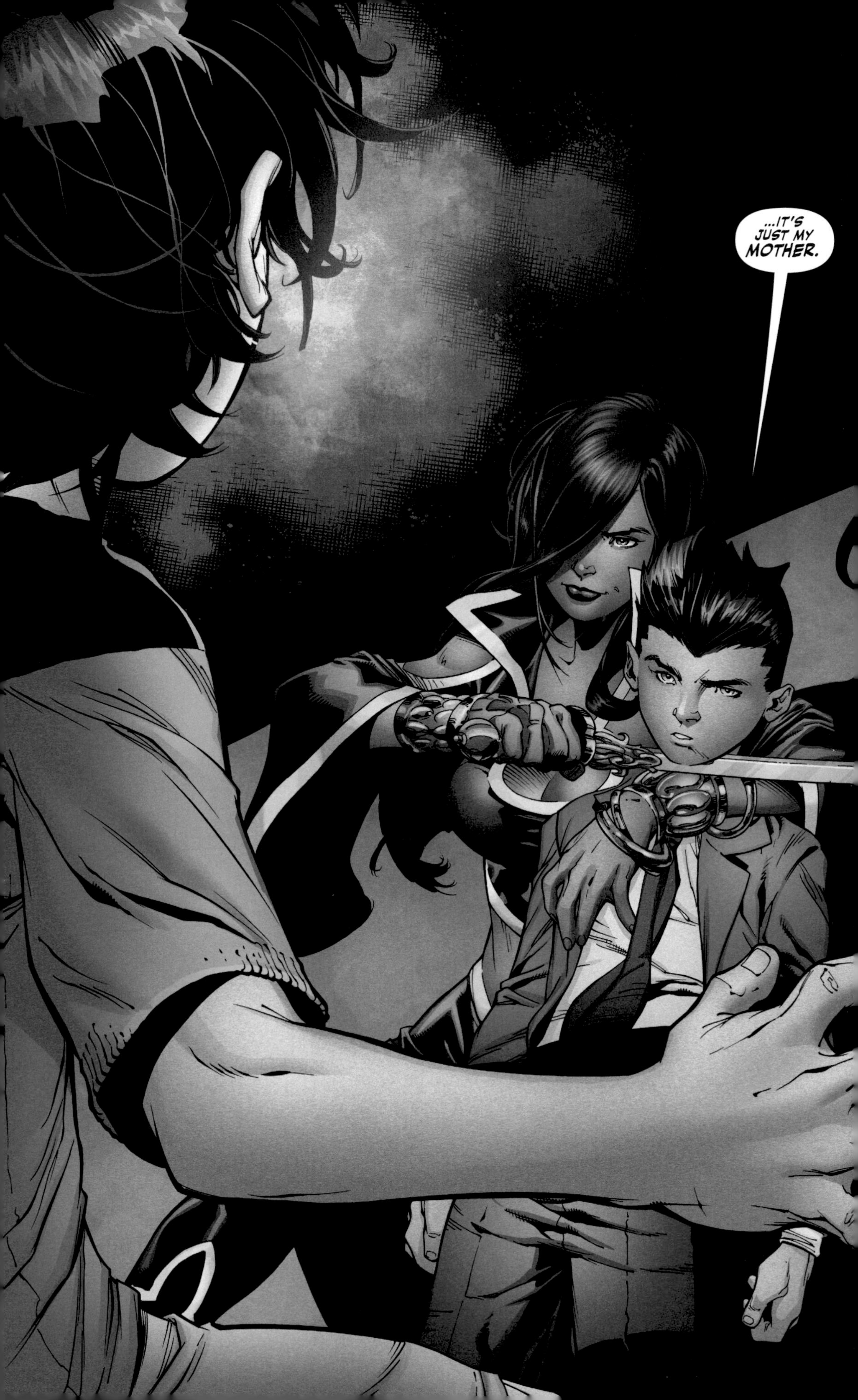
...IT'S JUST MY MOTHER.

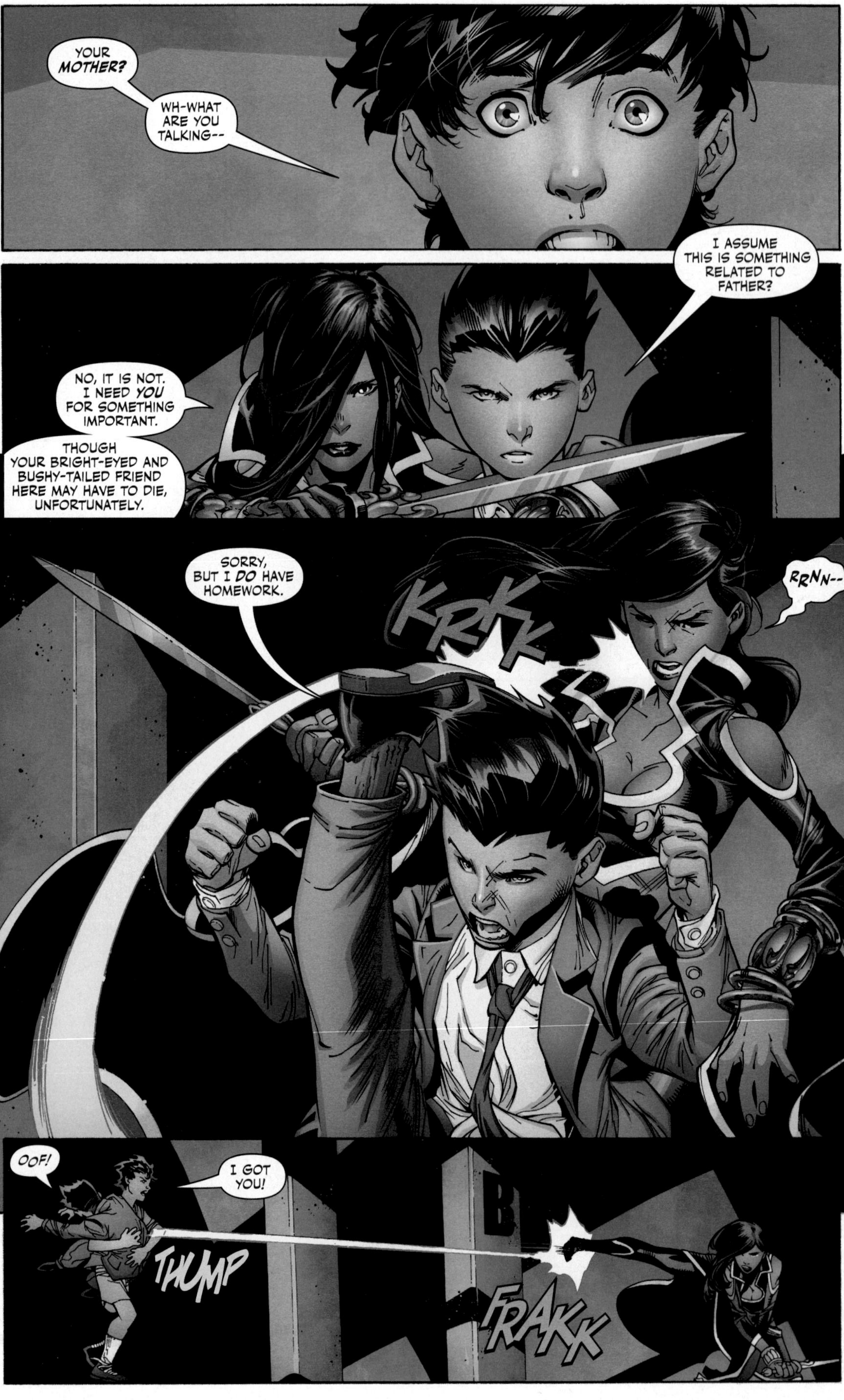
YOUR MOTHER?
WH-WHAT ARE YOU TALKING--
I ASSUME THIS IS SOMETHING RELATED TO FATHER?
NO, IT IS NOT. I NEED YOU FOR SOMETHING IMPORTANT.
THOUGH YOUR BRIGHT-EYED AND BUSHY-TAILED FRIEND HERE MAY HAVE TO DIE, UNFORTUNATELY.
SORRY, BUT I DO HAVE HOMEWORK.
KRKK
RRNN--
OOF!
I GOT YOU!
THUMP
FRAKK

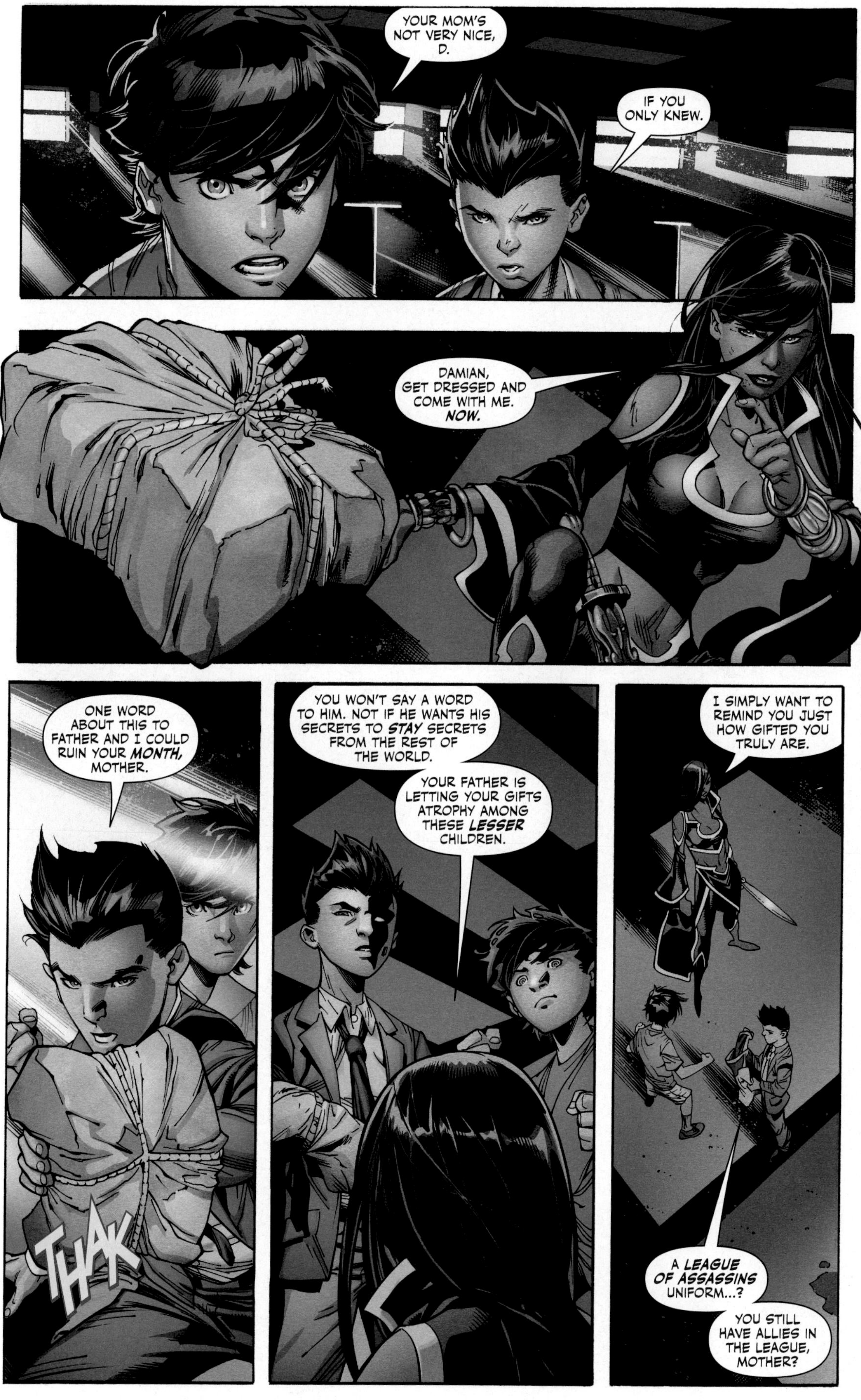
YOUR MOM'S NOT VERY NICE, D.
IF YOU ONLY KNEW.
DAMIAN, GET DRESSED AND COME WITH ME. *NOW.*
ONE WORD ABOUT THIS TO FATHER AND I COULD RUIN YOUR *MONTH,* MOTHER.
THAK
YOU WON'T SAY A WORD TO HIM. NOT IF HE WANTS HIS SECRETS TO *STAY* SECRETS FROM THE REST OF THE WORLD.
YOUR FATHER IS LETTING YOUR GIFTS ATROPHY AMONG THESE *LESSER* CHILDREN.
I SIMPLY WANT TO REMIND YOU JUST HOW GIFTED YOU TRULY ARE.
A *LEAGUE OF ASSASSINS* UNIFORM...?
YOU STILL HAVE ALLIES IN THE LEAGUE, MOTHER?

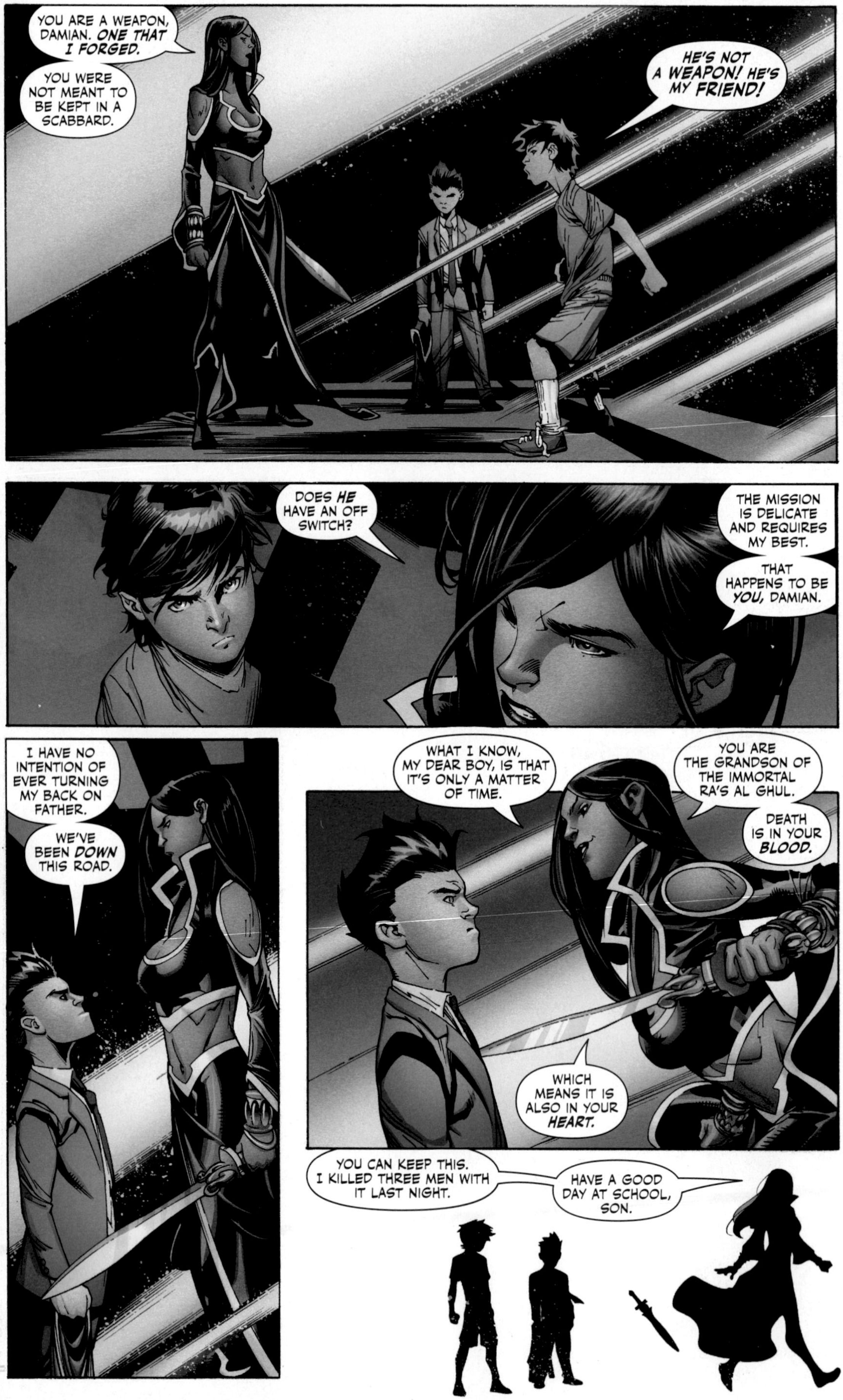
YOU ARE A WEAPON, DAMIAN. ONE THAT I FORGED.
YOU WERE NOT MEANT TO BE KEPT IN A SCABBARD.
HE'S NOT A WEAPON! HE'S MY FRIEND!
DOES HE HAVE AN OFF SWITCH?
THE MISSION IS DELICATE AND REQUIRES MY BEST.
THAT HAPPENS TO BE YOU, DAMIAN.
I HAVE NO INTENTION OF EVER TURNING MY BACK ON FATHER.
WE'VE BEEN DOWN THIS ROAD.
WHAT I KNOW, MY DEAR BOY, IS THAT IT'S ONLY A MATTER OF TIME.
YOU ARE THE GRANDSON OF THE IMMORTAL RA'S AL GHUL.
DEATH IS IN YOUR BLOOD.
WHICH MEANS IT IS ALSO IN YOUR HEART.
YOU CAN KEEP THIS. I KILLED THREE MEN WITH IT LAST NIGHT.
HAVE A GOOD DAY AT SCHOOL, SON.

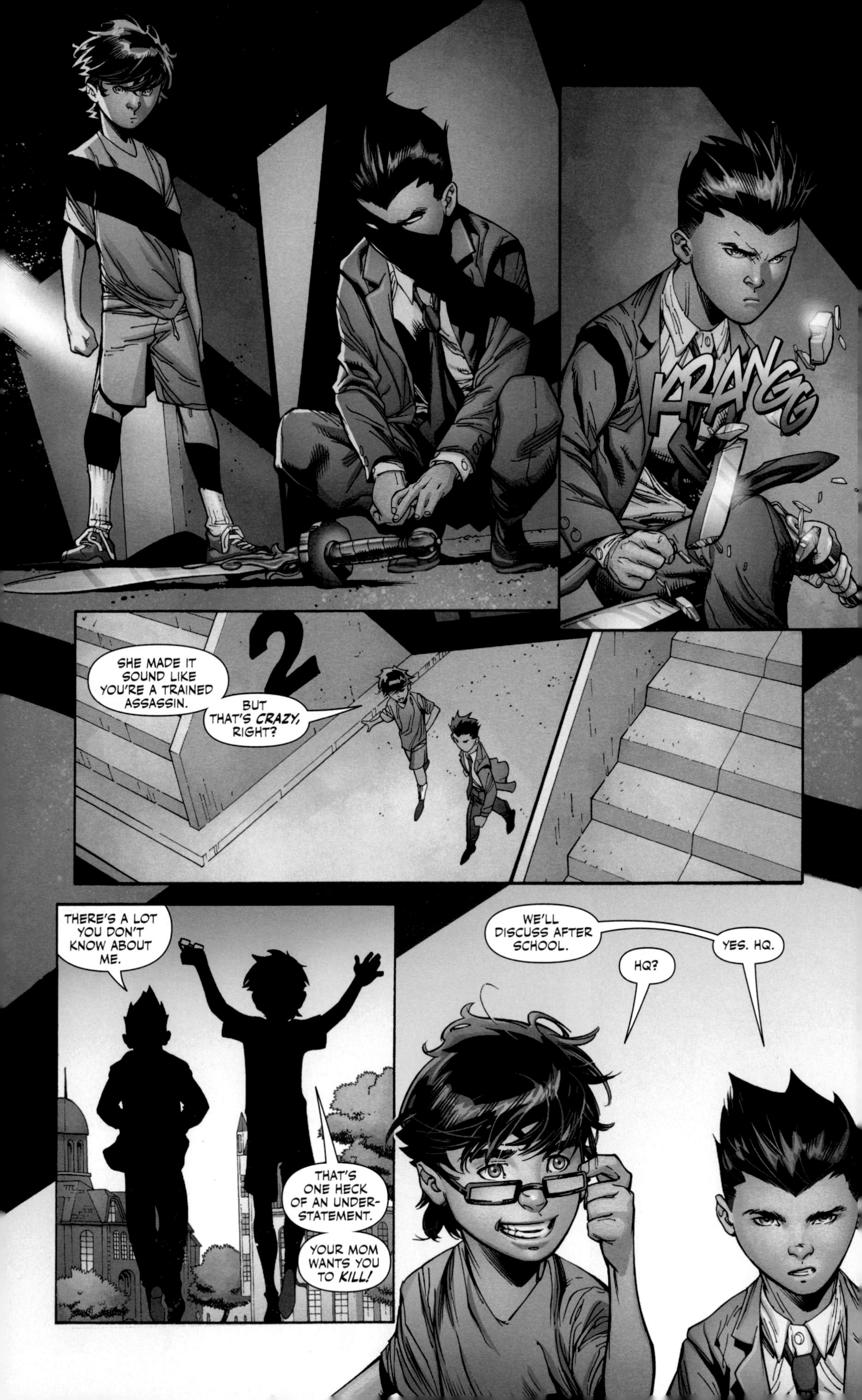
KRANGG
SHE MADE IT SOUND LIKE YOU'RE A TRAINED ASSASSIN.
BUT THAT'S *CRAZY,* RIGHT?
THERE'S A LOT YOU DON'T KNOW ABOUT ME.
THAT'S ONE HECK OF AN UNDER-STATEMENT.
YOUR MOM WANTS YOU TO ***KILL!***
WE'LL DISCUSS AFTER SCHOOL.
HQ?
YES. HQ.

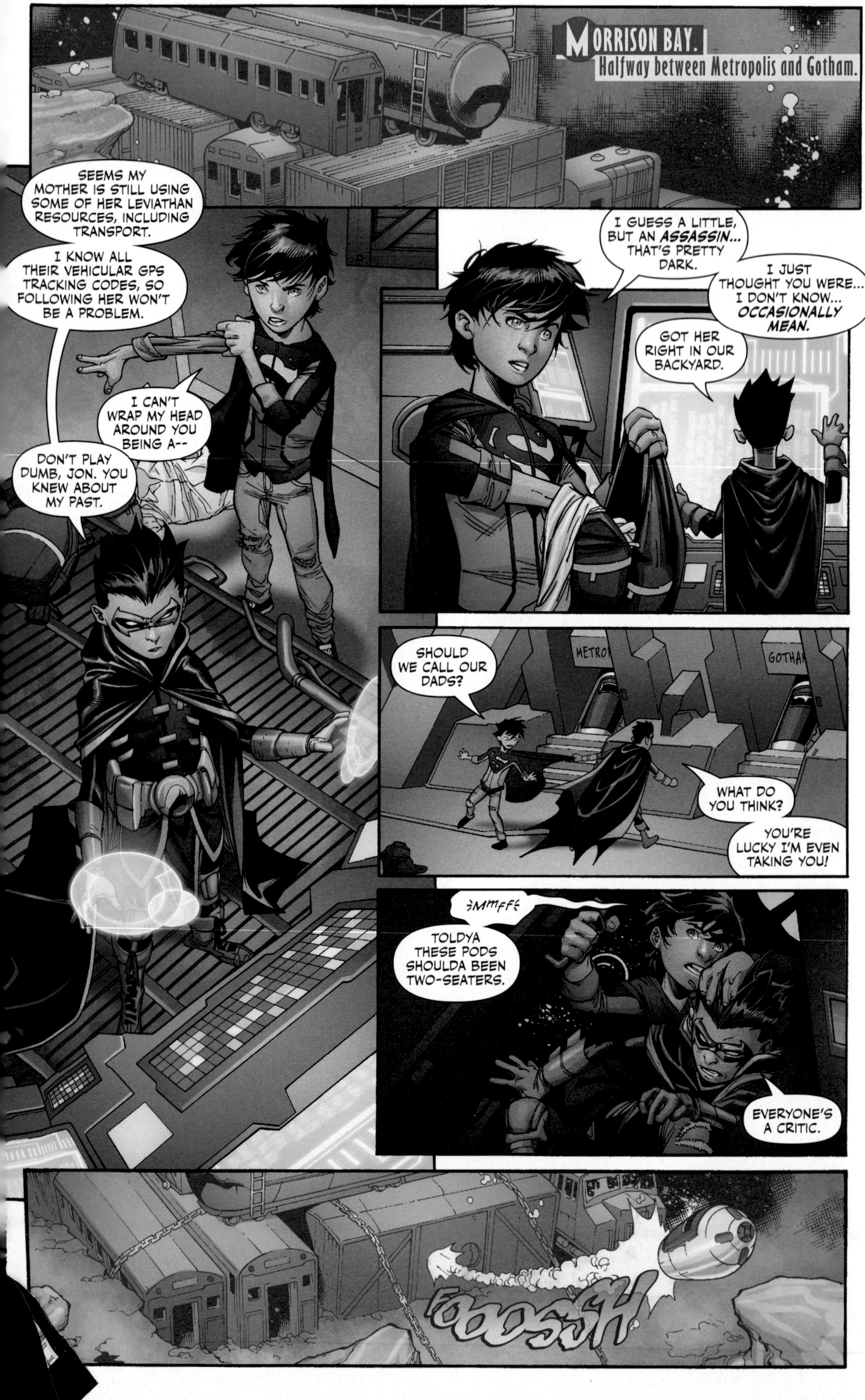
MORRISON BAY.
Halfway between Metropolis and Gotham.
SEEMS MY MOTHER IS STILL USING SOME OF HER LEVIATHAN RESOURCES, INCLUDING TRANSPORT.
I KNOW ALL THEIR VEHICULAR GPS TRACKING CODES, SO FOLLOWING HER WON'T BE A PROBLEM.
I CAN'T WRAP MY HEAD AROUND YOU BEING A--
DON'T PLAY DUMB, JON. YOU KNEW ABOUT MY PAST.
I GUESS A LITTLE, BUT AN ASSASSIN... THAT'S PRETTY DARK.
I JUST THOUGHT YOU WERE... I DON'T KNOW... OCCASIONALLY MEAN.
GOT HER RIGHT IN OUR BACKYARD.
SHOULD WE CALL OUR DADS?
METRO
GOTHAM
WHAT DO YOU THINK?
YOU'RE LUCKY I'M EVEN TAKING YOU!
MMFF
TOLDYA THESE PODS SHOULDA BEEN TWO-SEATERS.
EVERYONE'S A CRITIC.
FOOOSSH

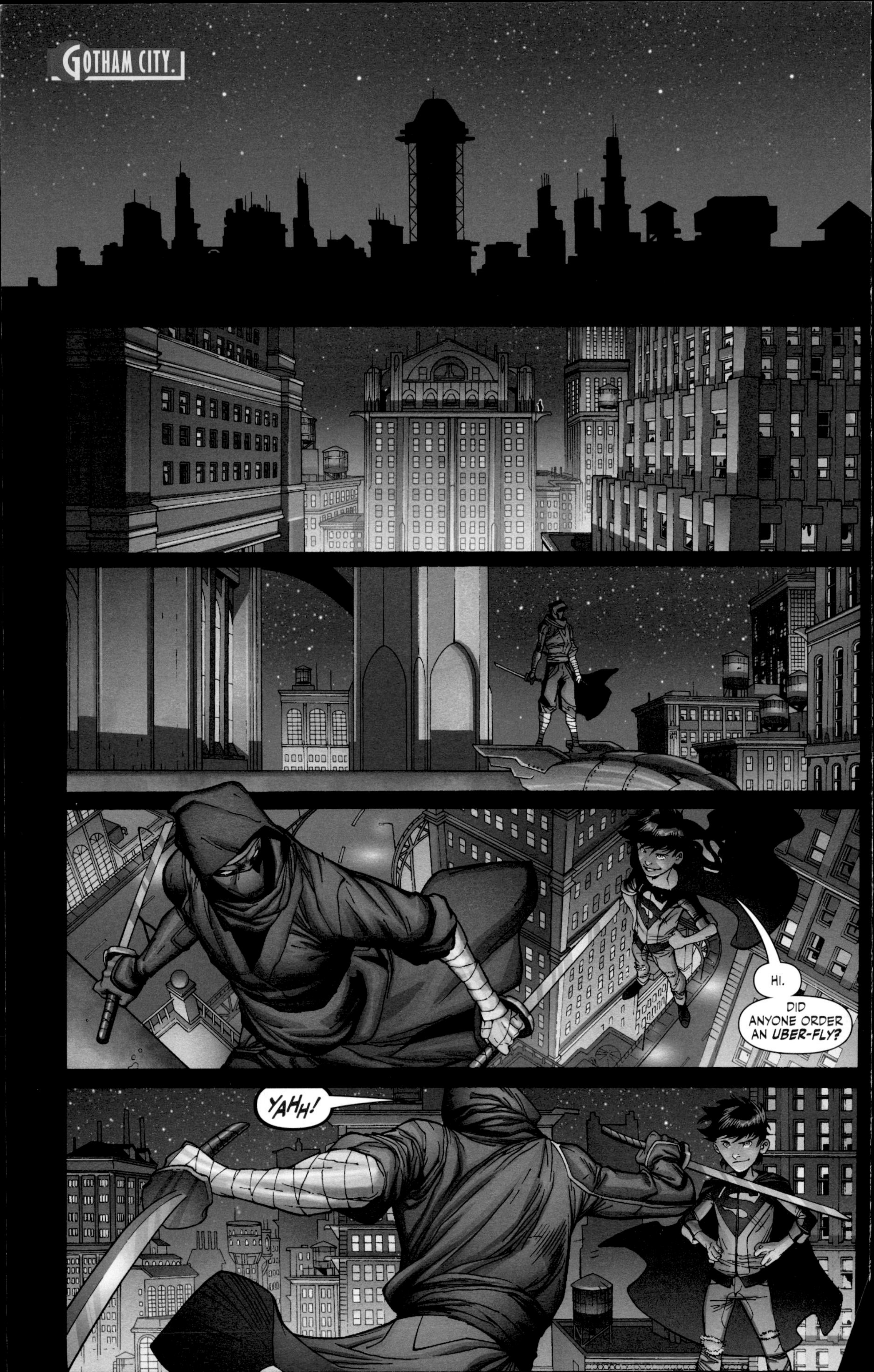
GOTHAM CITY.
HI.
DID ANYONE ORDER AN UBER-FLY?
YAHH!

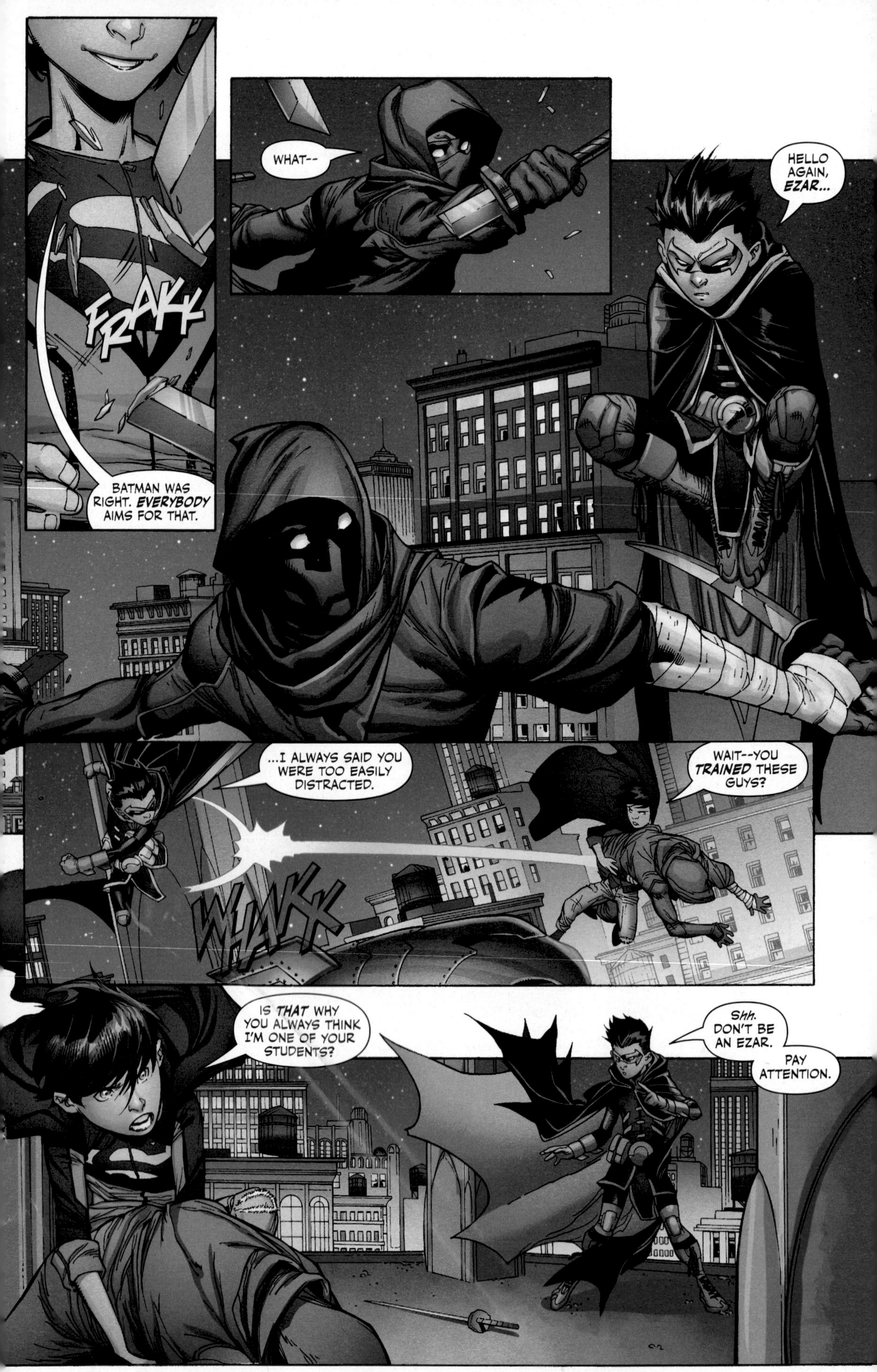
WHAT--
FRAKK
BATMAN WAS RIGHT. EVERYBODY AIMS FOR THAT.
HELLO AGAIN, EZAR...
...I ALWAYS SAID YOU WERE TOO EASILY DISTRACTED.
WHAKK
WAIT--YOU TRAINED THESE GUYS?
IS THAT WHY YOU ALWAYS THINK I'M ONE OF YOUR STUDENTS?
Shh. DON'T BE AN EZAR.
PAY ATTENTION.

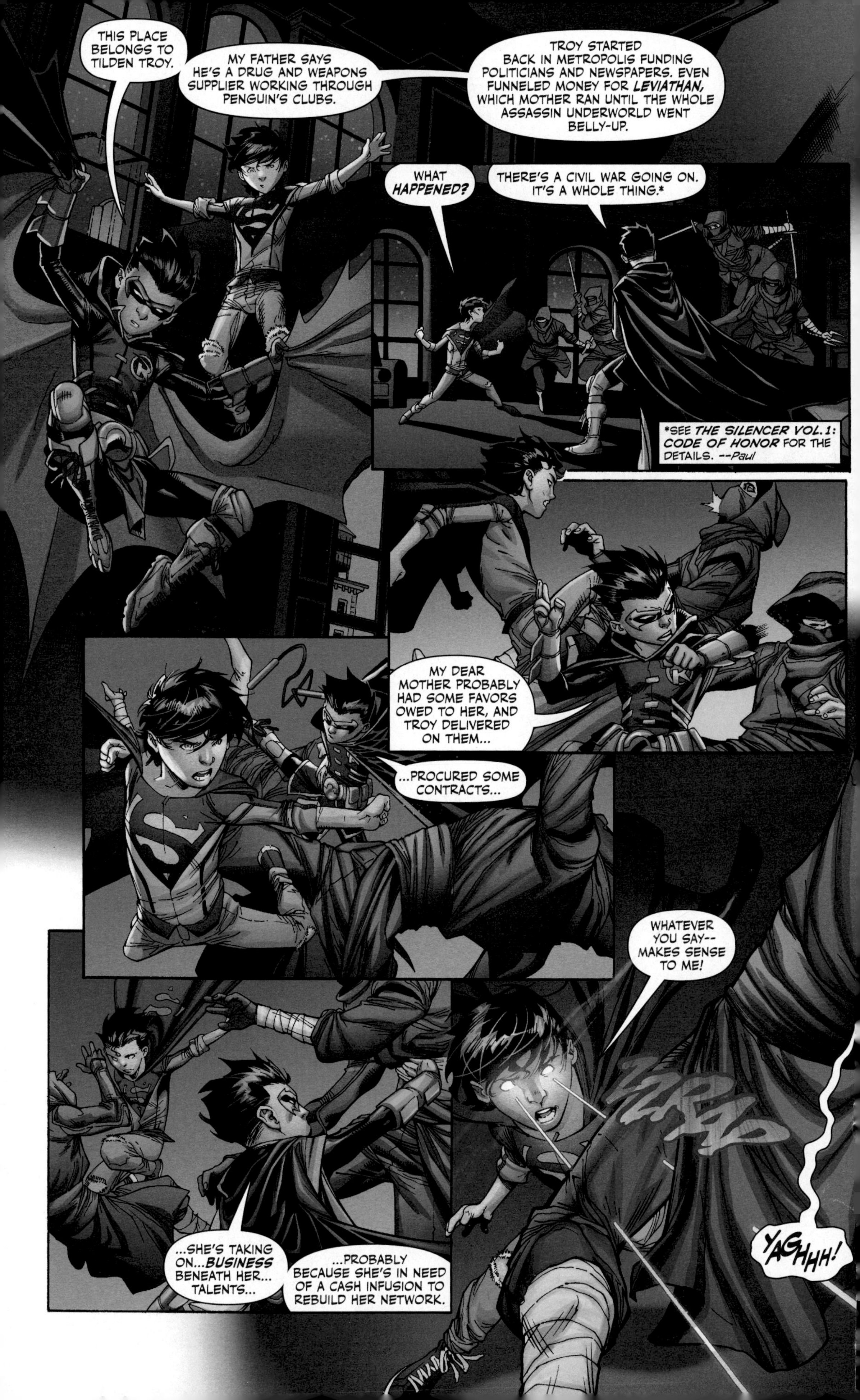

THIS PLACE BELONGS TO TILDEN TROY.
MY FATHER SAYS HE'S A DRUG AND WEAPONS SUPPLIER WORKING THROUGH PENGUIN'S CLUBS.
TROY STARTED BACK IN METROPOLIS FUNDING POLITICIANS AND NEWSPAPERS. EVEN FUNNELED MONEY FOR LEVIATHAN, WHICH MOTHER RAN UNTIL THE WHOLE ASSASSIN UNDERWORLD WENT BELLY-UP.
WHAT HAPPENED?
THERE'S A CIVIL WAR GOING ON. IT'S A WHOLE THING.*
*SEE THE SILENCER VOL.1: CODE OF HONOR FOR THE DETAILS. --Paul
MY DEAR MOTHER PROBABLY HAD SOME FAVORS OWED TO HER, AND TROY DELIVERED ON THEM...
...PROCURED SOME CONTRACTS...
...SHE'S TAKING ON...BUSINESS BENEATH HER... TALENTS...
...PROBABLY BECAUSE SHE'S IN NEED OF A CASH INFUSION TO REBUILD HER NETWORK.
WHATEVER YOU SAY-- MAKES SENSE TO ME!
YAGHHH!

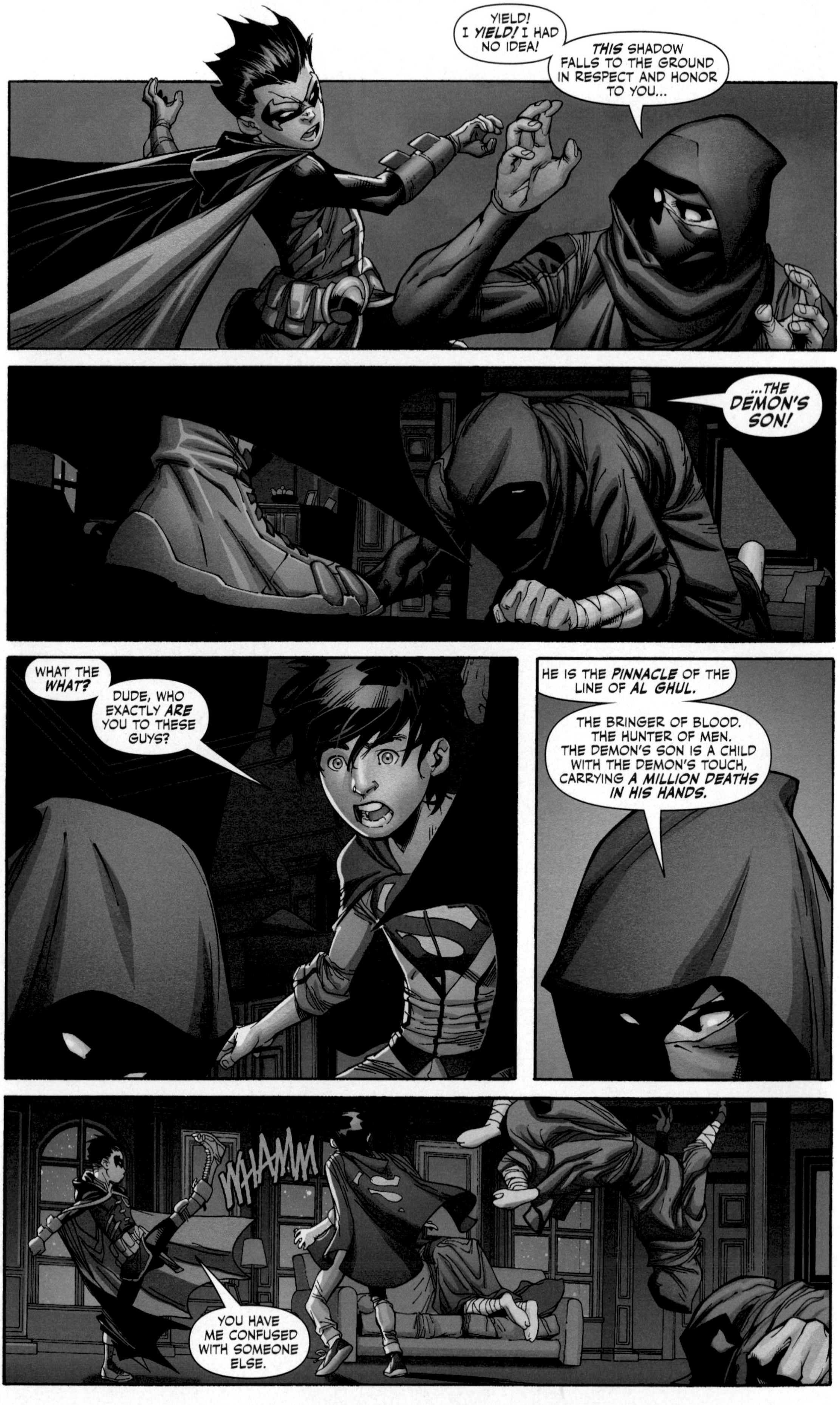
YIELD! I *YIELD!* I HAD NO IDEA!
THIS SHADOW FALLS TO THE GROUND IN RESPECT AND HONOR TO YOU...
...THE *DEMON'S SON!*
WHAT THE *WHAT?*
DUDE, WHO EXACTLY *ARE* YOU TO THESE GUYS?
HE IS THE *PINNACLE* OF THE LINE OF *AL GHUL.*
THE BRINGER OF BLOOD. THE HUNTER OF MEN. THE DEMON'S SON IS A CHILD WITH THE DEMON'S TOUCH, CARRYING *A MILLION DEATHS IN HIS HANDS.*
WHAMM
YOU HAVE ME CONFUSED WITH SOMEONE ELSE.

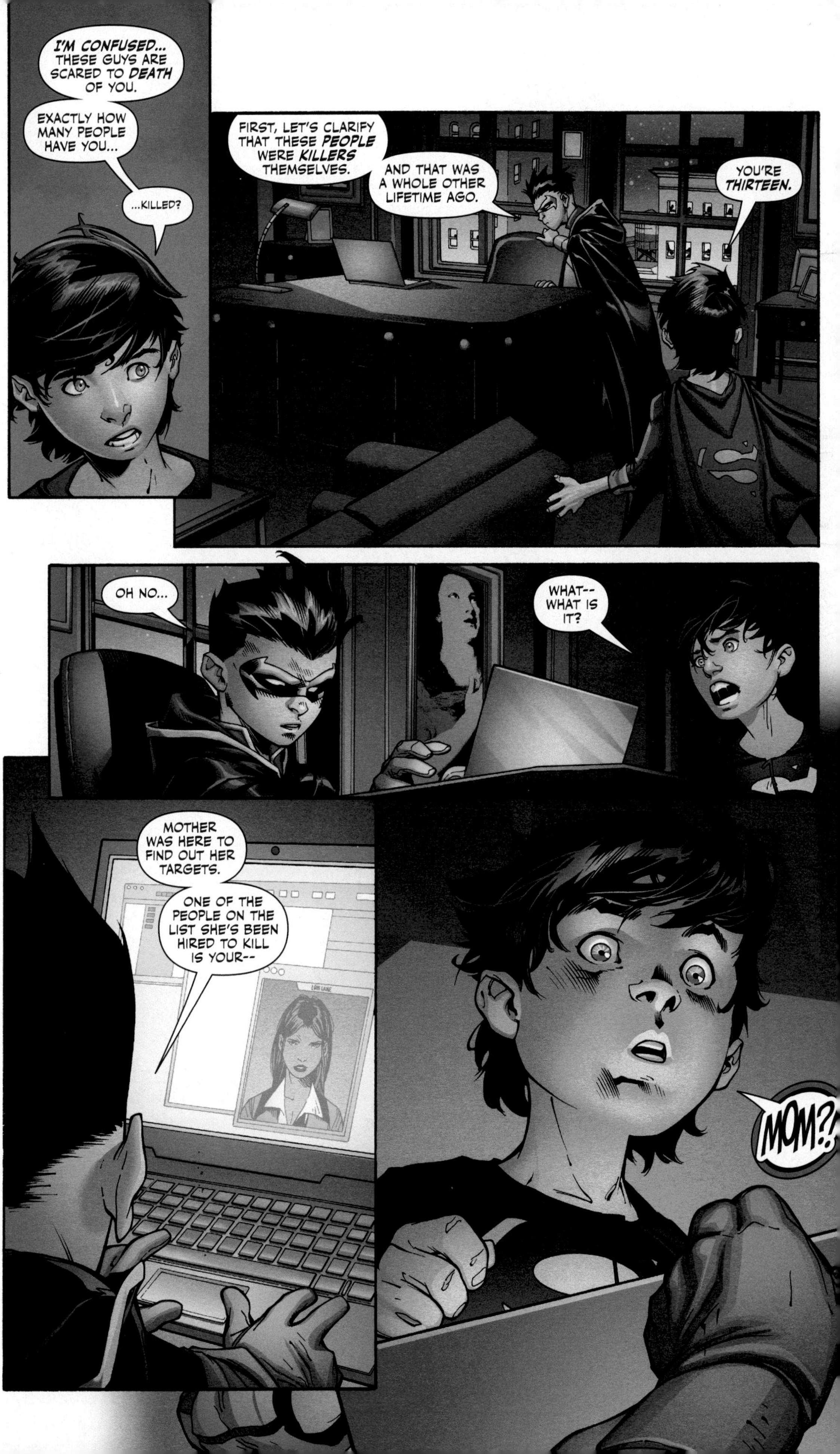
I'M CONFUSED... THESE GUYS ARE SCARED TO DEATH OF YOU.
EXACTLY HOW MANY PEOPLE HAVE YOU...
...KILLED?
FIRST, LET'S CLARIFY THAT THESE PEOPLE WERE KILLERS THEMSELVES.
AND THAT WAS A WHOLE OTHER LIFETIME AGO.
YOU'RE THIRTEEN.
OH NO...
WHAT-- WHAT IS IT?
MOTHER WAS HERE TO FIND OUT HER TARGETS.
ONE OF THE PEOPLE ON THE LIST SHE'S BEEN HIRED TO KILL IS YOUR--
MOM?!

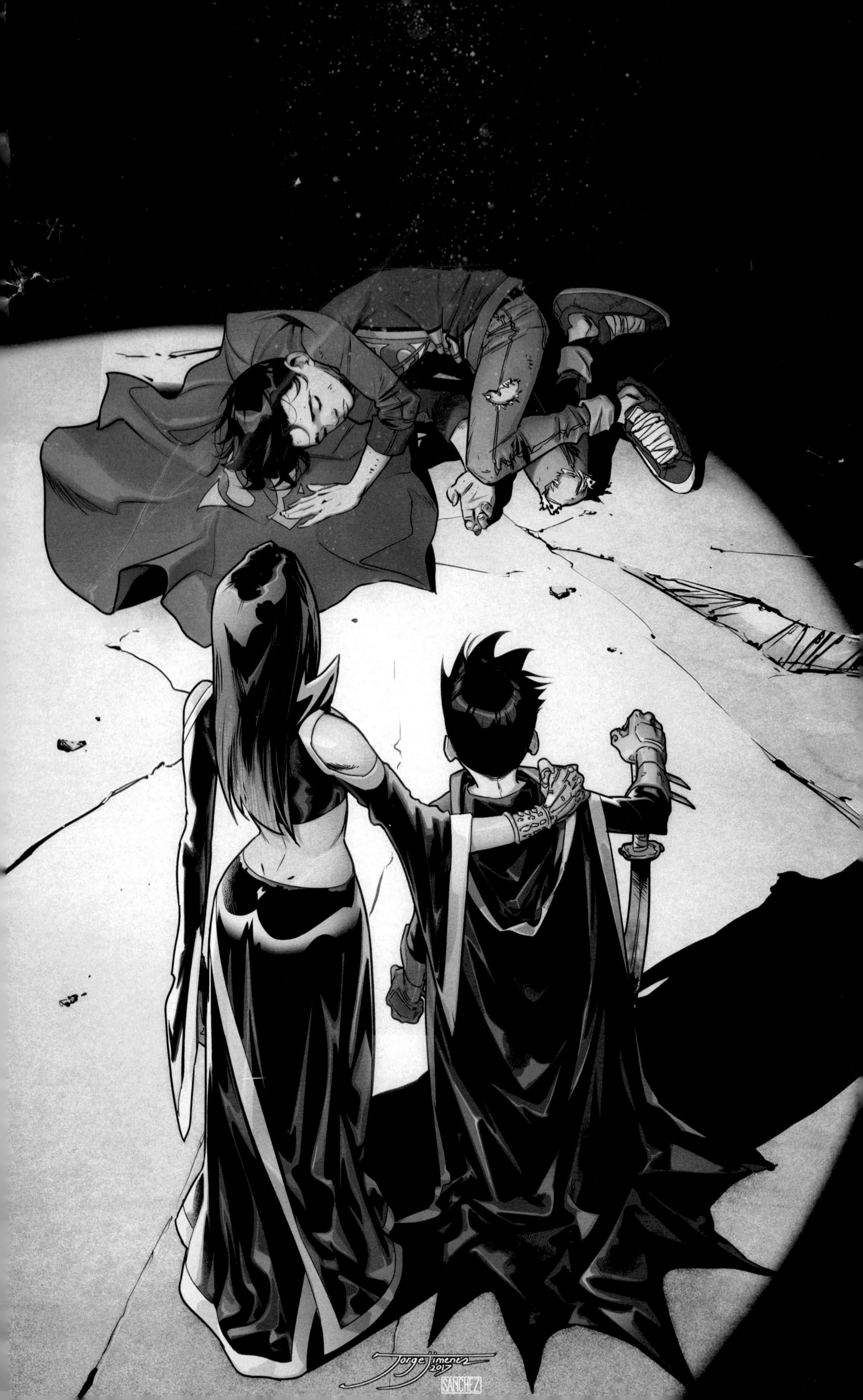

Jorge Jimenez 2017
SÁNCHEZ

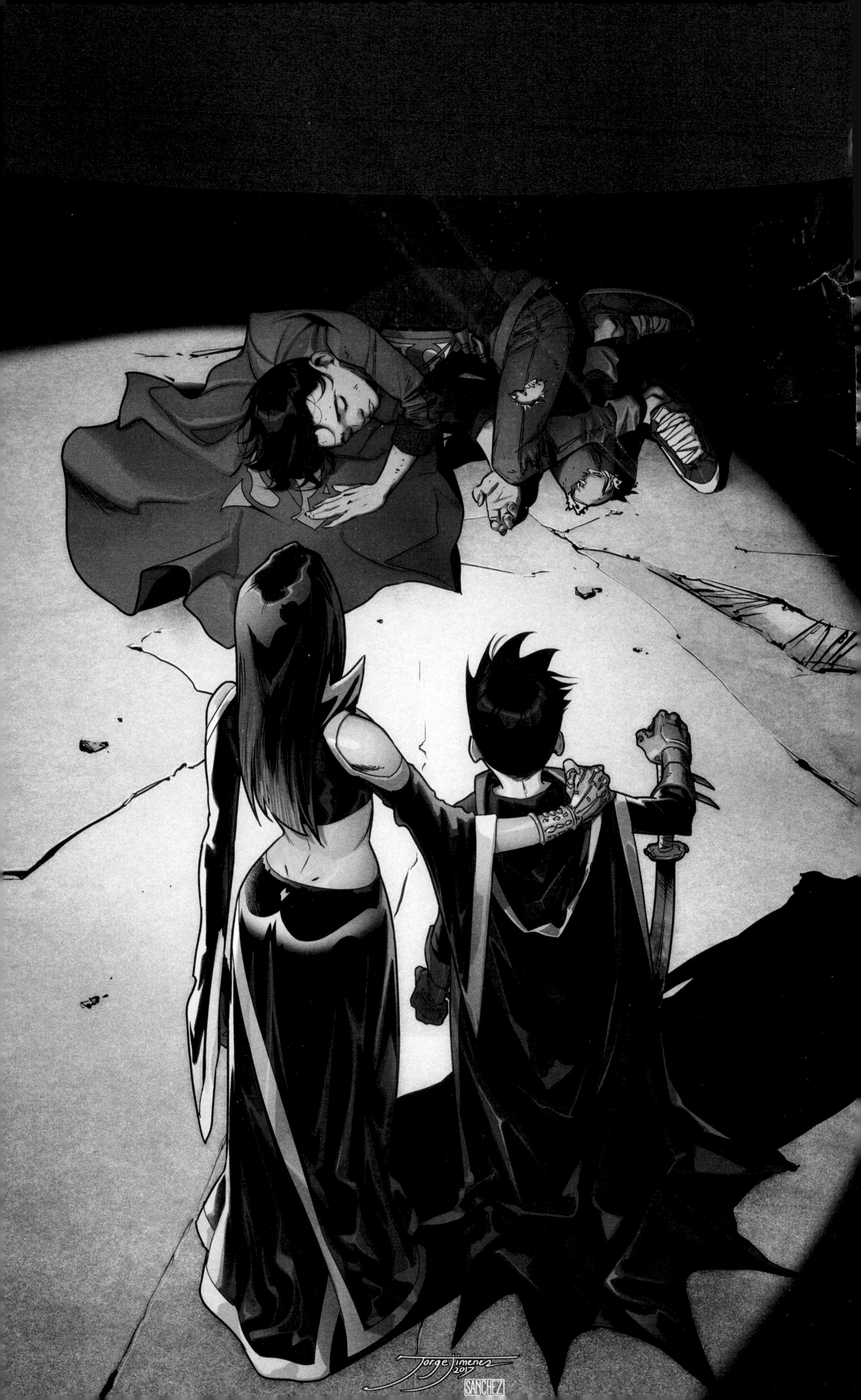
Jorge Jimenez 2017
SANCHEZ

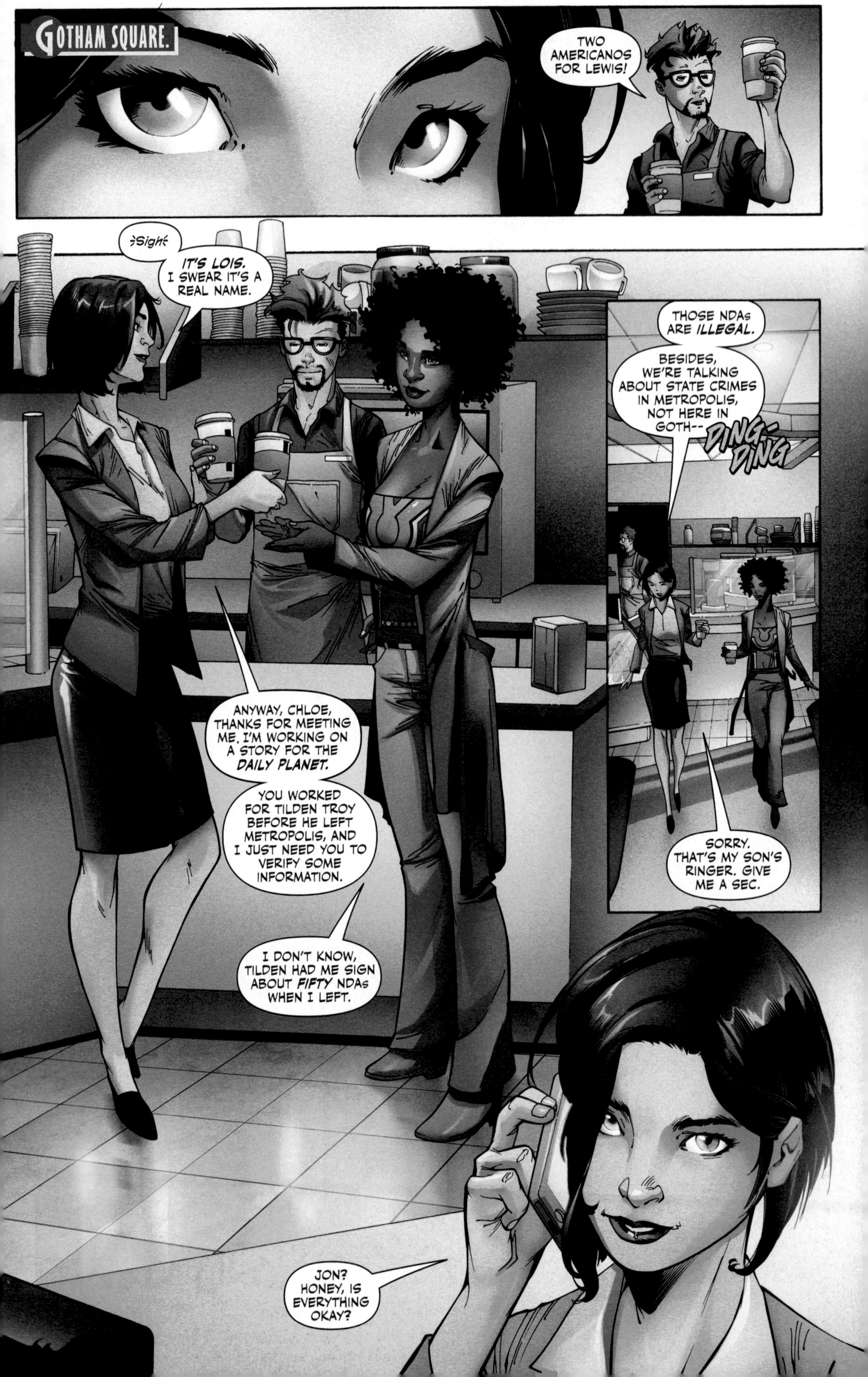
GOTHAM SQUARE.
TWO AMERICANOS FOR LEWIS!
Sigh
IT'S LOIS. I SWEAR IT'S A REAL NAME.
ANYWAY, CHLOE, THANKS FOR MEETING ME. I'M WORKING ON A STORY FOR THE DAILY PLANET.
YOU WORKED FOR TILDEN TROY BEFORE HE LEFT METROPOLIS, AND I JUST NEED YOU TO VERIFY SOME INFORMATION.
I DON'T KNOW, TILDEN HAD ME SIGN ABOUT FIFTY NDAs WHEN I LEFT.
THOSE NDAs ARE ILLEGAL.
BESIDES, WE'RE TALKING ABOUT STATE CRIMES IN METROPOLIS, NOT HERE IN GOTH--
DING-DING
SORRY. THAT'S MY SON'S RINGER. GIVE ME A SEC.
JON? HONEY, IS EVERYTHING OKAY?

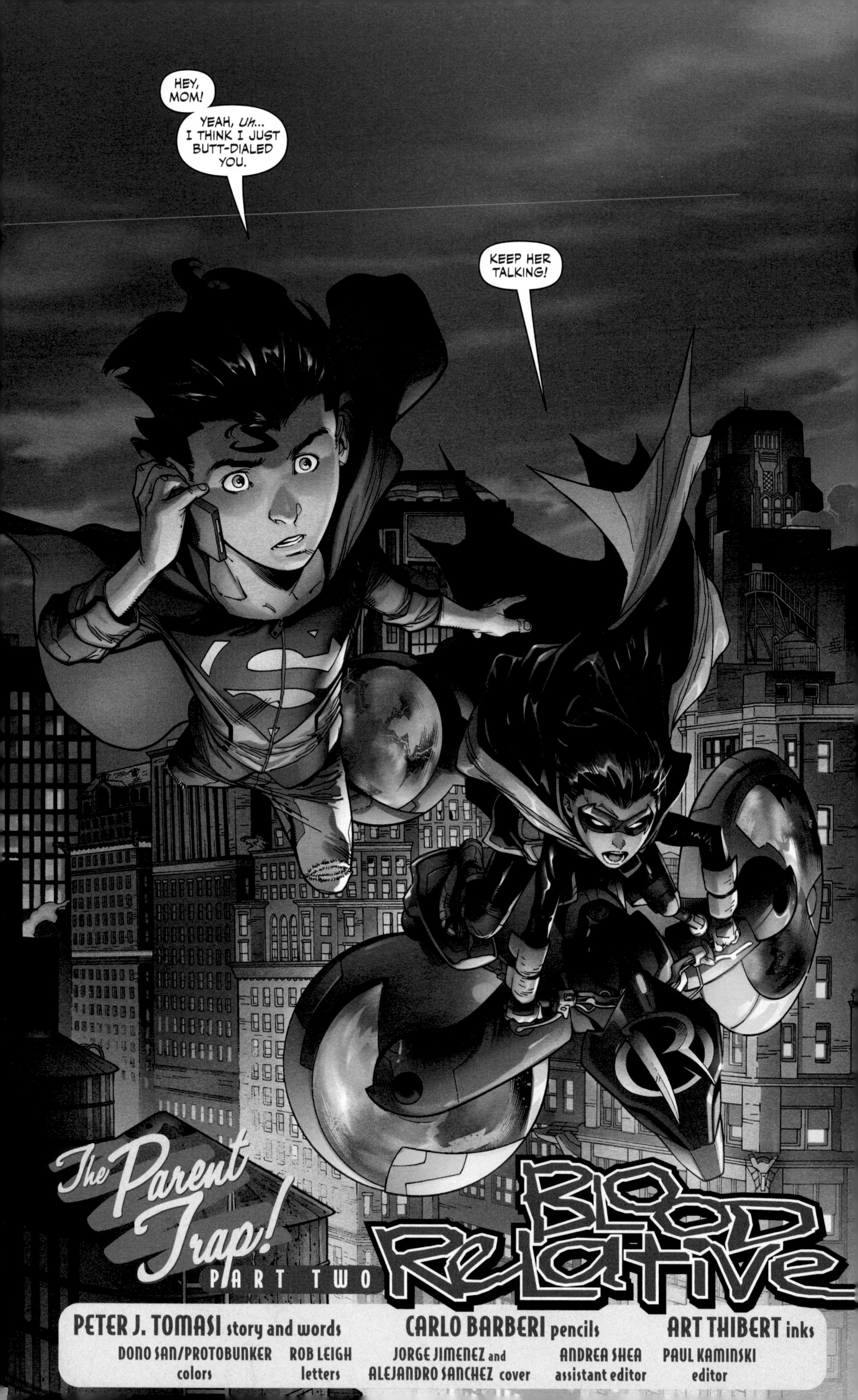
HEY, MOM!
YEAH, UH... I THINK I JUST BUTT-DIALED YOU.
KEEP HER TALKING!
The Parent Trap! PART TWO
BLOOD Relative
PETER J. TOMASI story and words
CARLO BARBERI pencils
ART THIBERT inks
DONO SAN/PROTOBUNKER colors
ROB LEIGH letters
JORGE JIMENEZ and ALEJANDRO SANCHEZ cover
ANDREA SHEA assistant editor
PAUL KAMINSKI editor

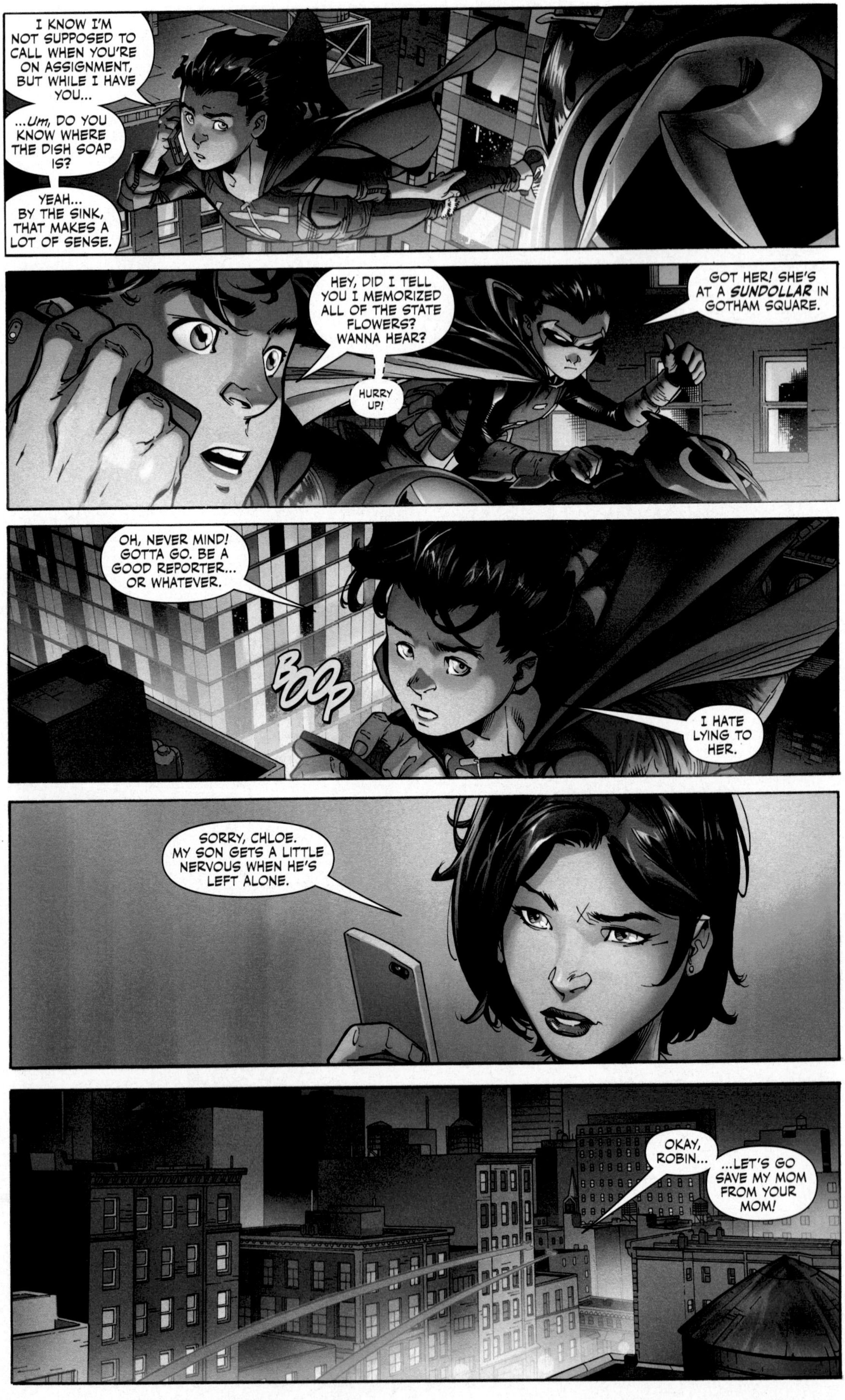
I KNOW I'M NOT SUPPOSED TO CALL WHEN YOU'RE ON ASSIGNMENT, BUT WHILE I HAVE YOU...
...*Um,* DO YOU KNOW WHERE THE DISH SOAP IS?
YEAH... BY THE SINK, THAT MAKES A LOT OF SENSE.
HEY, DID I TELL YOU I MEMORIZED ALL OF THE STATE FLOWERS? WANNA HEAR?
HURRY UP!
GOT HER! SHE'S AT A ***SUNDOLLAR*** IN GOTHAM SQUARE.
OH, NEVER MIND! GOTTA GO. BE A GOOD REPORTER... OR WHATEVER.
BOOP
I HATE LYING TO HER.
SORRY, CHLOE. MY SON GETS A LITTLE NERVOUS WHEN HE'S LEFT ALONE.
OKAY, ROBIN...
...LET'S GO SAVE MY MOM FROM YOUR MOM!

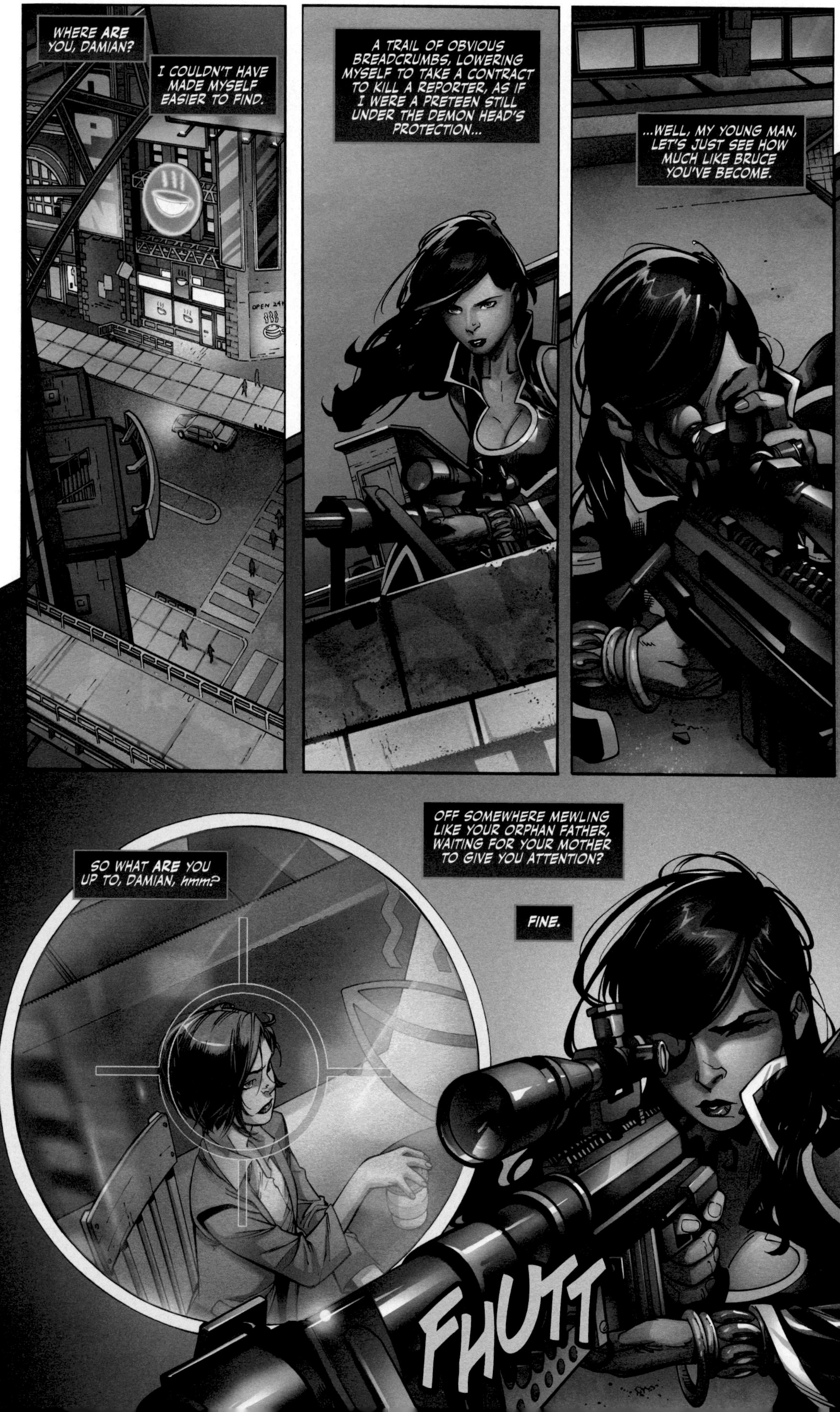
WHERE ARE YOU, DAMIAN?
I COULDN'T HAVE MADE MYSELF EASIER TO FIND.
OPEN 24H
A TRAIL OF OBVIOUS BREADCRUMBS, LOWERING MYSELF TO TAKE A CONTRACT TO KILL A REPORTER, AS IF I WERE A PRETEEN STILL UNDER THE DEMON HEAD'S PROTECTION...
...WELL, MY YOUNG MAN, LET'S JUST SEE HOW MUCH LIKE BRUCE YOU'VE BECOME.
SO WHAT ARE YOU UP TO, DAMIAN, hmm?
OFF SOMEWHERE MEWLING LIKE YOUR ORPHAN FATHER, WAITING FOR YOUR MOTHER TO GIVE YOU ATTENTION?
FINE.
FHUTT

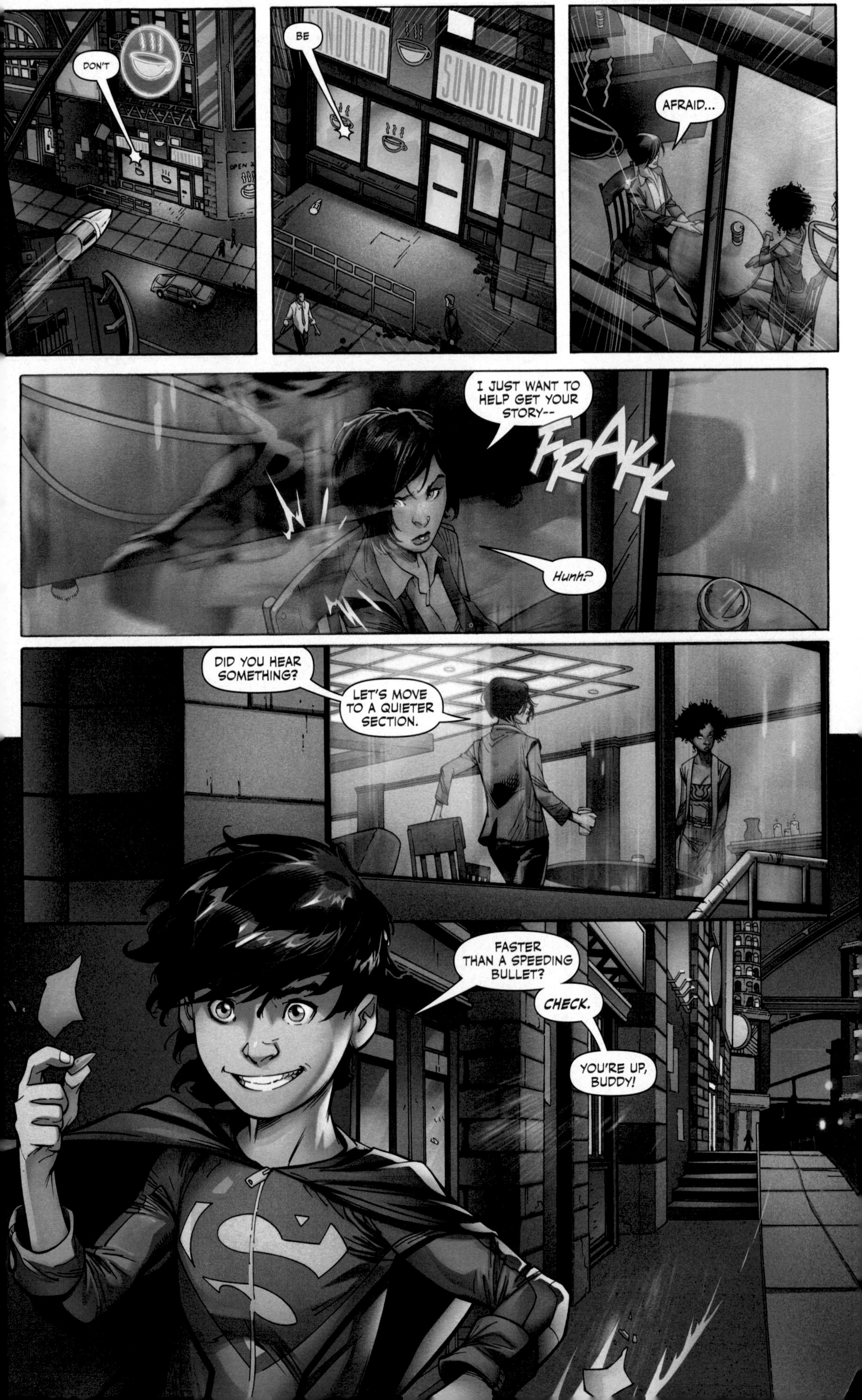
DON'T
BE
AFRAID...
I JUST WANT TO HELP GET YOUR STORY--
FRAKK
Hunh?
DID YOU HEAR SOMETHING?
LET'S MOVE TO A QUIETER SECTION.
FASTER THAN A SPEEDING BULLET?
CHECK.
YOU'RE UP, BUDDY!

Hmm?

BZZT

SOMETHING OR SOMEONE DEFLECTED MY SHOT.

FIND IT.

KILL IT.

AND TELL ME--

--IF YOU SEE--

--MY SON--

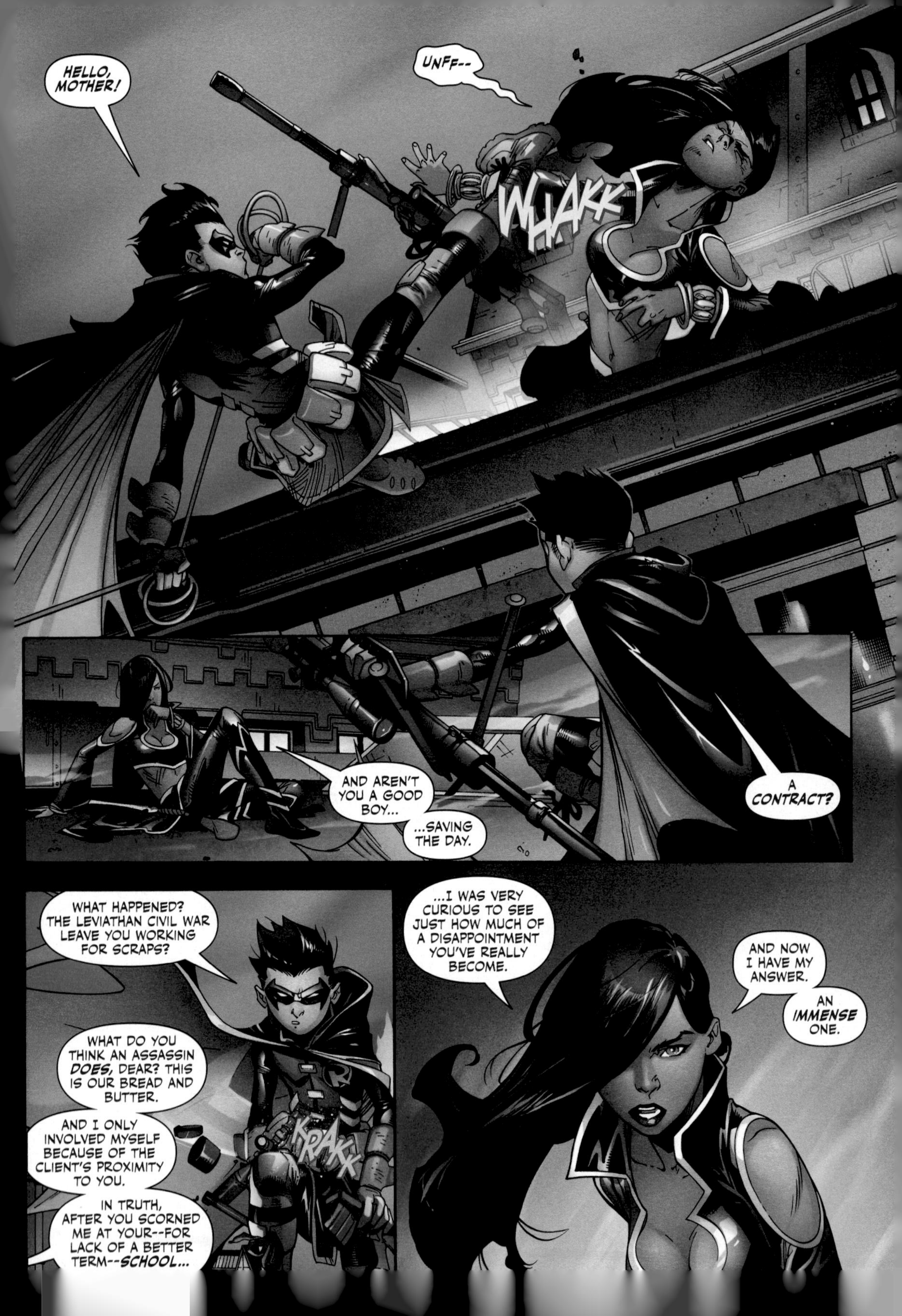
HELLO, MOTHER!
UNFF--
WHAKK
AND AREN'T YOU A GOOD BOY...
...SAVING THE DAY.
A CONTRACT?
WHAT HAPPENED? THE LEVIATHAN CIVIL WAR LEAVE YOU WORKING FOR SCRAPS?
WHAT DO YOU THINK AN ASSASSIN DOES, DEAR? THIS IS OUR BREAD AND BUTTER.
AND I ONLY INVOLVED MYSELF BECAUSE OF THE CLIENT'S PROXIMITY TO YOU.
IN TRUTH, AFTER YOU SCORNED ME AT YOUR--FOR LACK OF A BETTER TERM--SCHOOL...
KRAKK
...I WAS VERY CURIOUS TO SEE JUST HOW MUCH OF A DISAPPOINTMENT YOU'VE REALLY BECOME.
AND NOW I HAVE MY ANSWER.
AN IMMENSE ONE.

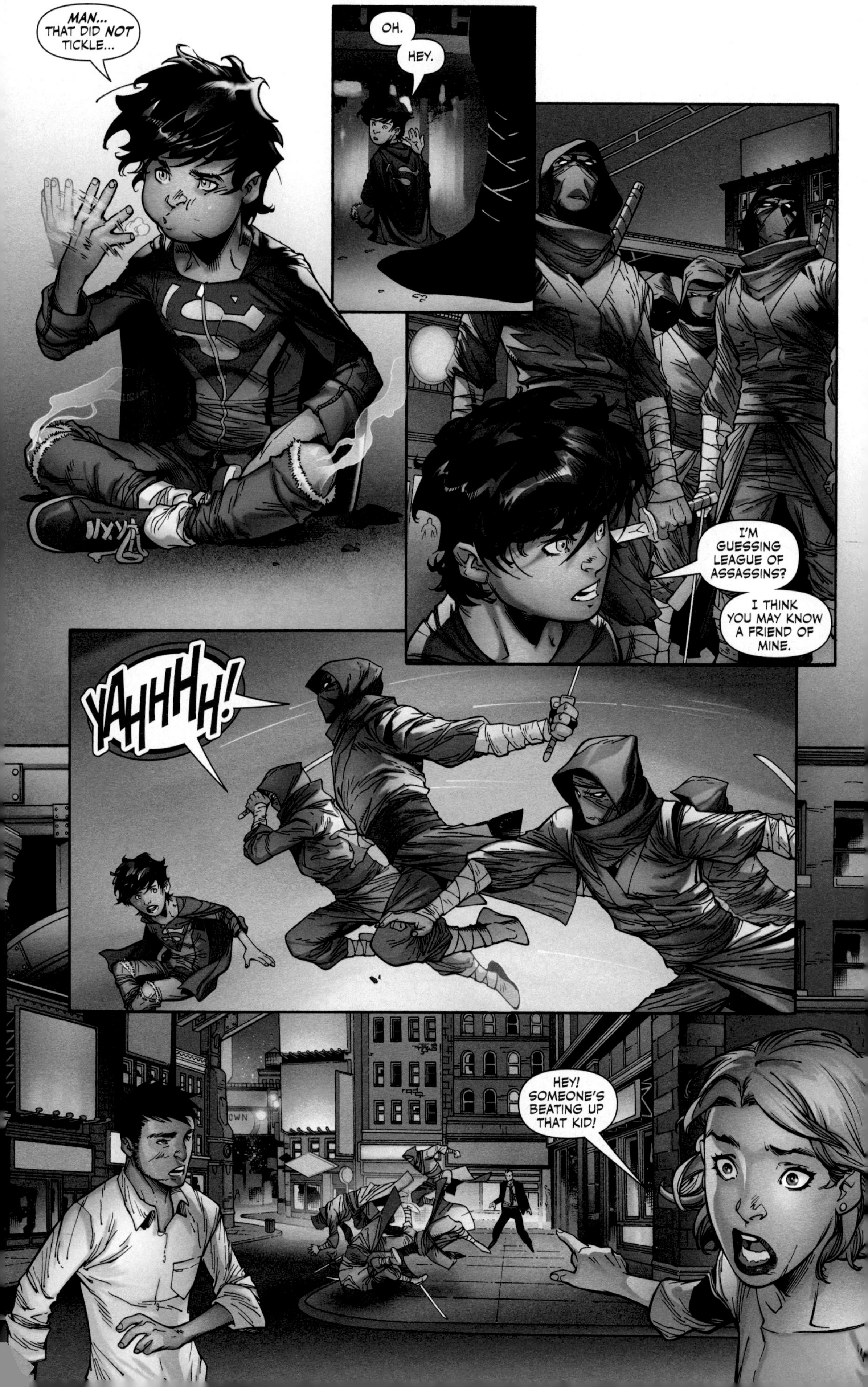
MAN... THAT DID NOT TICKLE...
OH.
HEY.
I'M GUESSING LEAGUE OF ASSASSINS?
I THINK YOU MAY KNOW A FRIEND OF MINE.
YAHHHH!
HEY! SOMEONE'S BEATING UP THAT KID!

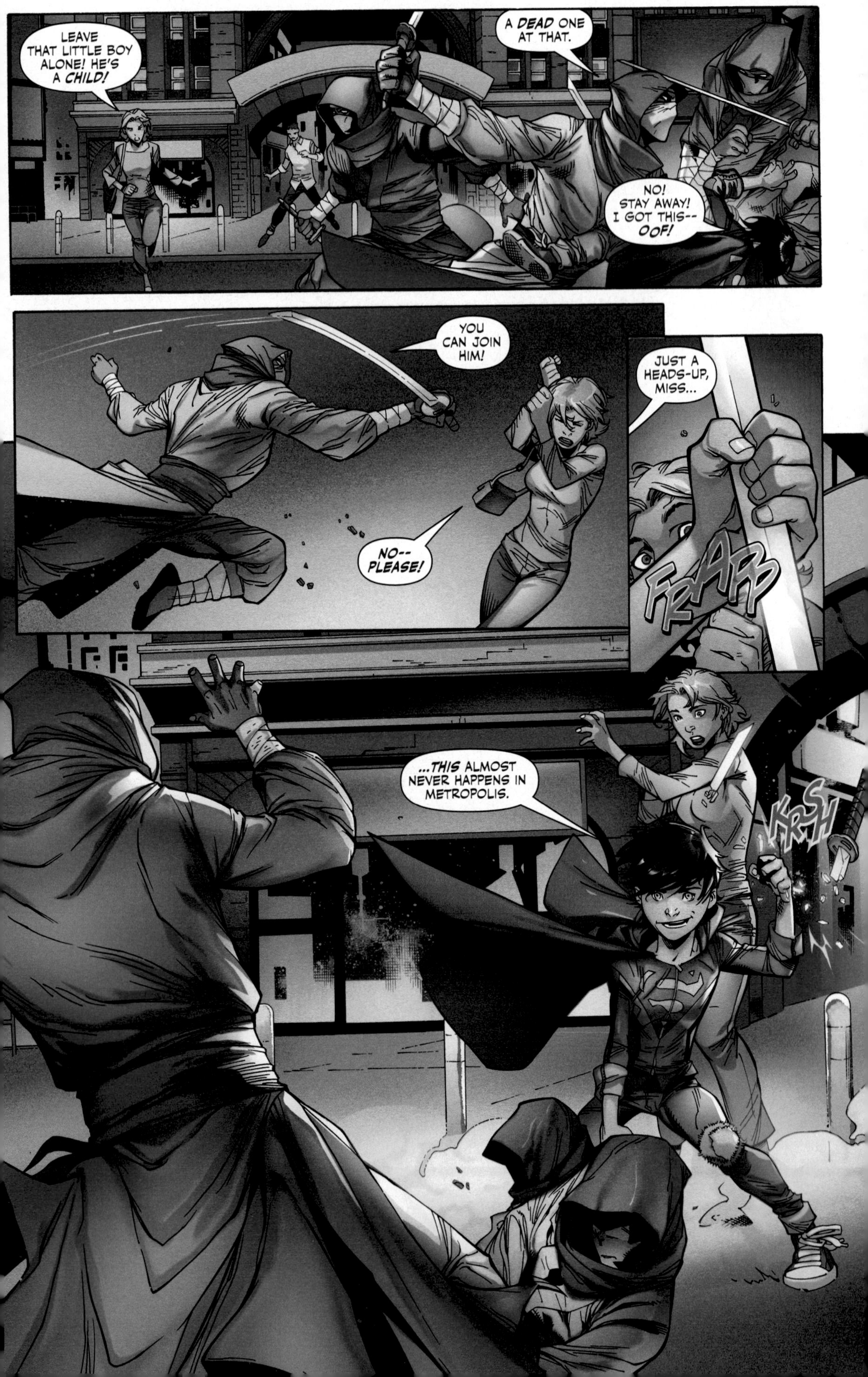
LEAVE THAT LITTLE BOY ALONE! HE'S A CHILD!
A DEAD ONE AT THAT.
NO! STAY AWAY! I GOT THIS-- OOF!
YOU CAN JOIN HIM!
NO-- PLEASE!
JUST A HEADS-UP, MISS...
FRAPP
...THIS ALMOST NEVER HAPPENS IN METROPOLIS.
KRSH

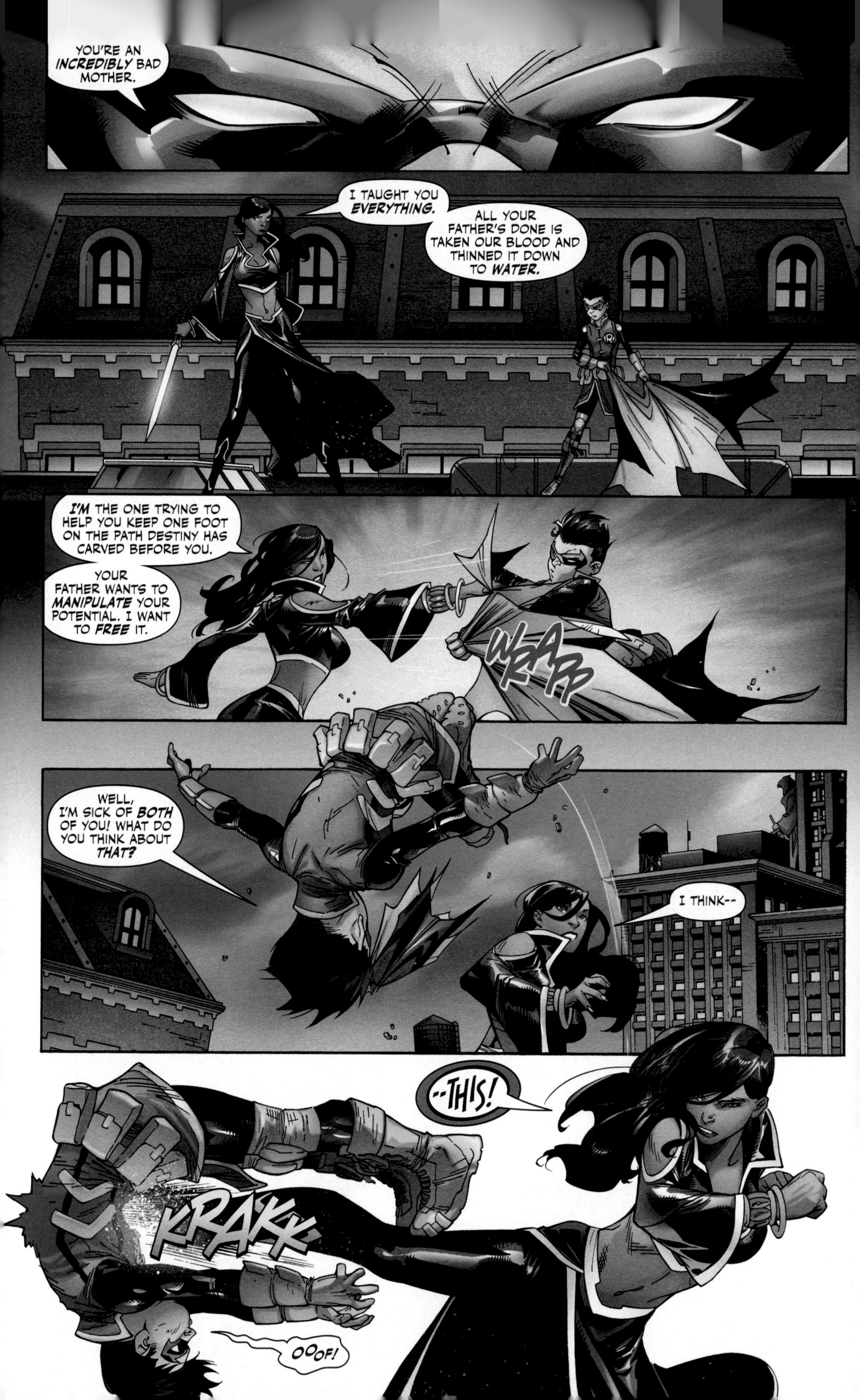
YOU'RE AN INCREDIBLY BAD MOTHER.
I TAUGHT YOU EVERYTHING.
ALL YOUR FATHER'S DONE IS TAKEN OUR BLOOD AND THINNED IT DOWN TO WATER.
I'M THE ONE TRYING TO HELP YOU KEEP ONE FOOT ON THE PATH DESTINY HAS CARVED BEFORE YOU.
YOUR FATHER WANTS TO MANIPULATE YOUR POTENTIAL. I WANT TO FREE IT.
WRAPP
WELL, I'M SICK OF BOTH OF YOU! WHAT DO YOU THINK ABOUT THAT?
I THINK--
--THIS!
KRAKK
OOOF!

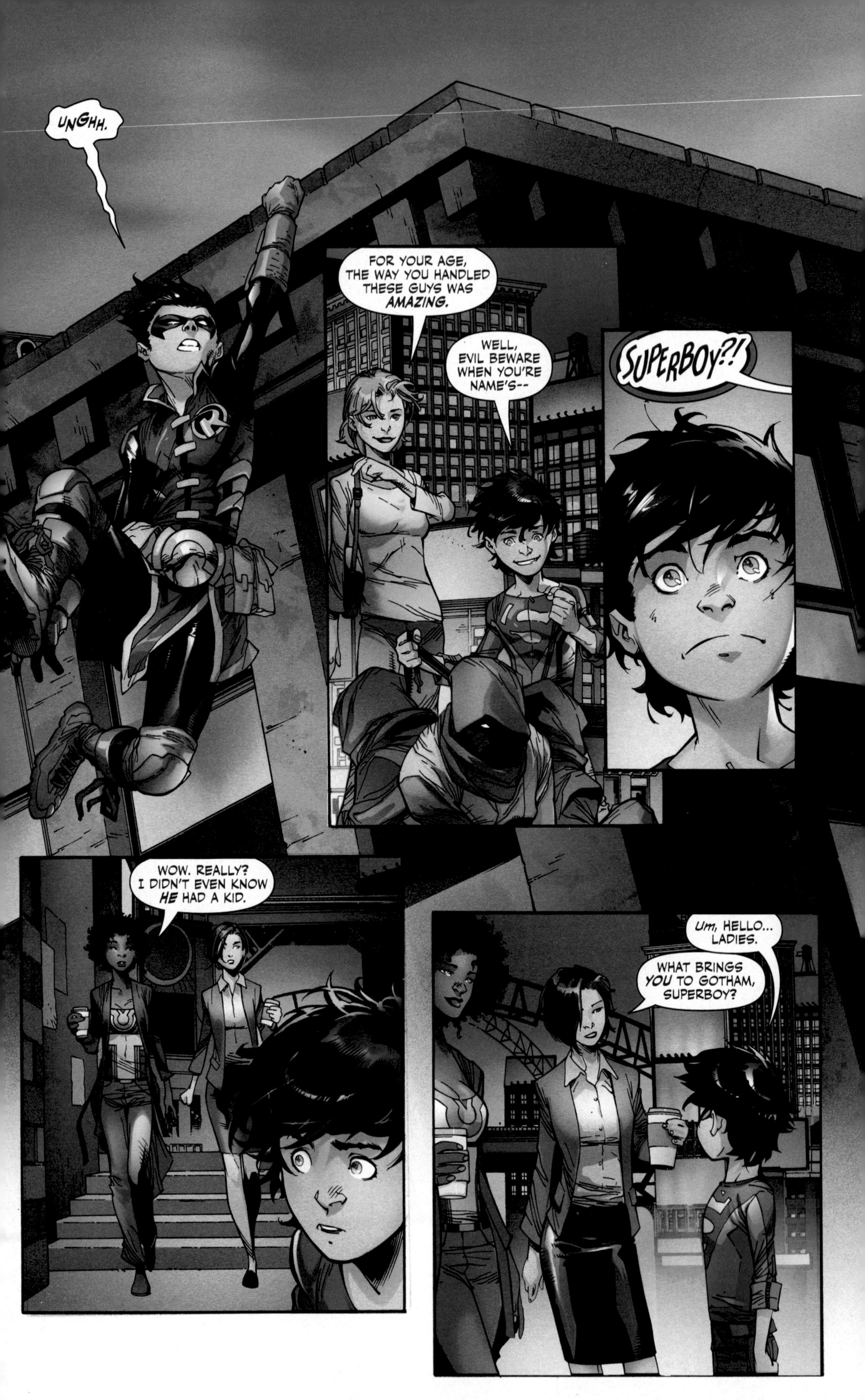
UNGHH.
FOR YOUR AGE, THE WAY YOU HANDLED THESE GUYS WAS *AMAZING.*
WELL, EVIL BEWARE WHEN YOU'RE NAME'S--
SUPERBOY?!
WOW. REALLY? I DIDN'T EVEN KNOW *HE* HAD A KID.
Um, HELLO... LADIES.
WHAT BRINGS *YOU* TO GOTHAM, SUPERBOY?

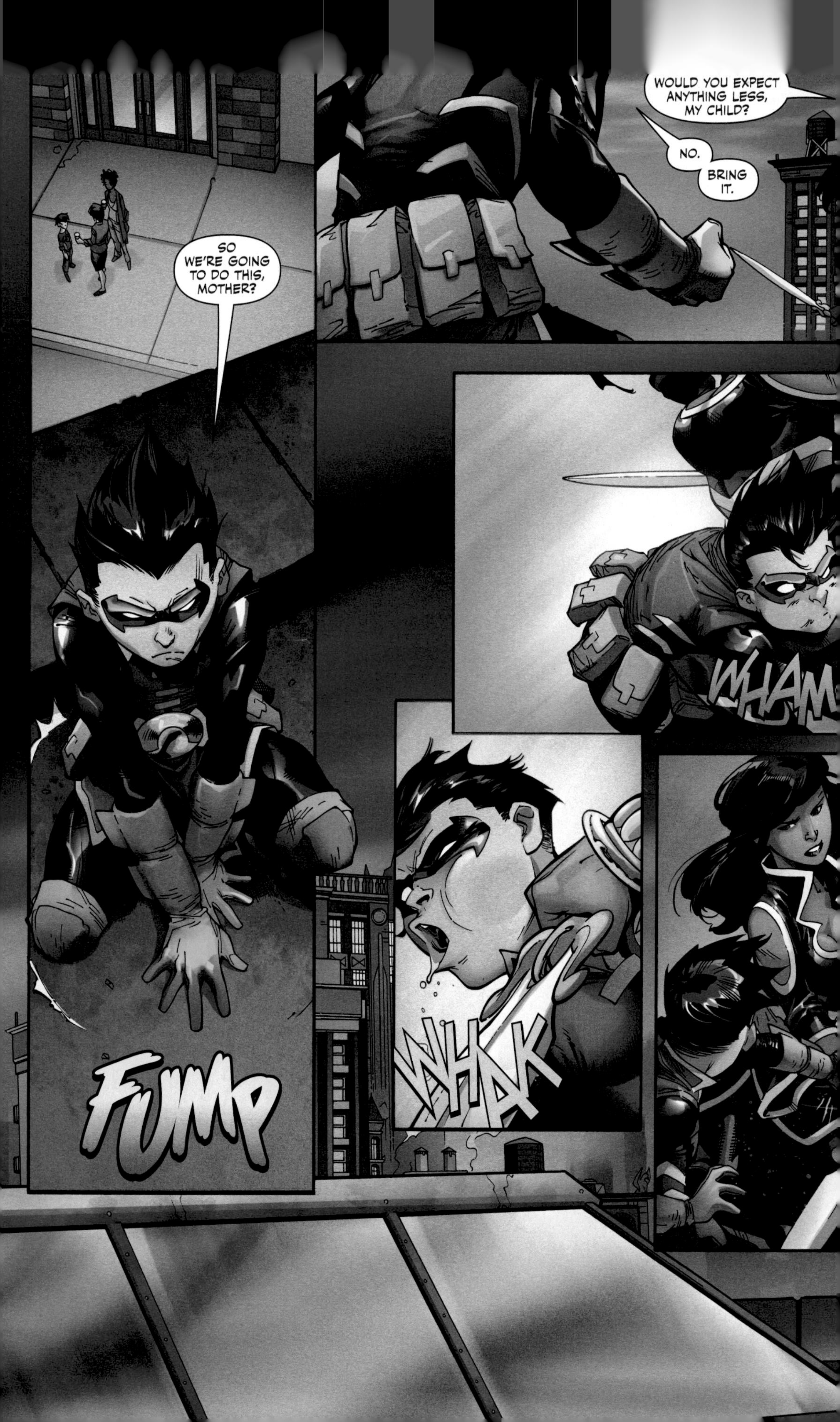
SO WE'RE GOING TO DO THIS, MOTHER?
WOULD YOU EXPECT ANYTHING LESS, MY CHILD?
NO.
BRING IT.
FUMP
WHAM
WHAK

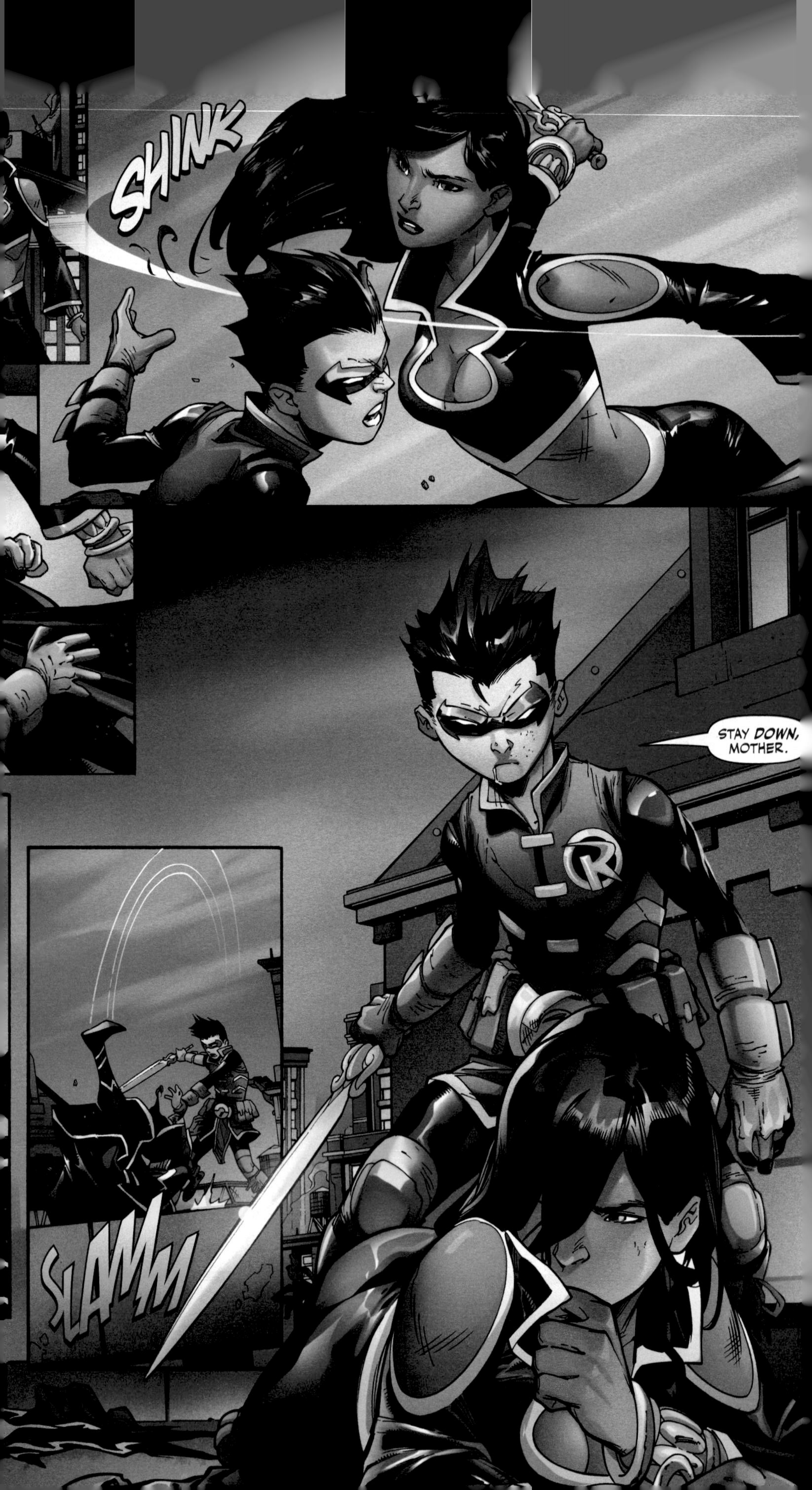
SHINK
SLAMM
STAY DOWN, MOTHER.

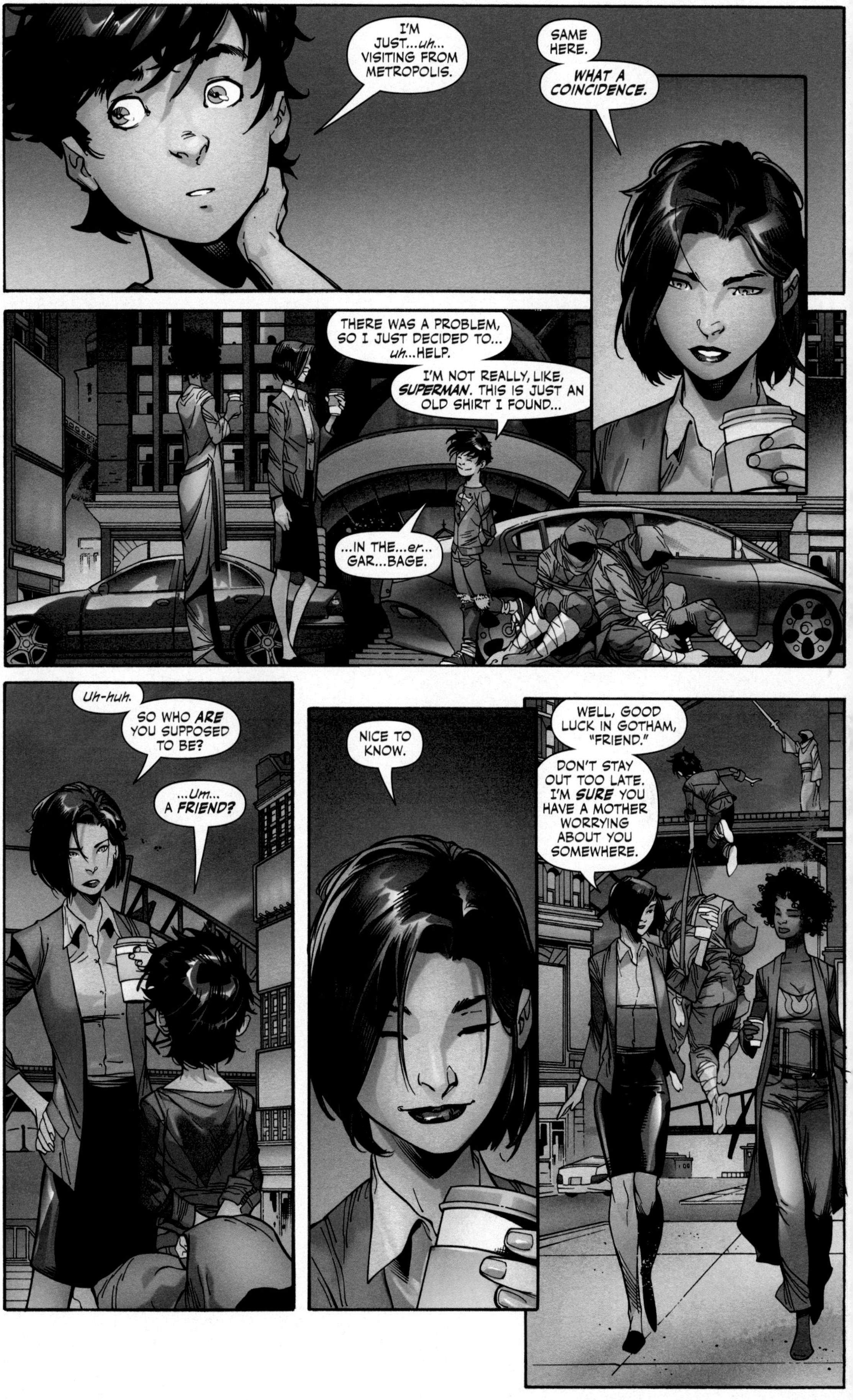
I'M JUST...*uh*... VISITING FROM METROPOLIS.
SAME HERE.
WHAT A COINCIDENCE.
THERE WAS A PROBLEM, SO I JUST DECIDED TO... *uh*...HELP.
I'M NOT REALLY, LIKE, *SUPERMAN*. THIS IS JUST AN OLD SHIRT I FOUND...
...IN THE...*er*... GAR...BAGE.
Uh-huh.
SO WHO *ARE* YOU SUPPOSED TO BE?
...*Um*... A *FRIEND?*
NICE TO KNOW.
WELL, GOOD LUCK IN GOTHAM, "FRIEND."
DON'T STAY OUT TOO LATE. I'M *SURE* YOU HAVE A MOTHER WORRYING ABOUT YOU SOMEWHERE.

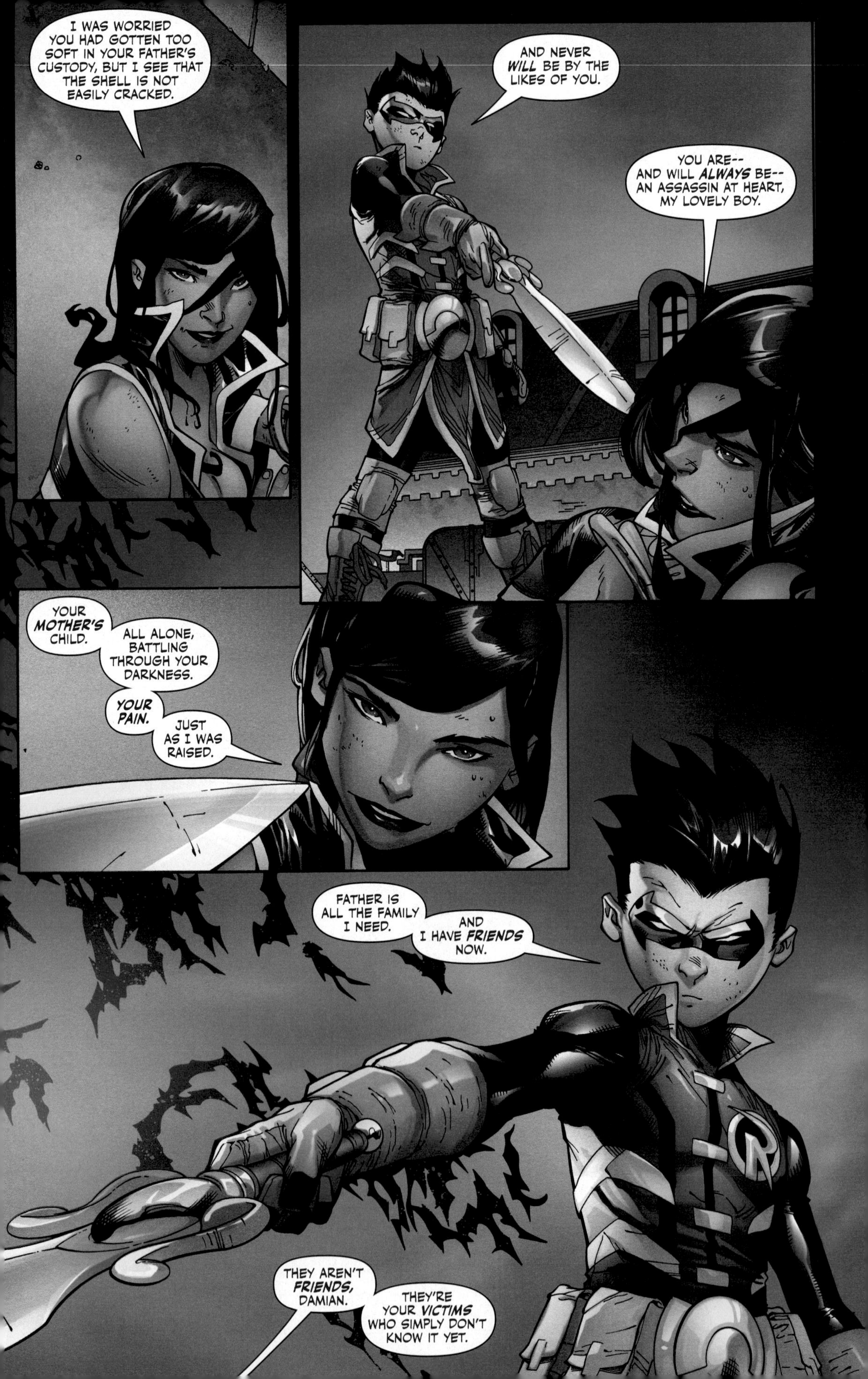
I WAS WORRIED YOU HAD GOTTEN TOO SOFT IN YOUR FATHER'S CUSTODY, BUT I SEE THAT THE SHELL IS NOT EASILY CRACKED.
AND NEVER WILL BE BY THE LIKES OF YOU.
YOU ARE-- AND WILL ALWAYS BE-- AN ASSASSIN AT HEART, MY LOVELY BOY.
YOUR MOTHER'S CHILD.
ALL ALONE, BATTLING THROUGH YOUR DARKNESS.
YOUR PAIN.
JUST AS I WAS RAISED.
FATHER IS ALL THE FAMILY I NEED.
AND I HAVE FRIENDS NOW.
THEY AREN'T FRIENDS, DAMIAN.
THEY'RE YOUR VICTIMS WHO SIMPLY DON'T KNOW IT YET.

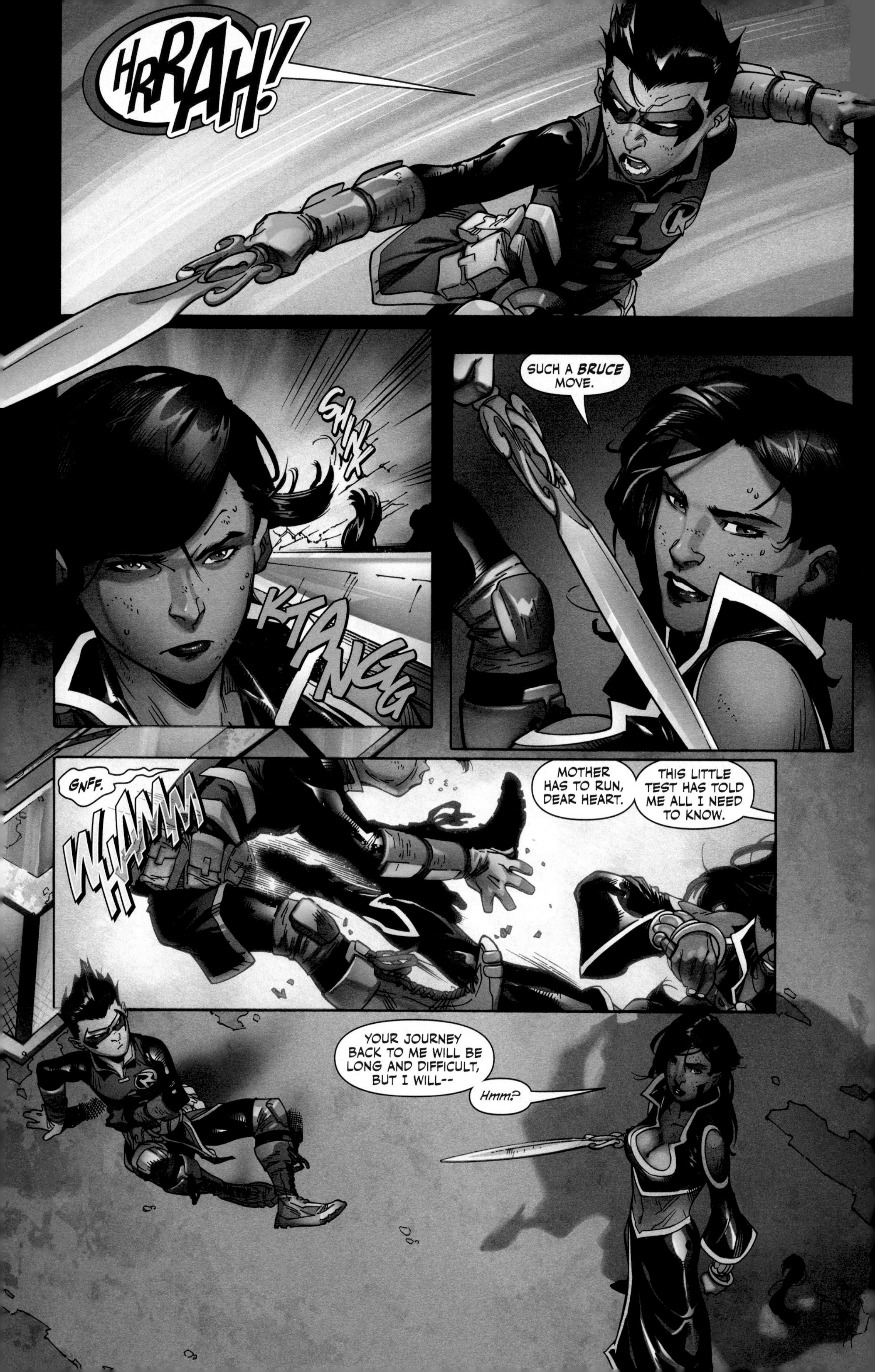
HRRAH!
SHINK
KTANGG
SUCH A BRUCE MOVE.
GNFF.
WHAMM
MOTHER HAS TO RUN, DEAR HEART.
THIS LITTLE TEST HAS TOLD ME ALL I NEED TO KNOW.
YOUR JOURNEY BACK TO ME WILL BE LONG AND DIFFICULT, BUT I WILL--
Hmm?

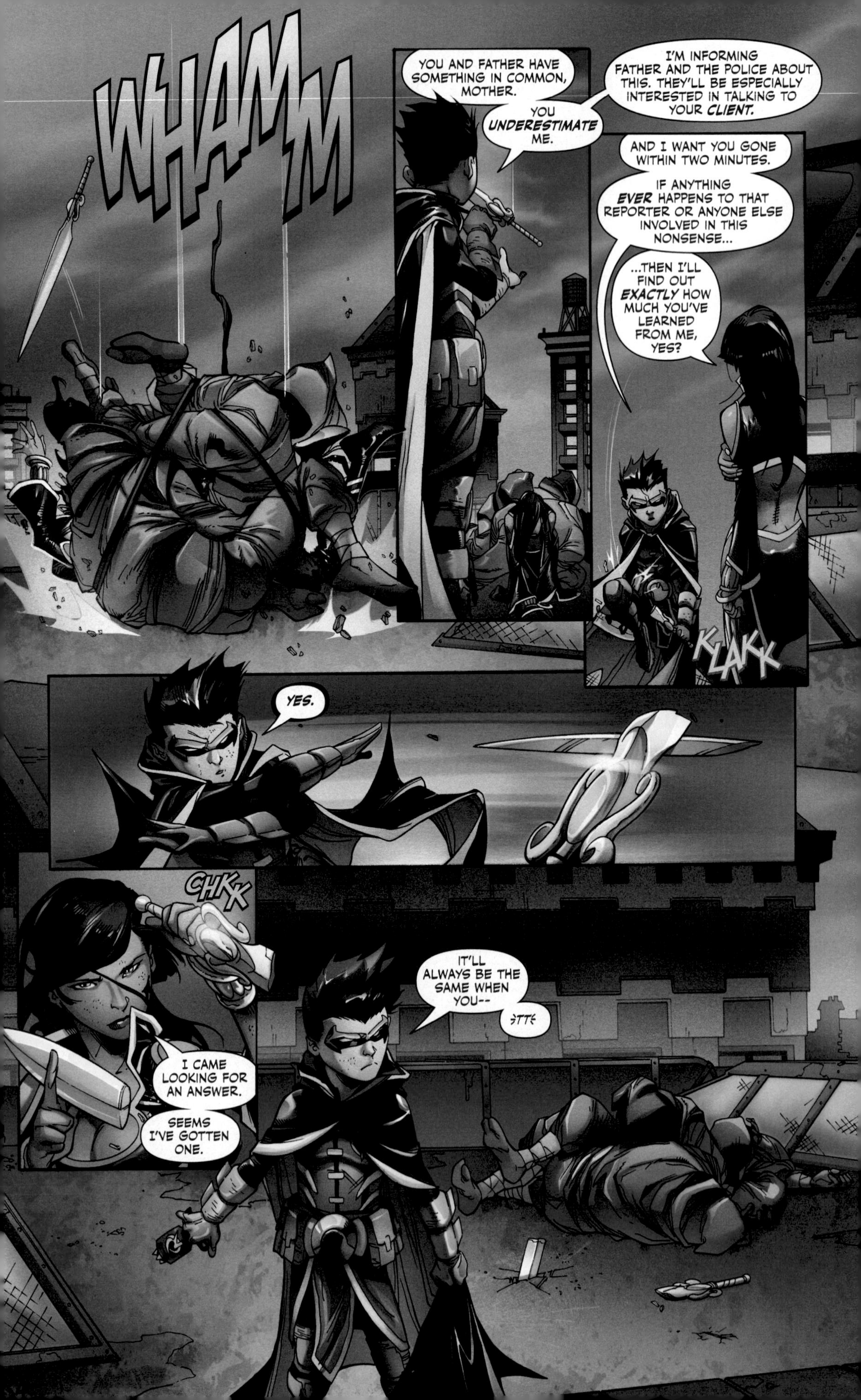
WHAMM
YOU AND FATHER HAVE SOMETHING IN COMMON, MOTHER.
YOU UNDERESTIMATE ME.
I'M INFORMING FATHER AND THE POLICE ABOUT THIS. THEY'LL BE ESPECIALLY INTERESTED IN TALKING TO YOUR CLIENT.
AND I WANT YOU GONE WITHIN TWO MINUTES.
IF ANYTHING EVER HAPPENS TO THAT REPORTER OR ANYONE ELSE INVOLVED IN THIS NONSENSE...
...THEN I'LL FIND OUT EXACTLY HOW MUCH YOU'VE LEARNED FROM ME, YES?
KLAKK
YES.
CHKK
IT'LL ALWAYS BE THE SAME WHEN YOU--
TT
I CAME LOOKING FOR AN ANSWER.
SEEMS I'VE GOTTEN ONE.

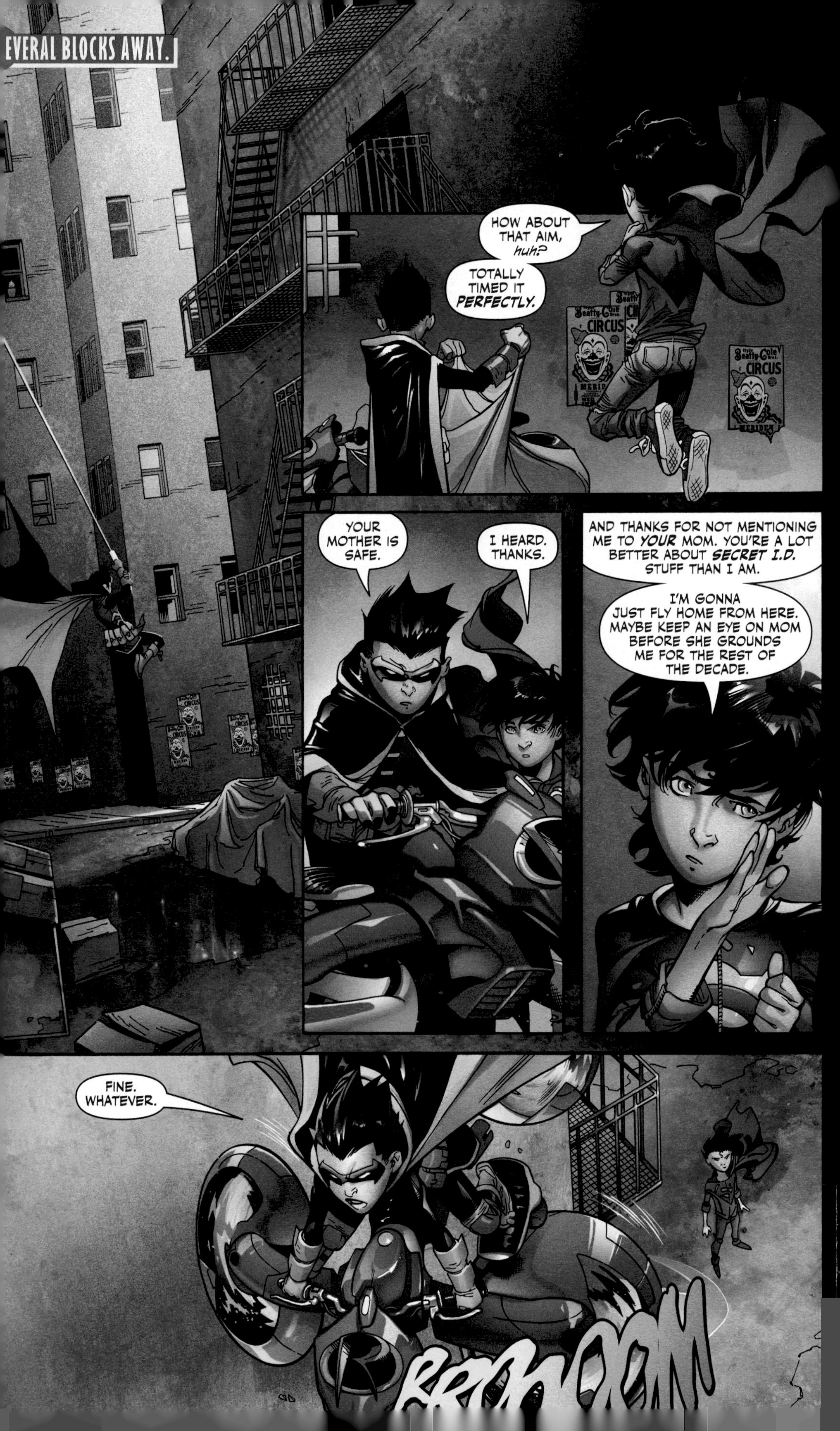
EVERAL BLOCKS AWAY.
HOW ABOUT THAT AIM, *huh?*
TOTALLY TIMED IT *PERFECTLY.*
YOUR MOTHER IS SAFE.
I HEARD. THANKS.
AND THANKS FOR NOT MENTIONING ME TO *YOUR* MOM. YOU'RE A LOT BETTER ABOUT *SECRET I.D.* STUFF THAN I AM.
I'M GONNA JUST FLY HOME FROM HERE. MAYBE KEEP AN EYE ON MOM BEFORE SHE GROUNDS ME FOR THE REST OF THE DECADE.
FINE. WHATEVER.

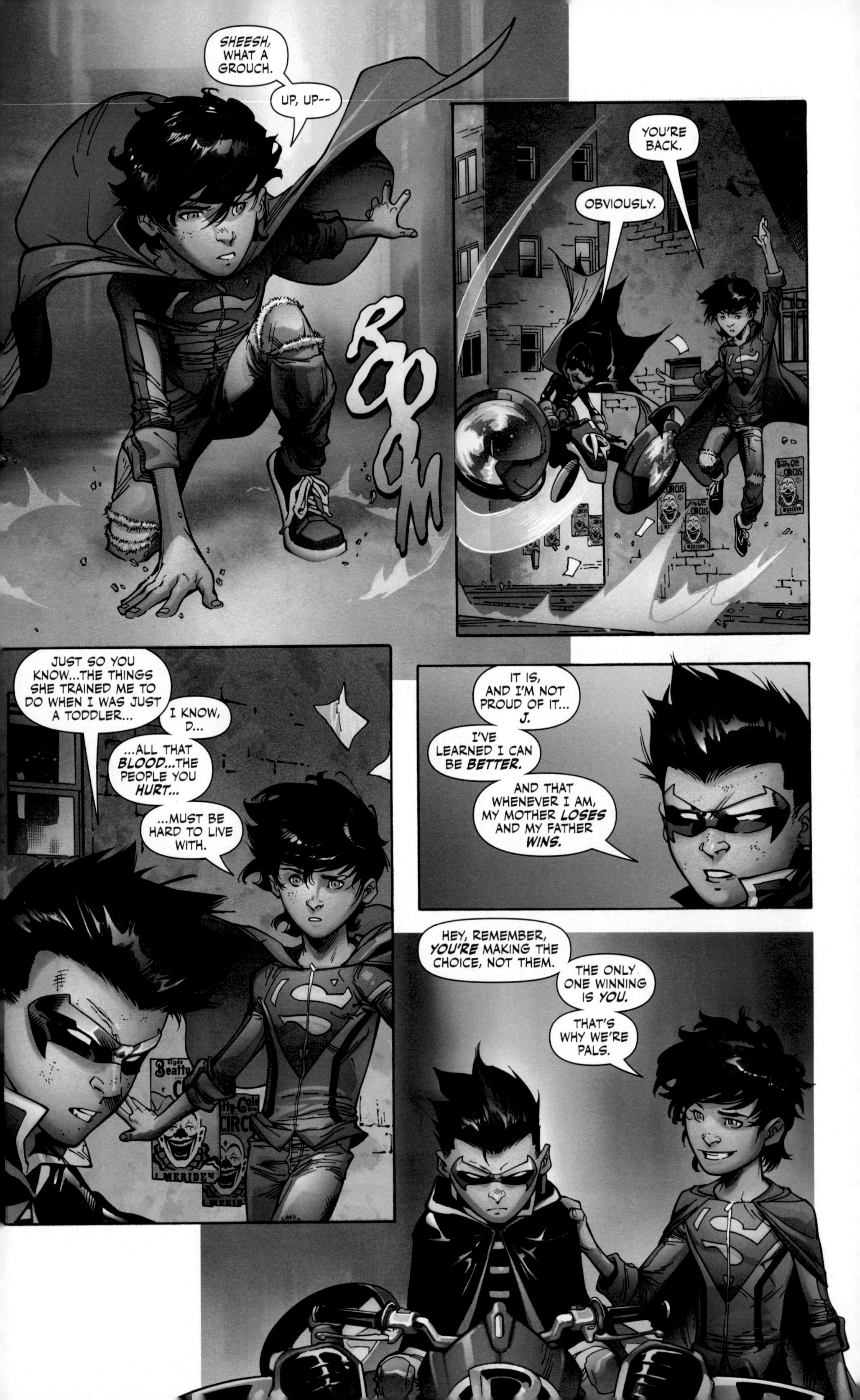
SHEESH, WHAT A GROUCH.
UP, UP--
ROOOM
YOU'RE BACK.
OBVIOUSLY.
JUST SO YOU KNOW...THE THINGS SHE TRAINED ME TO DO WHEN I WAS JUST A TODDLER...
I KNOW, D...
...ALL THAT BLOOD...THE PEOPLE YOU HURT...
...MUST BE HARD TO LIVE WITH.
IT IS, AND I'M NOT PROUD OF IT... J.
I'VE LEARNED I CAN BE BETTER.
AND THAT WHENEVER I AM, MY MOTHER LOSES AND MY FATHER WINS.
HEY, REMEMBER, YOU'RE MAKING THE CHOICE, NOT THEM.
THE ONLY ONE WINNING IS YOU.
THAT'S WHY WE'RE PALS.

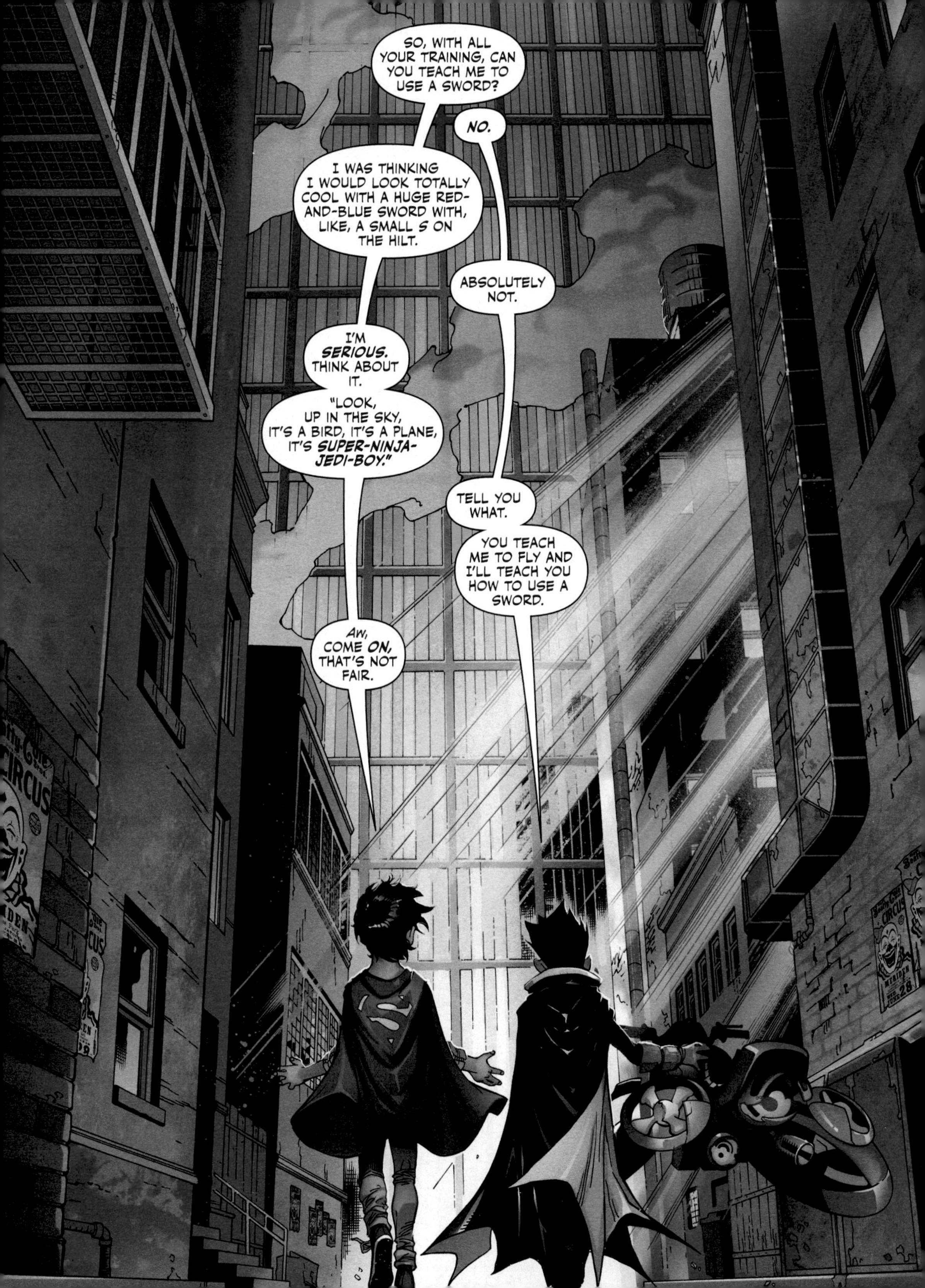
SO, WITH ALL YOUR TRAINING, CAN YOU TEACH ME TO USE A SWORD?
NO.
I WAS THINKING I WOULD LOOK TOTALLY COOL WITH A HUGE RED-AND-BLUE SWORD WITH, LIKE, A SMALL S ON THE HILT.
ABSOLUTELY NOT.
I'M SERIOUS. THINK ABOUT IT.
"LOOK, UP IN THE SKY, IT'S A BIRD, IT'S A PLANE, IT'S SUPER-NINJA-JEDI-BOY."
TELL YOU WHAT.
YOU TEACH ME TO FLY AND I'LL TEACH YOU HOW TO USE A SWORD.
AW, COME ON, THAT'S NOT FAIR.
CIRCUS

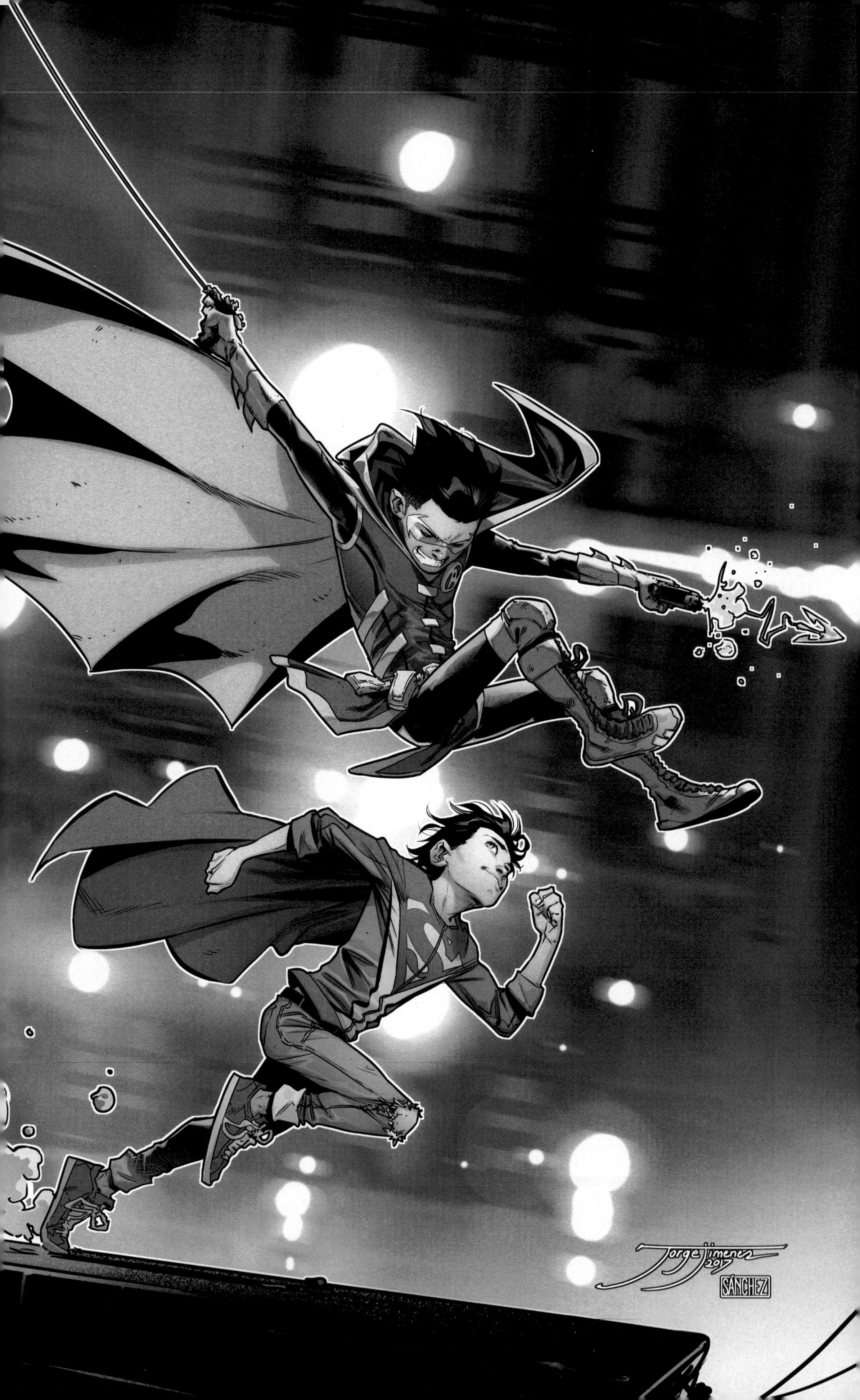
Jorge Jimenez 2017
SÁNCHEZ

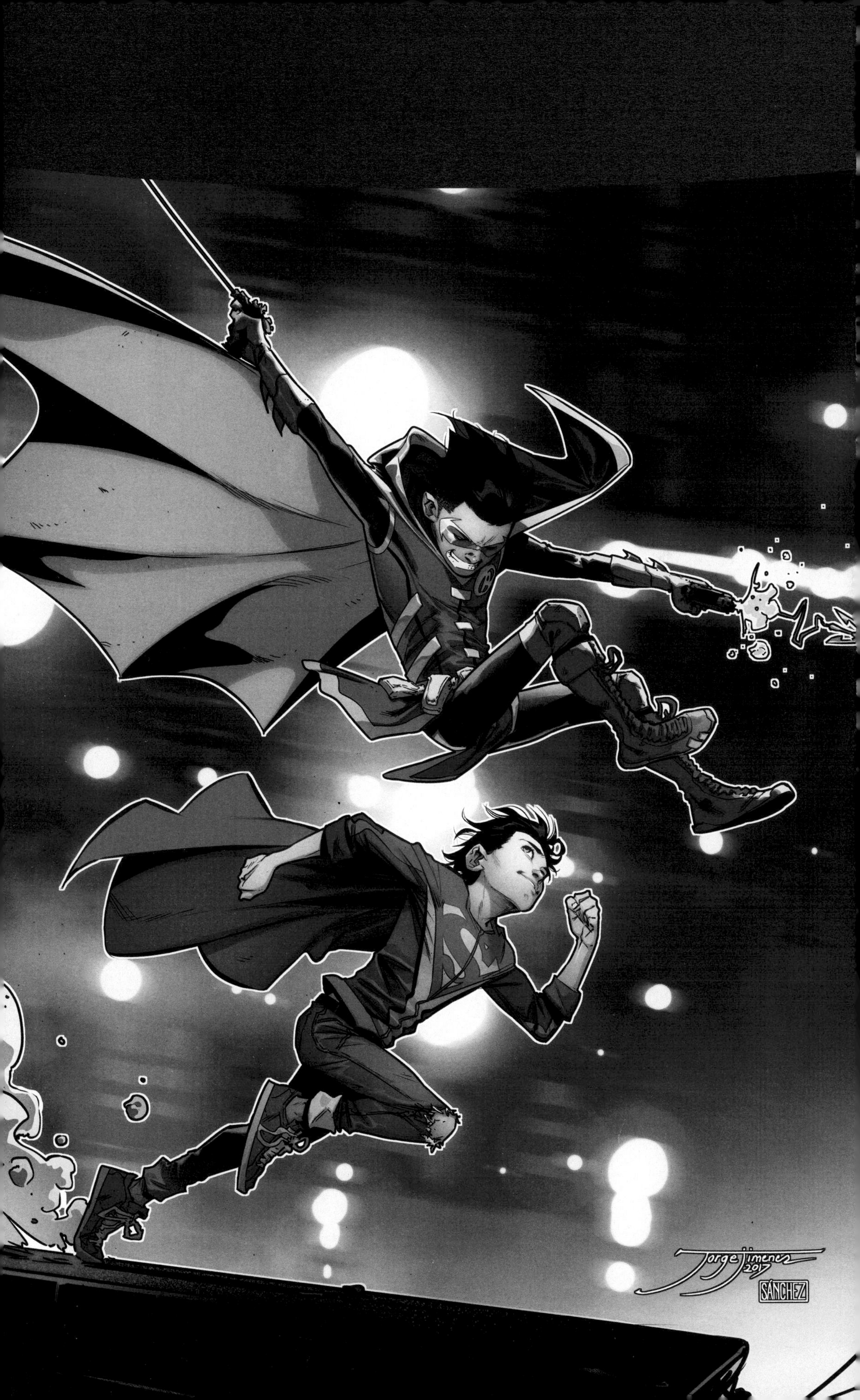
Jorge Jimenez 2017
SÁNCHEZ

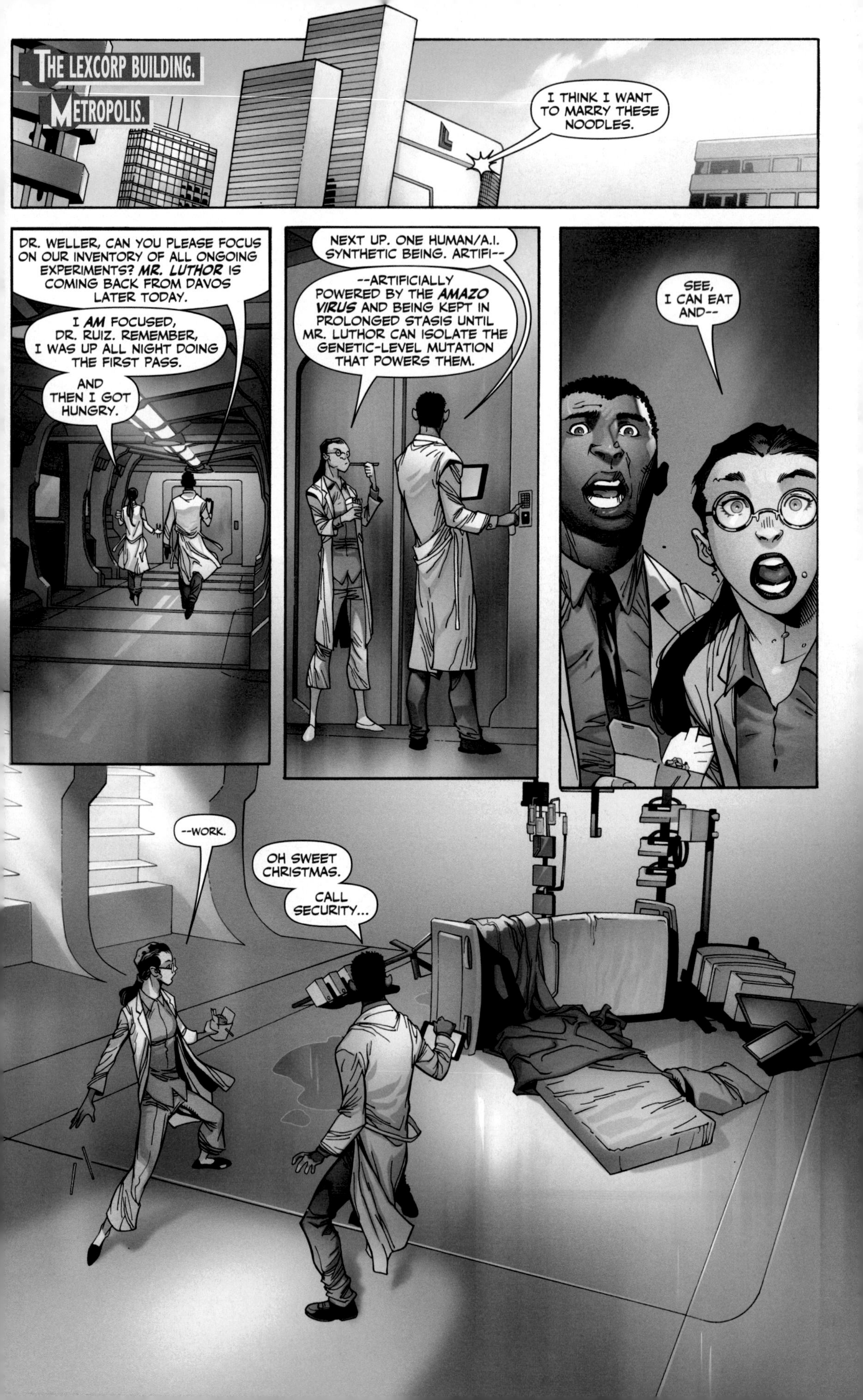
THE LEXCORP BUILDING.
METROPOLIS.
I THINK I WANT TO MARRY THESE NOODLES.
DR. WELLER, CAN YOU PLEASE FOCUS ON OUR INVENTORY OF ALL ONGOING EXPERIMENTS? MR. LUTHOR IS COMING BACK FROM DAVOS LATER TODAY.
I AM FOCUSED, DR. RUIZ. REMEMBER, I WAS UP ALL NIGHT DOING THE FIRST PASS.
AND THEN I GOT HUNGRY.
NEXT UP. ONE HUMAN/A.I. SYNTHETIC BEING. ARTIFI--
--ARTIFICIALLY POWERED BY THE AMAZO VIRUS AND BEING KEPT IN PROLONGED STASIS UNTIL MR. LUTHOR CAN ISOLATE THE GENETIC-LEVEL MUTATION THAT POWERS THEM.
SEE, I CAN EAT AND--
--WORK.
OH SWEET CHRISTMAS.
CALL SECURITY...

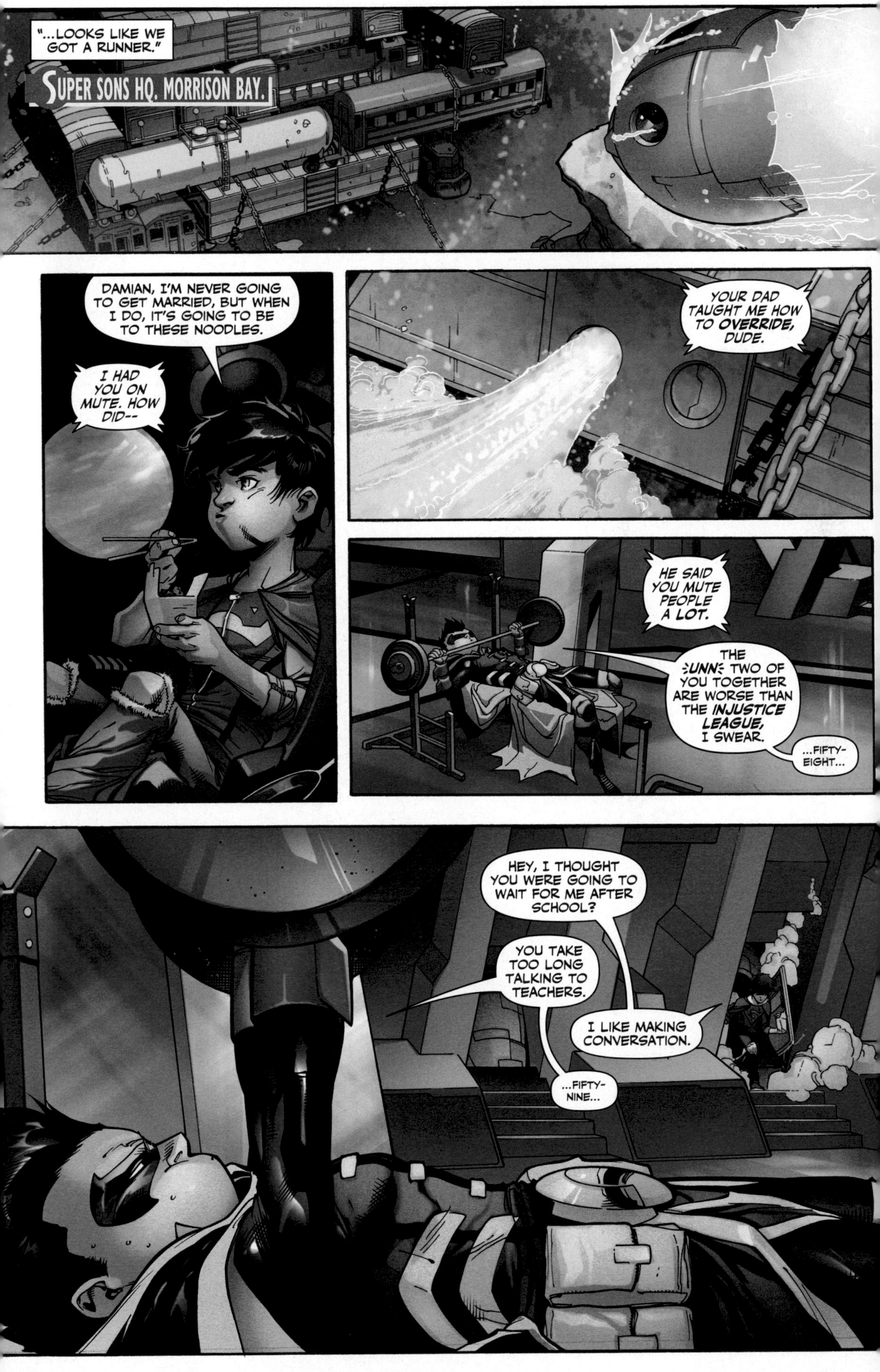
"...LOOKS LIKE WE GOT A RUNNER."
SUPER SONS HQ. MORRISON BAY.
DAMIAN, I'M NEVER GOING TO GET MARRIED, BUT WHEN I DO, IT'S GOING TO BE TO THESE NOODLES.
I HAD YOU ON MUTE. HOW DID--
YOUR DAD TAUGHT ME HOW TO OVERRIDE, DUDE.
HE SAID YOU MUTE PEOPLE A LOT.
THE UNN TWO OF YOU TOGETHER ARE WORSE THAN THE INJUSTICE LEAGUE, I SWEAR.
...FIFTY-EIGHT...
HEY, I THOUGHT YOU WERE GOING TO WAIT FOR ME AFTER SCHOOL?
YOU TAKE TOO LONG TALKING TO TEACHERS.
I LIKE MAKING CONVERSATION.
...FIFTY-NINE...

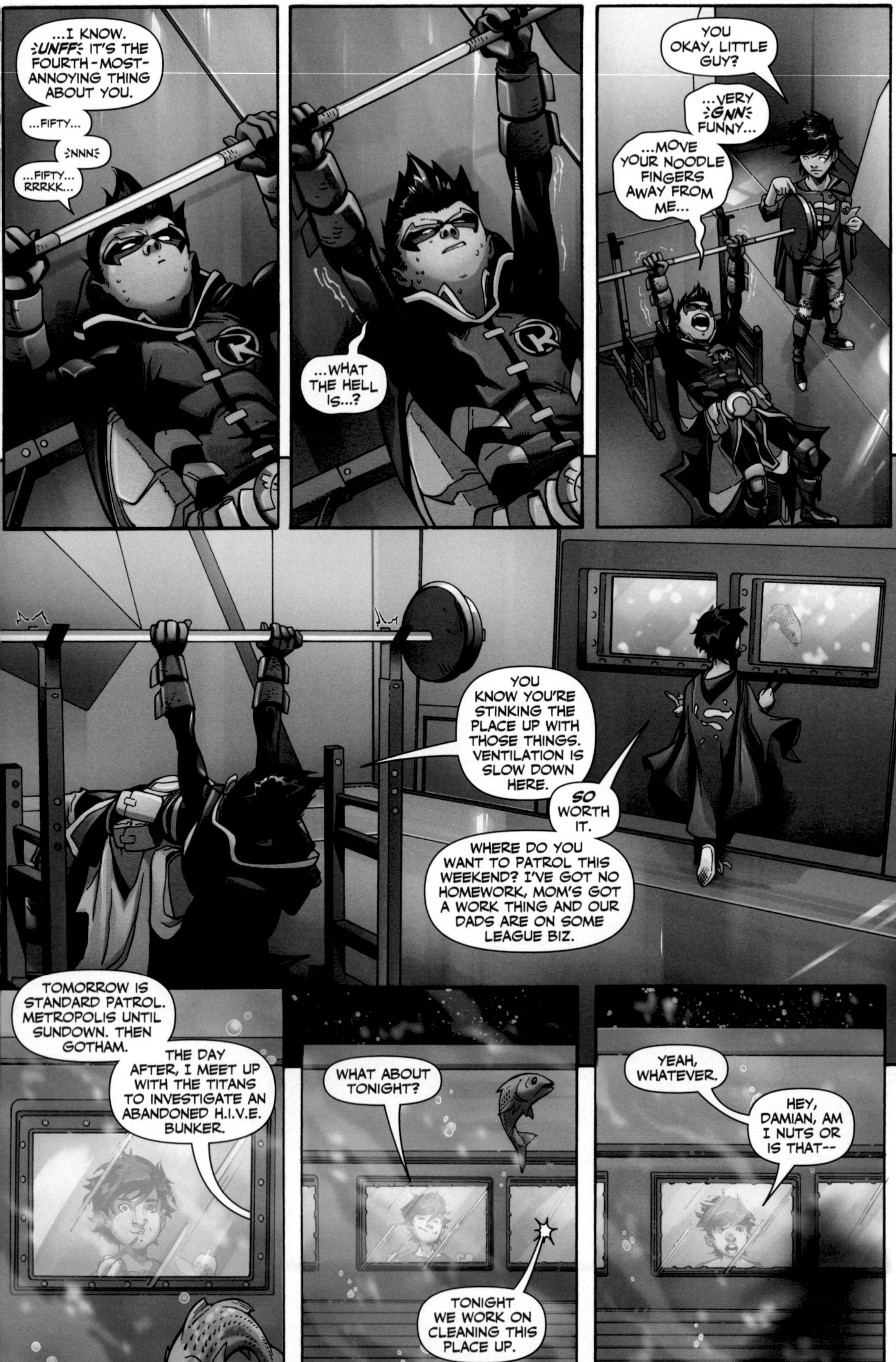

...I KNOW. UNFF IT'S THE FOURTH-MOST-ANNOYING THING ABOUT YOU.
...FIFTY...
NNN
...FIFTY... RRRKK...
...WHAT THE HELL IS...?
YOU OKAY, LITTLE GUY?
...VERY GNN FUNNY...
...MOVE YOUR NOODLE FINGERS AWAY FROM ME...
YOU KNOW YOU'RE STINKING THE PLACE UP WITH THOSE THINGS. VENTILATION IS SLOW DOWN HERE.
SO WORTH IT.
WHERE DO YOU WANT TO PATROL THIS WEEKEND? I'VE GOT NO HOMEWORK, MOM'S GOT A WORK THING AND OUR DADS ARE ON SOME LEAGUE BIZ.
TOMORROW IS STANDARD PATROL. METROPOLIS UNTIL SUNDOWN. THEN GOTHAM.
THE DAY AFTER, I MEET UP WITH THE TITANS TO INVESTIGATE AN ABANDONED H.I.V.E. BUNKER.
WHAT ABOUT TONIGHT?
TONIGHT WE WORK ON CLEANING THIS PLACE UP.
YEAH, WHATEVER.
HEY, DAMIAN, AM I NUTS OR IS THAT--

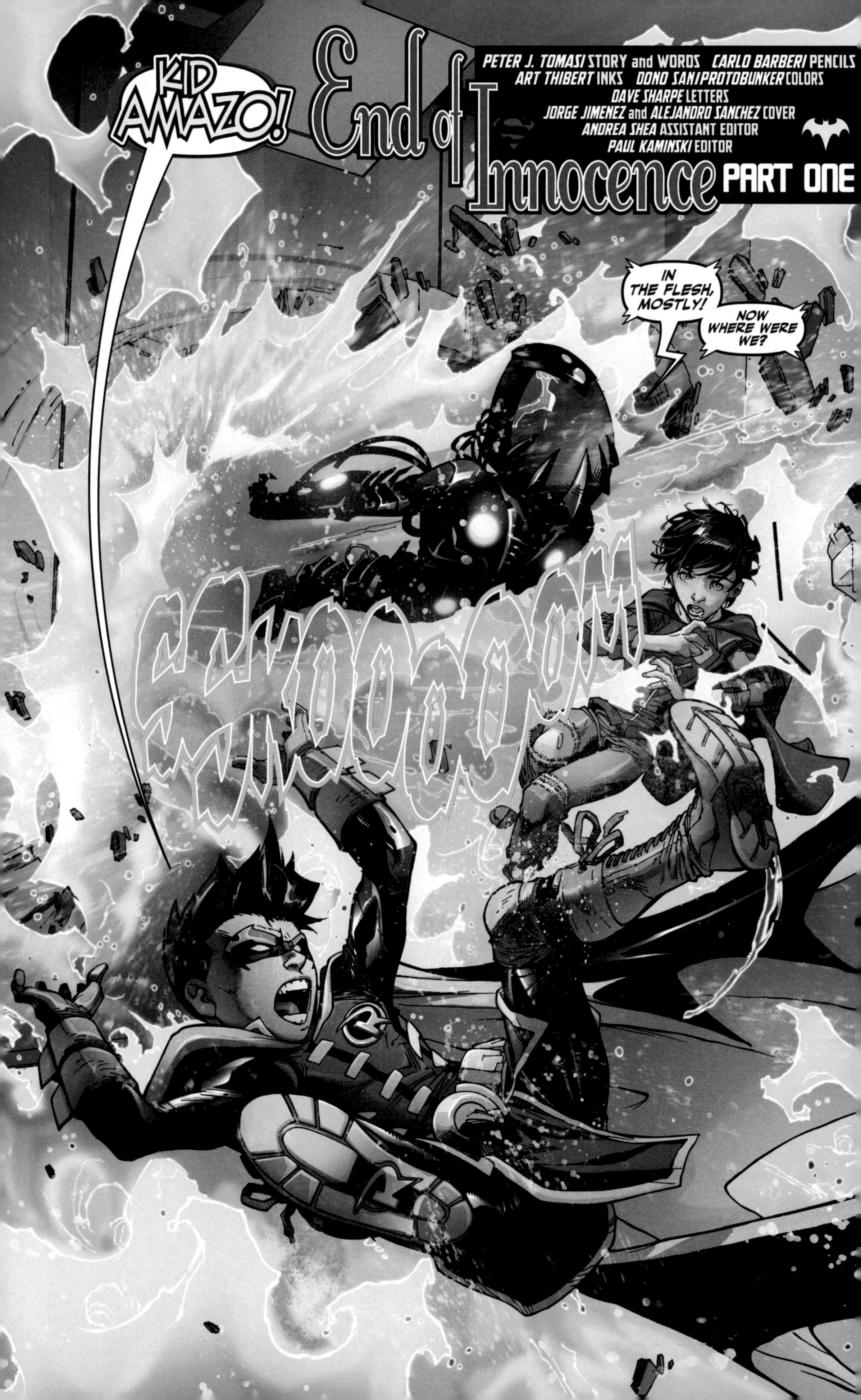
KID AMAZO!
End of Innocence PART ONE
PETER J. TOMASI STORY and WORDS CARLO BARBERI PENCILS
ART THIBERT INKS DONO SANI/PROTOBUNKER COLORS
DAVE SHARPE LETTERS
JORGE JIMENEZ and ALEJANDRO SANCHEZ COVER
ANDREA SHEA ASSISTANT EDITOR
PAUL KAMINSKI EDITOR
IN THE FLESH, MOSTLY!
NOW WHERE WERE WE?
SKWOOOOOOM

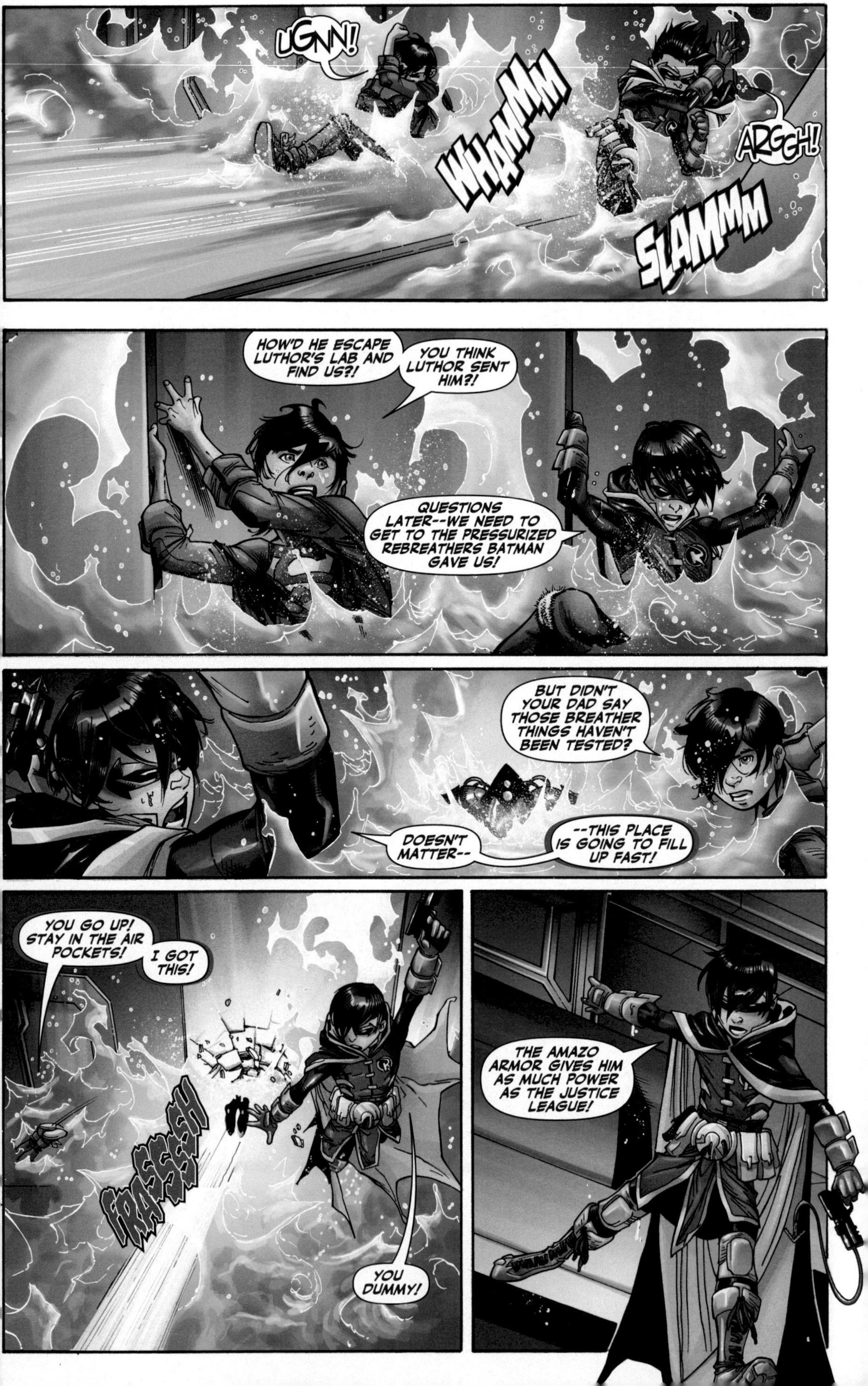
UGNN!
WHAMMM
ARGGH!
SLAMMM
HOW'D HE ESCAPE LUTHOR'S LAB AND FIND US?!
YOU THINK LUTHOR SENT HIM?!
QUESTIONS LATER--WE NEED TO GET TO THE PRESSURIZED REBREATHERS BATMAN GAVE US!
BUT DIDN'T YOUR DAD SAY THOSE BREATHER THINGS HAVEN'T BEEN TESTED?
DOESN'T MATTER--
--THIS PLACE IS GOING TO FILL UP FAST!
YOU GO UP! STAY IN THE AIR POCKETS!
I GOT THIS!
FRASSSH
YOU DUMMY!
THE AMAZO ARMOR GIVES HIM AS MUCH POWER AS THE JUSTICE LEAGUE!

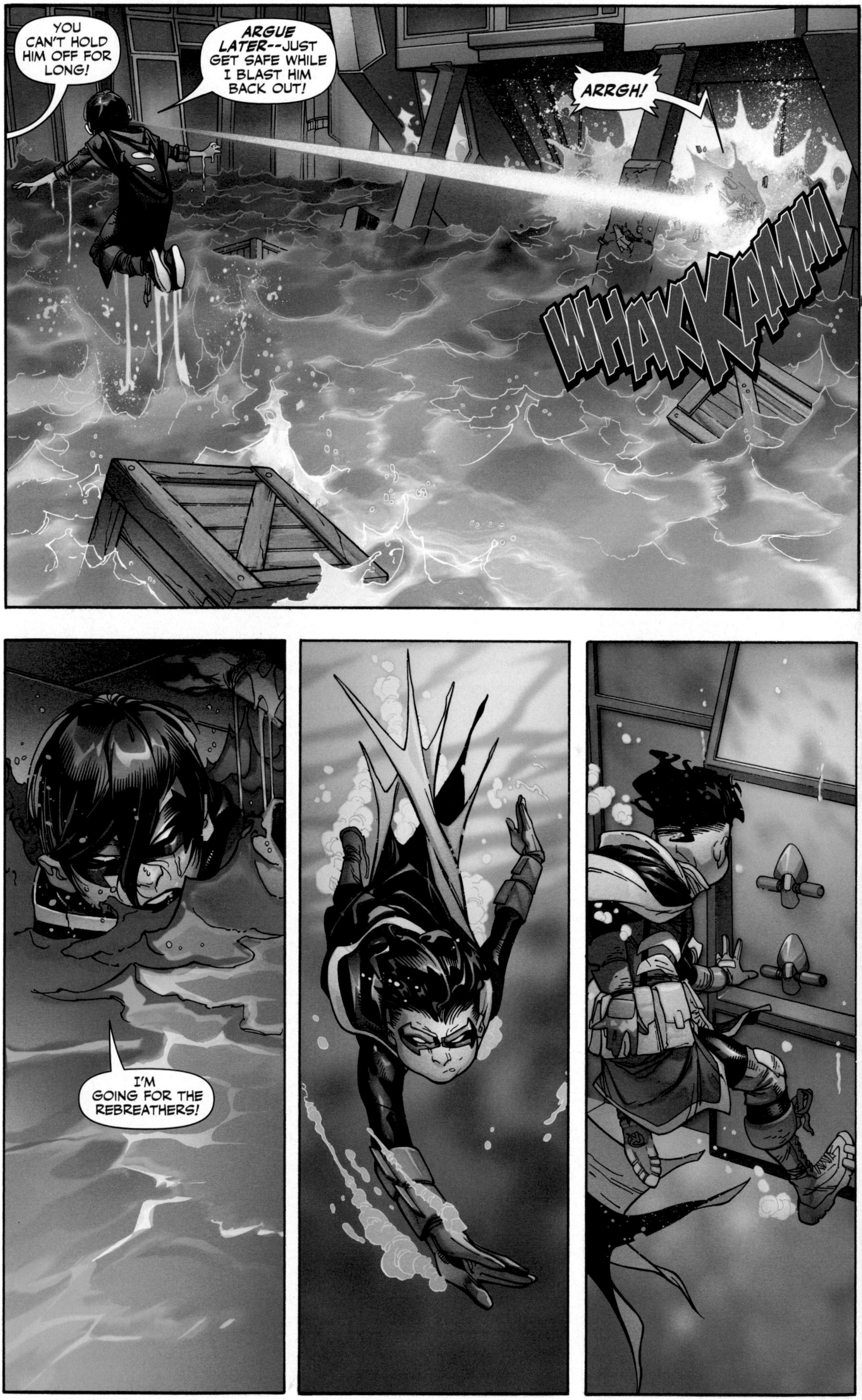
YOU CAN'T HOLD HIM OFF FOR LONG!
ARGUE LATER--JUST GET SAFE WHILE I BLAST HIM BACK OUT!
ARRGH!
WHAKKAMM
I'M GOING FOR THE REBREATHERS!

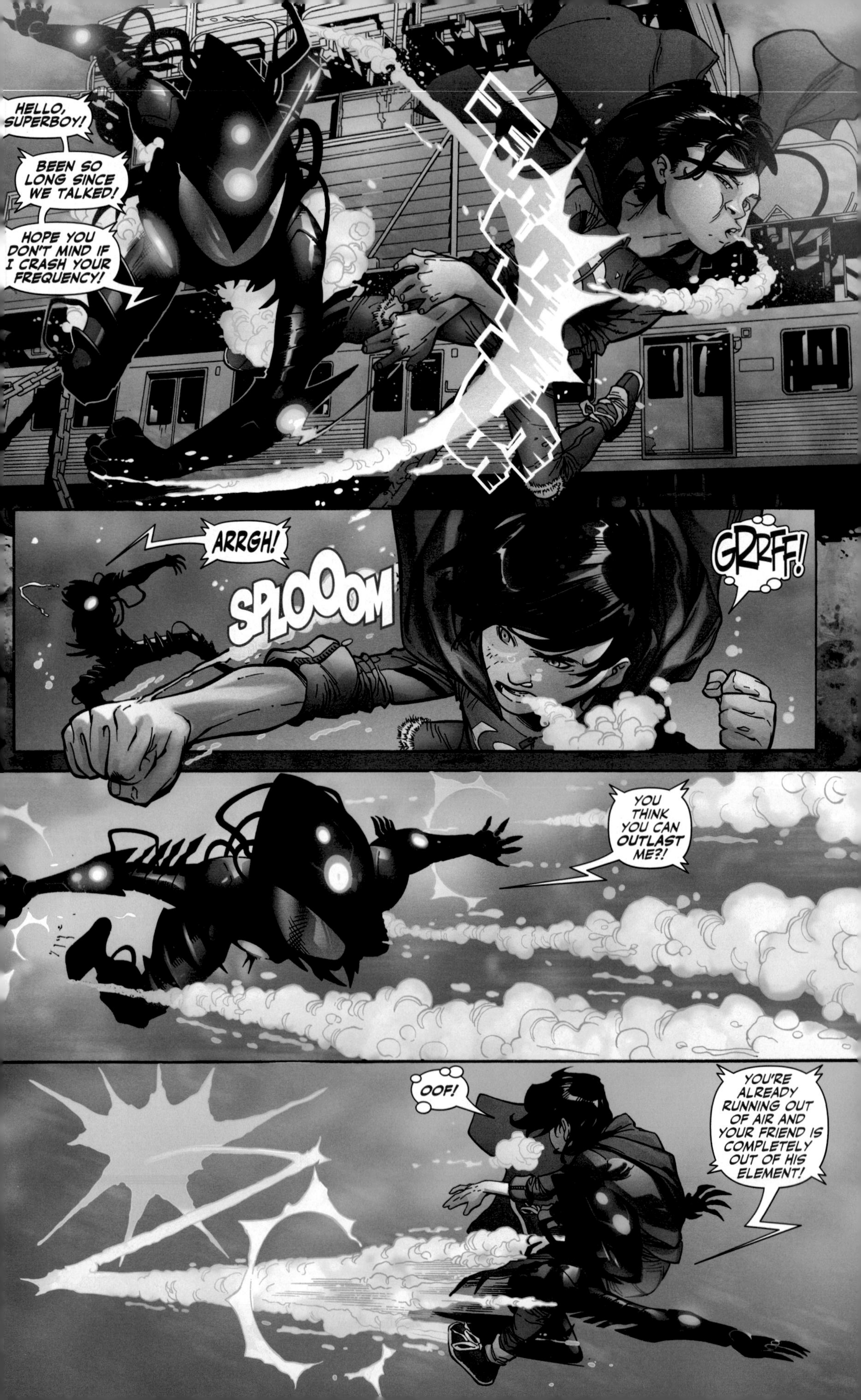
HELLO, SUPERBOY!
BEEN SO LONG SINCE WE TALKED!
HOPE YOU DON'T MIND IF I CRASH YOUR FREQUENCY!
ARRGH!
SPLOOOM
GRRFF!
YOU THINK YOU CAN OUTLAST ME?!
OOF!
YOU'RE ALREADY RUNNING OUT OF AIR AND YOUR FRIEND IS COMPLETELY OUT OF HIS ELEMENT!

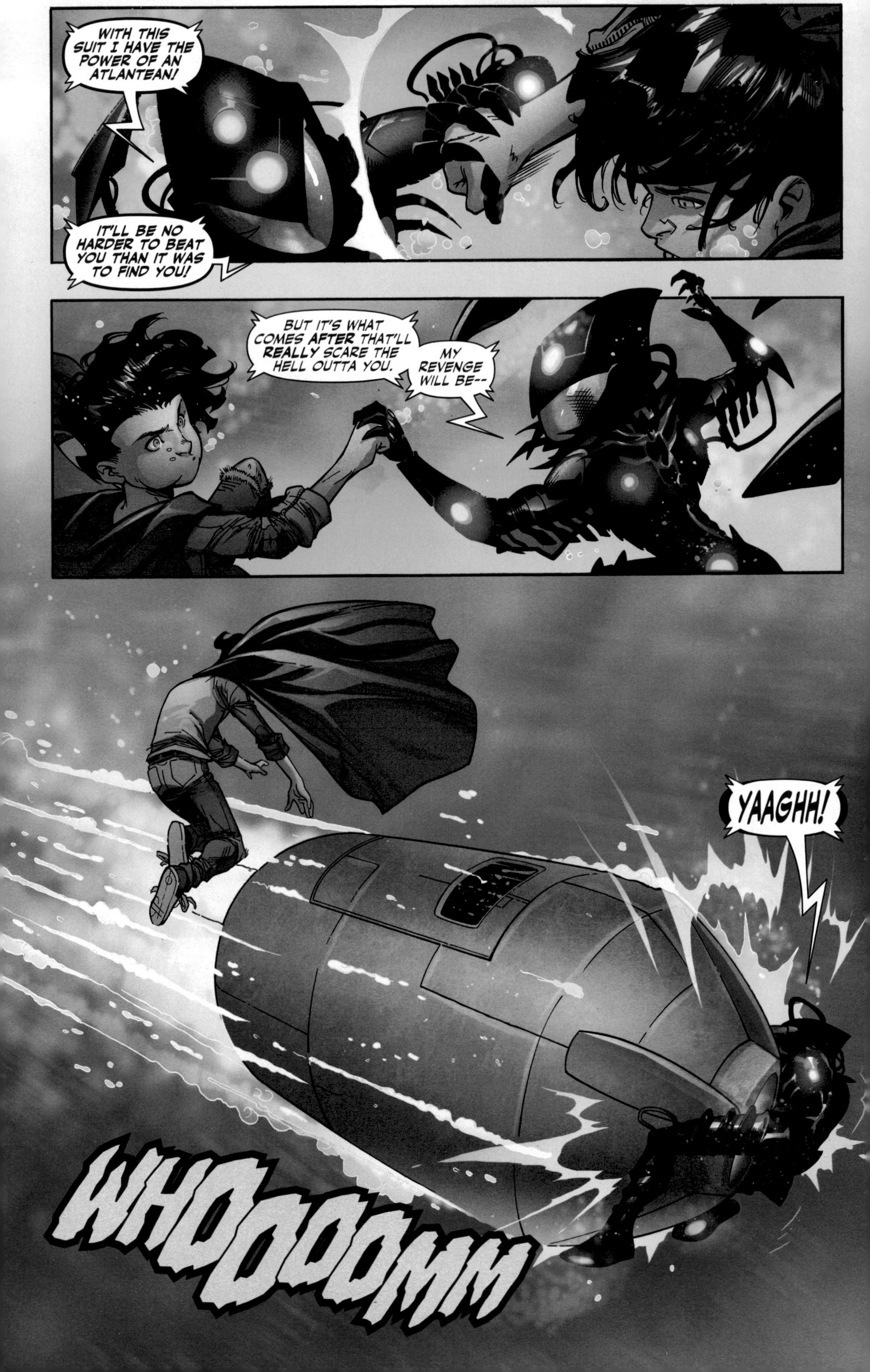
WITH THIS SUIT I HAVE THE POWER OF AN ATLANTEAN!
IT'LL BE NO HARDER TO BEAT YOU THAN IT WAS TO FIND YOU!
BUT IT'S WHAT COMES AFTER THAT'LL REALLY SCARE THE HELL OUTTA YOU.
MY REVENGE WILL BE--
YAAGHH!
WHOOOOMM

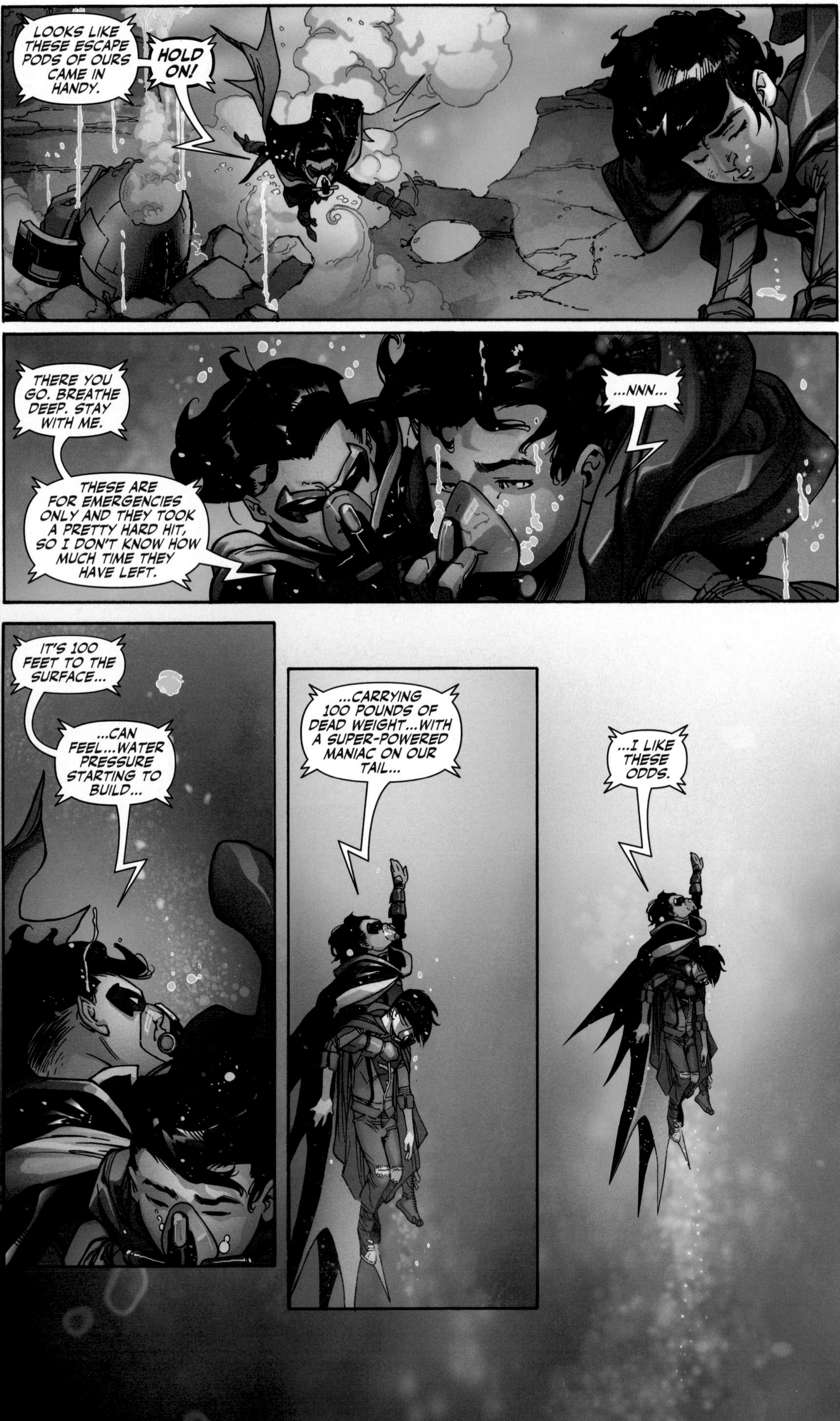
LOOKS LIKE THESE ESCAPE PODS OF OURS CAME IN HANDY.
HOLD ON!
THERE YOU GO. BREATHE DEEP. STAY WITH ME.
THESE ARE FOR EMERGENCIES ONLY AND THEY TOOK A PRETTY HARD HIT, SO I DON'T KNOW HOW MUCH TIME THEY HAVE LEFT.
...NNN...
IT'S 100 FEET TO THE SURFACE...
...CAN FEEL...WATER PRESSURE STARTING TO BUILD...
...CARRYING 100 POUNDS OF DEAD WEIGHT...WITH A SUPER-POWERED MANIAC ON OUR TAIL...
...I LIKE THESE ODDS.

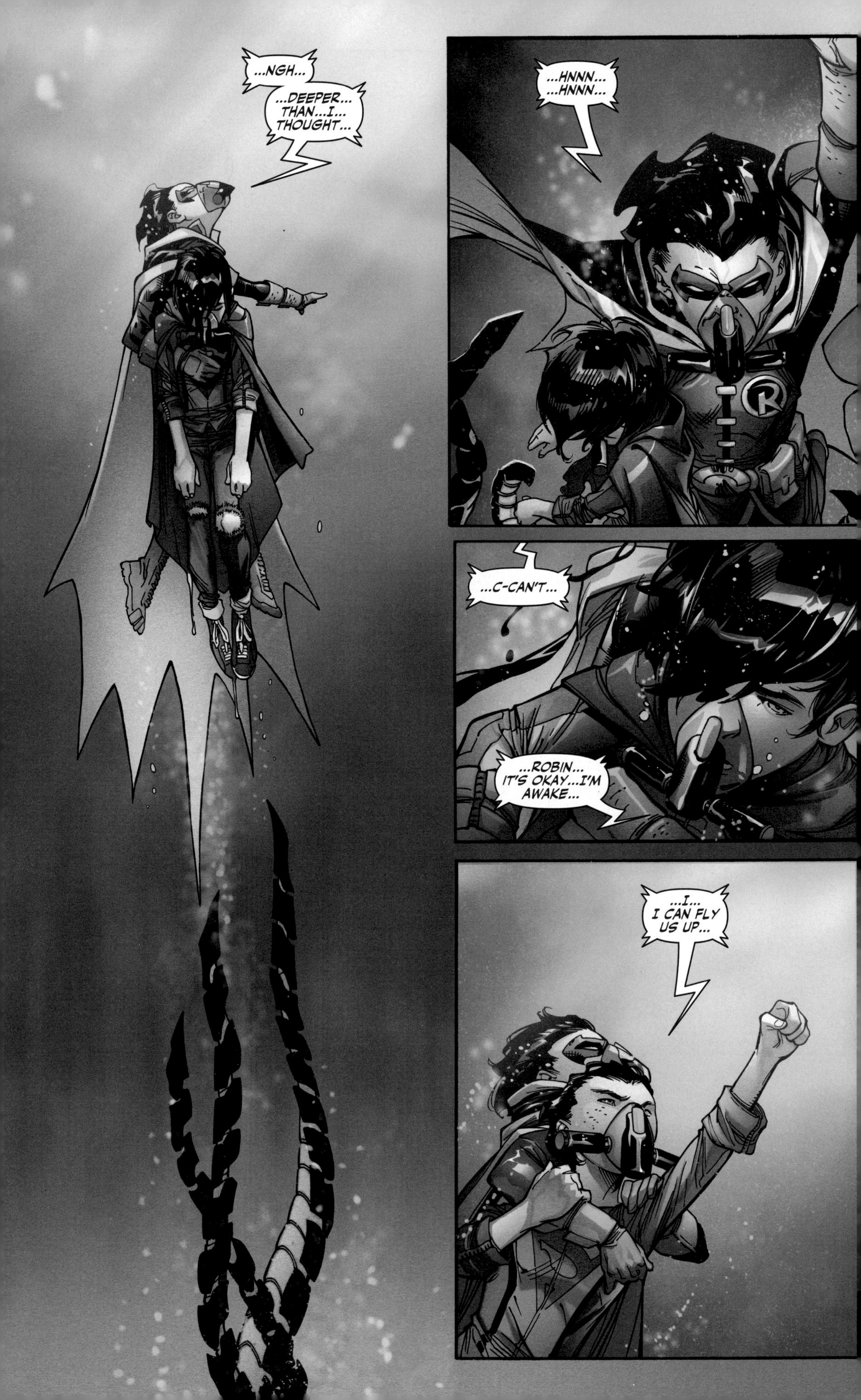
...NGH...
...DEEPER... THAN...I... THOUGHT...
...HNNN... ...HNNN...
...C-CAN'T...
...ROBIN... IT'S OKAY...I'M AWAKE...
...I... I CAN FLY US UP...

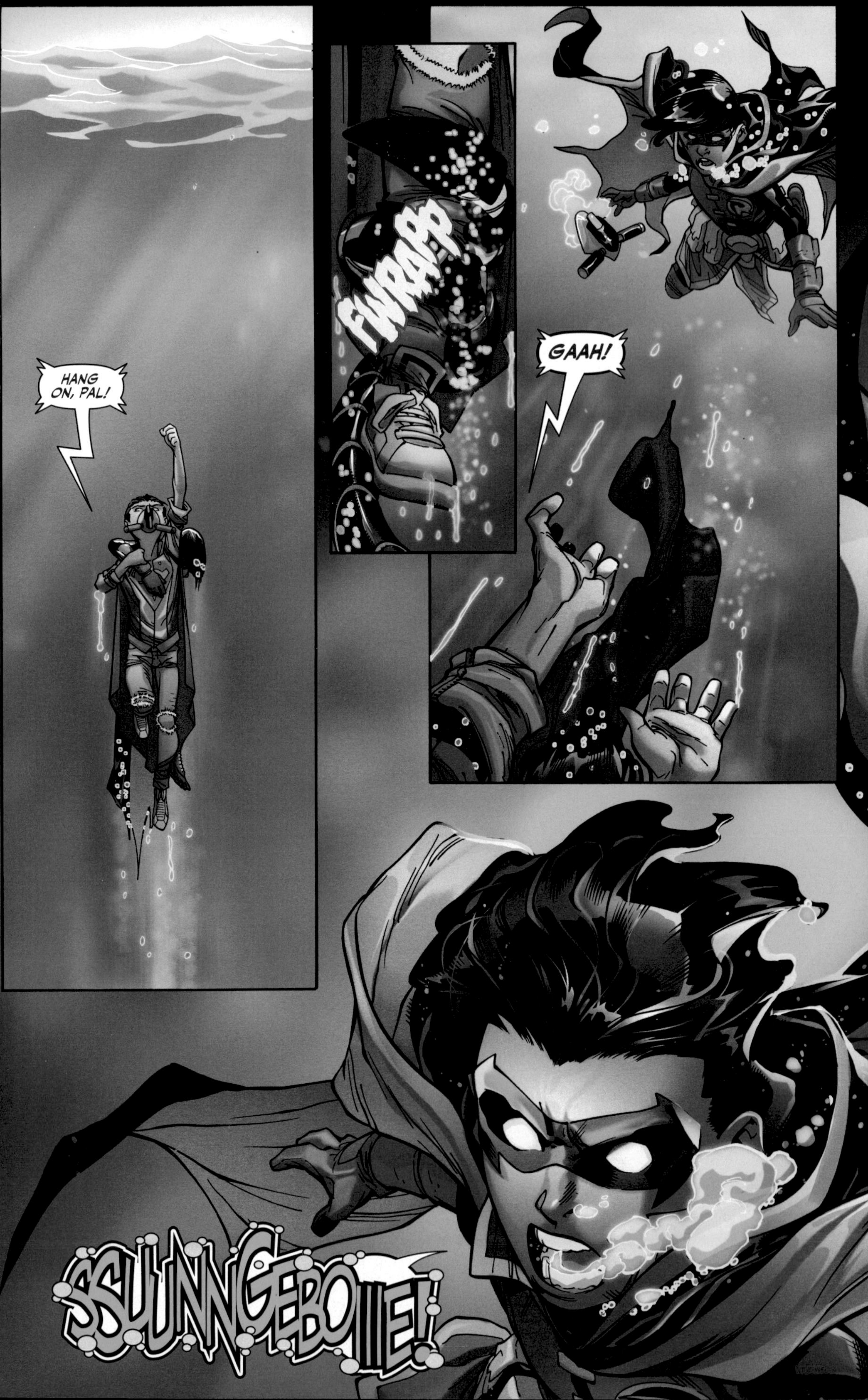
HANG ON, PAL!
FWAP
GAAH!
SSUUNNGEBOOIIE!

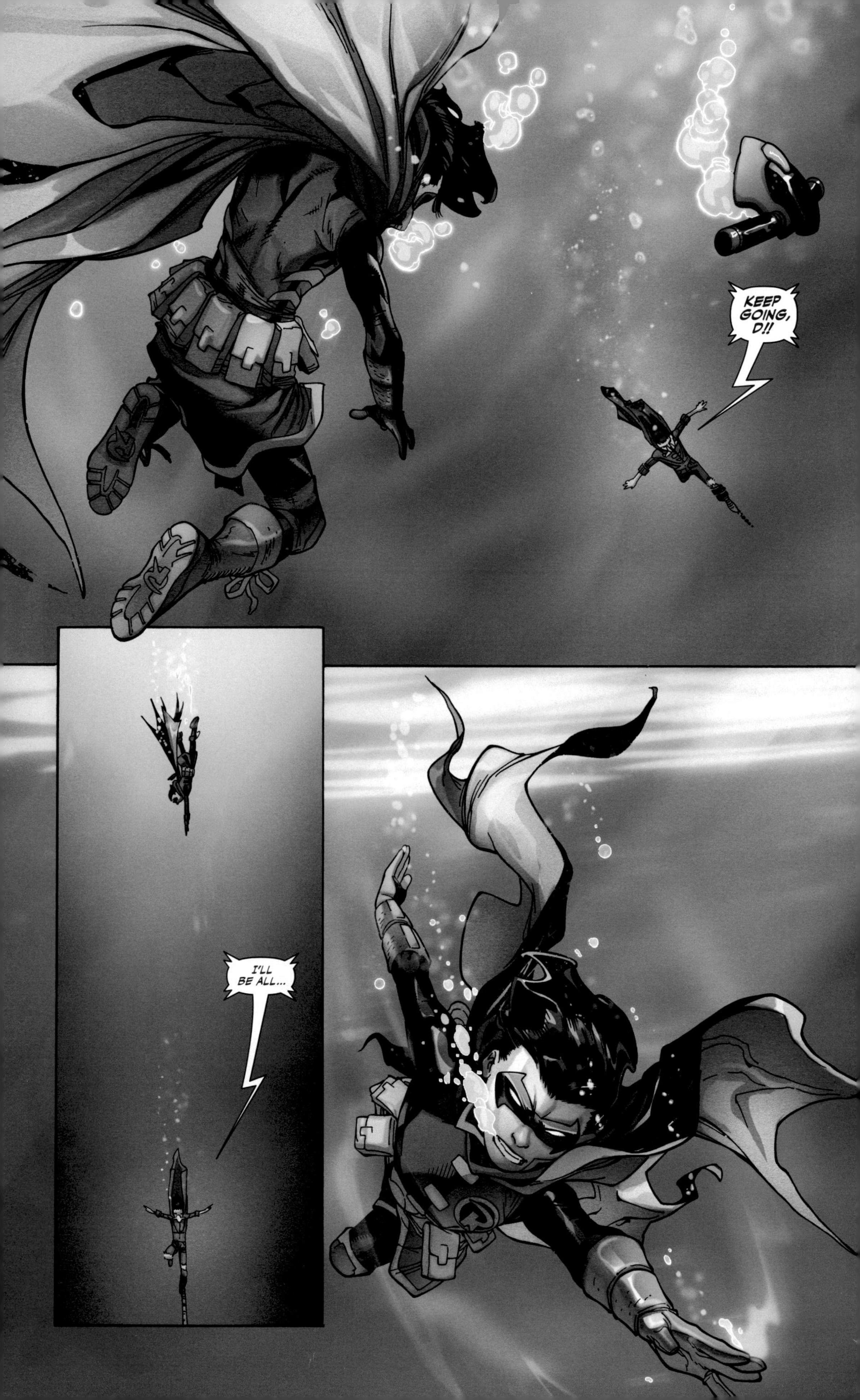
KEEP GOING, D!!
I'LL BE ALL...

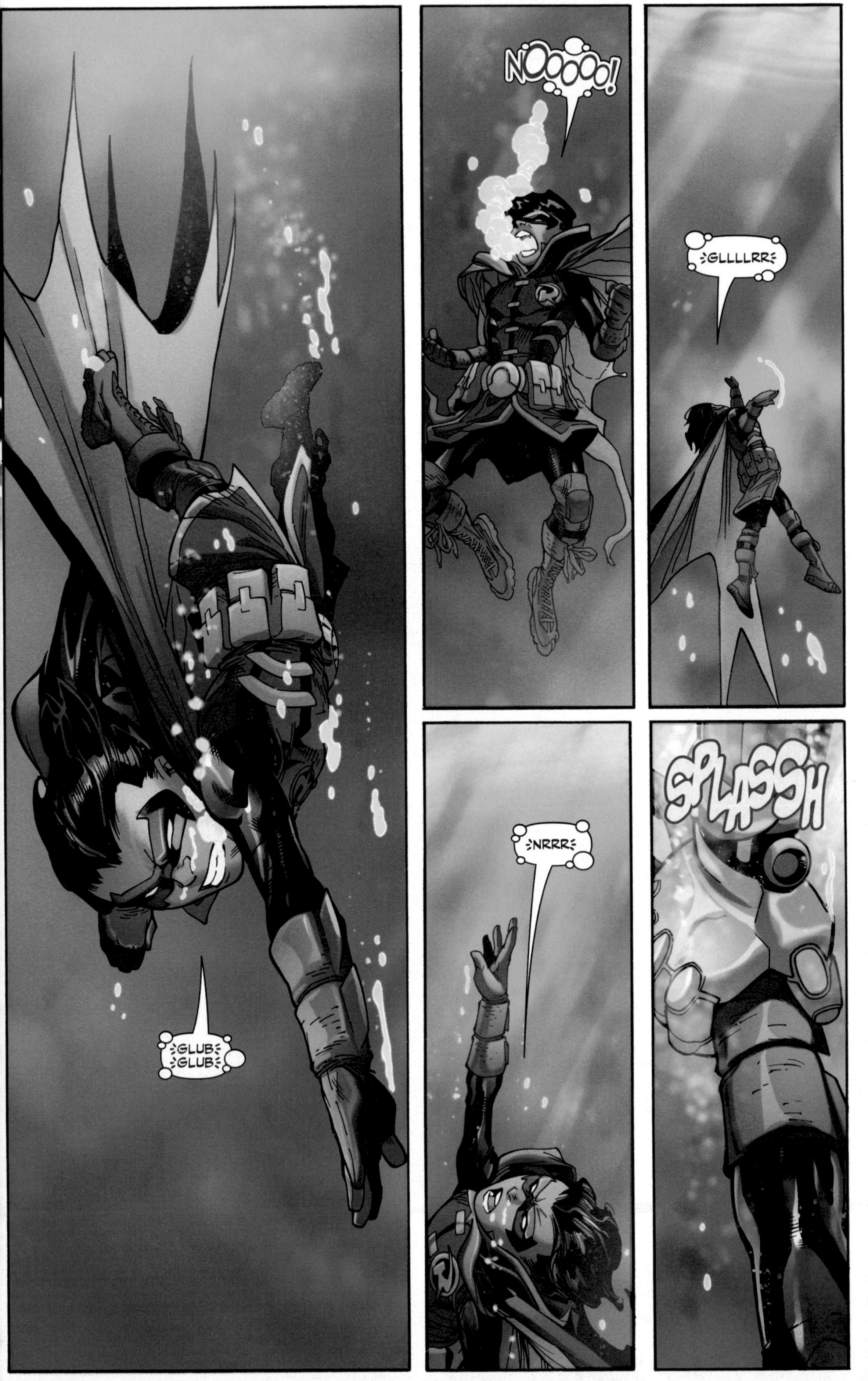
GLUB GLUB
NOOOOO!
GLLLLRR
NRRR
SPLASSH

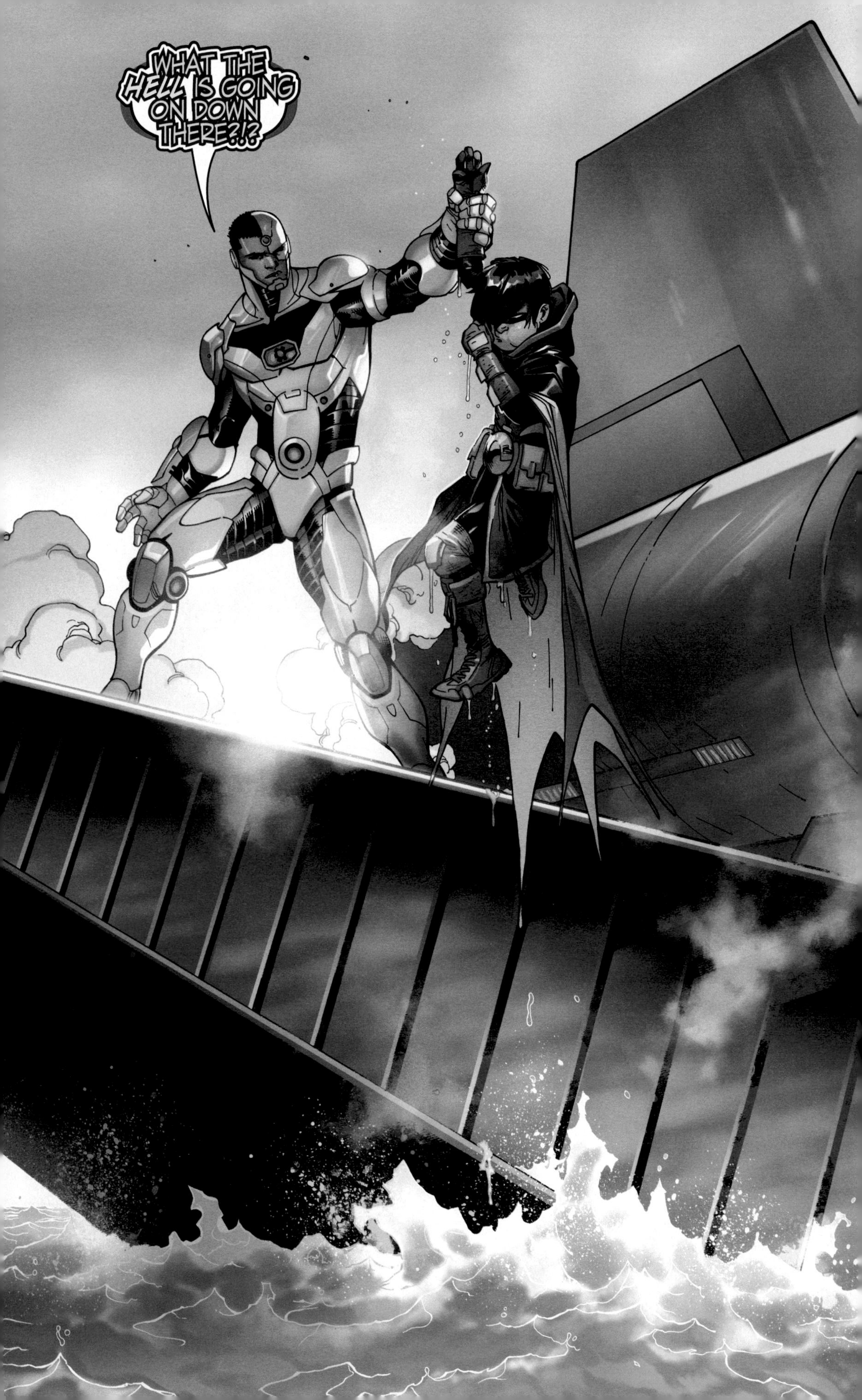
WHAT THE HELL IS GOING ON DOWN THERE?!?

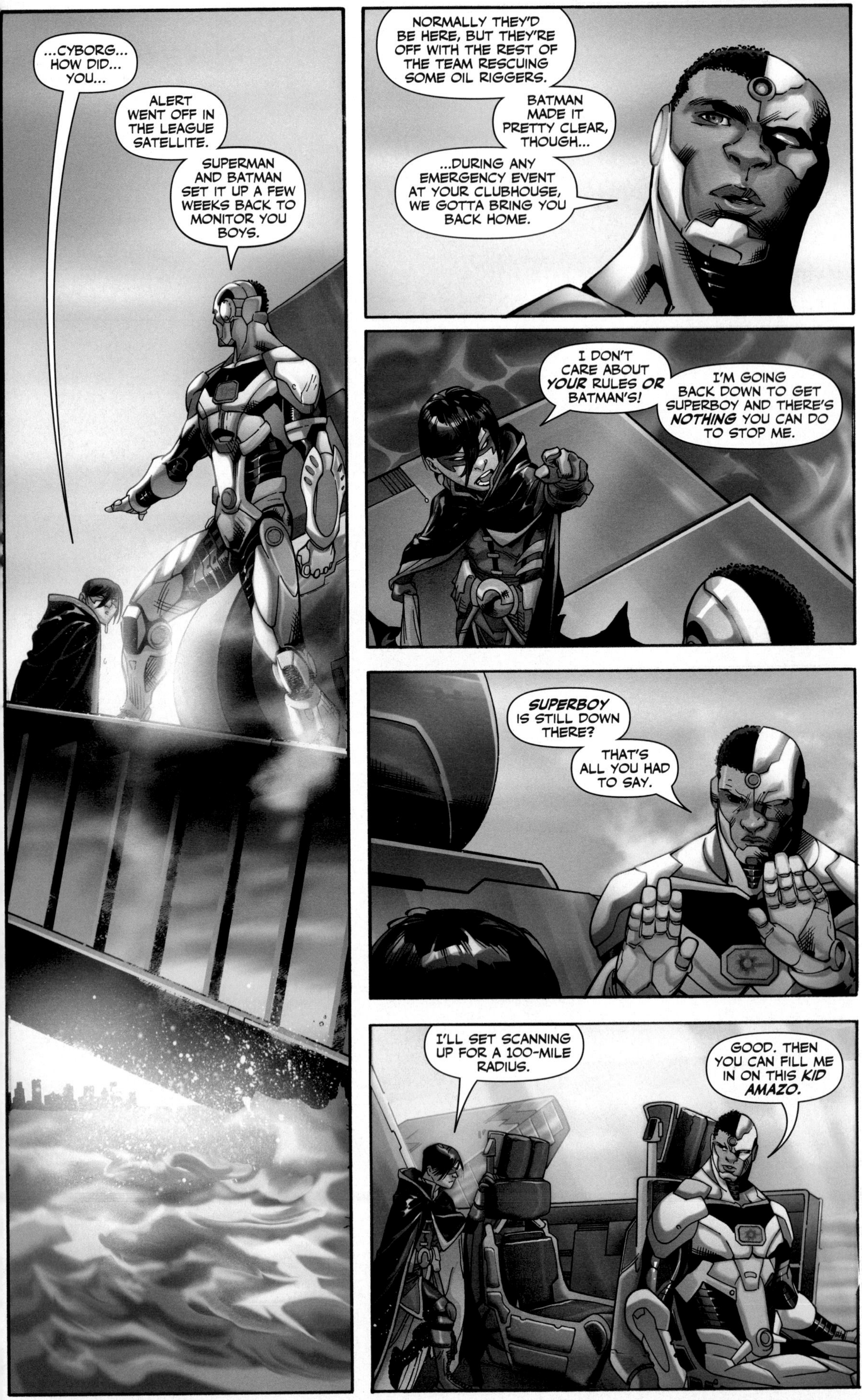
...CYBORG... HOW DID... YOU...
ALERT WENT OFF IN THE LEAGUE SATELLITE.
SUPERMAN AND BATMAN SET IT UP A FEW WEEKS BACK TO MONITOR YOU BOYS.
NORMALLY THEY'D BE HERE, BUT THEY'RE OFF WITH THE REST OF THE TEAM RESCUING SOME OIL RIGGERS.
BATMAN MADE IT PRETTY CLEAR, THOUGH...
...DURING ANY EMERGENCY EVENT AT YOUR CLUBHOUSE, WE GOTTA BRING YOU BACK HOME.
I DON'T CARE ABOUT YOUR RULES OR BATMAN'S!
I'M GOING BACK DOWN TO GET SUPERBOY AND THERE'S NOTHING YOU CAN DO TO STOP ME.
SUPERBOY IS STILL DOWN THERE?
THAT'S ALL YOU HAD TO SAY.
I'LL SET SCANNING UP FOR A 100-MILE RADIUS.
GOOD. THEN YOU CAN FILL ME IN ON THIS KID AMAZO.

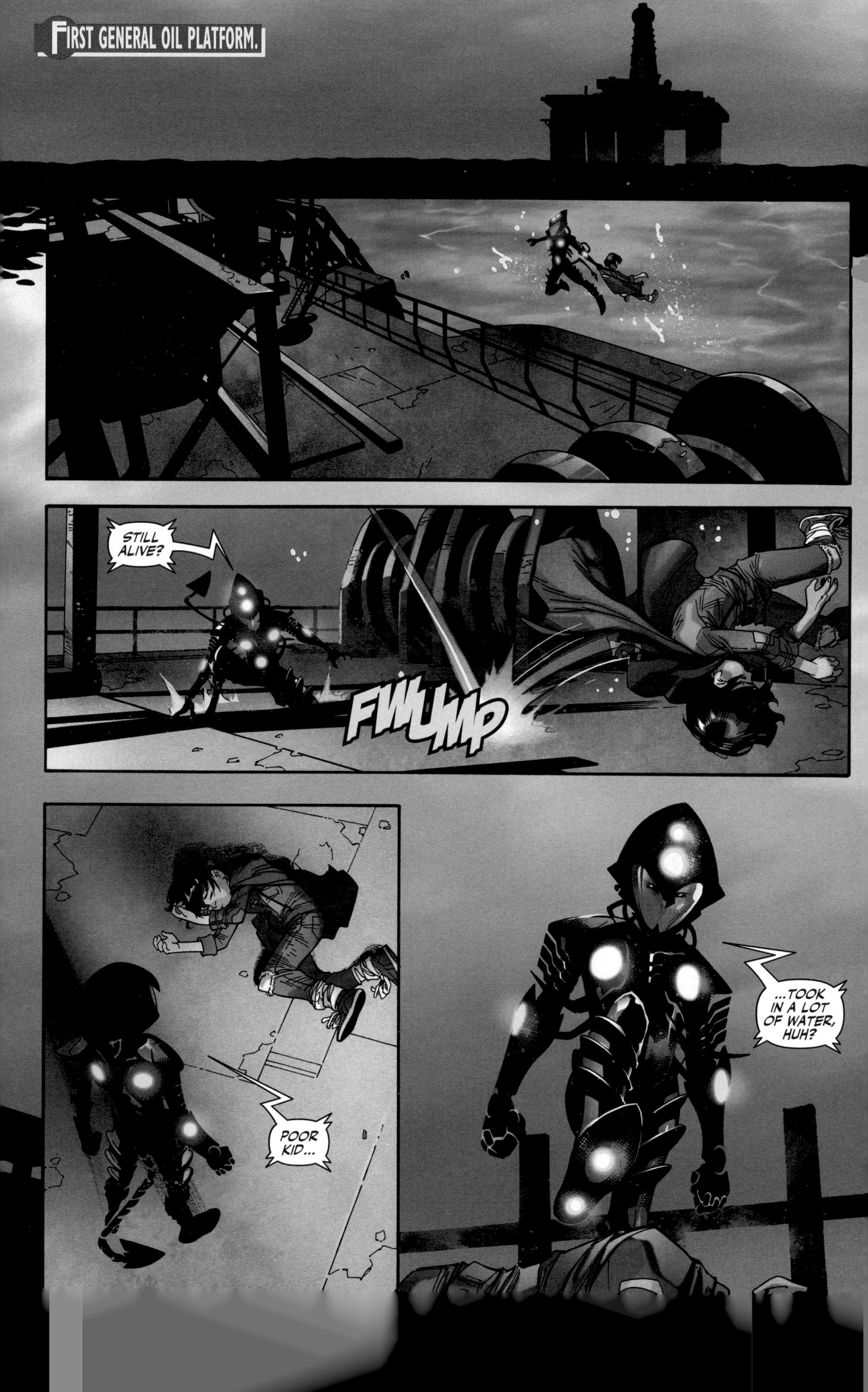
FIRST GENERAL OIL PLATFORM.
STILL ALIVE?
FWUMP
POOR KID...
...TOOK IN A LOT OF WATER, HUH?

LET'S GET IT OUT.

GRAM

GLLAAHKK

...REGGIE...

NOT ANYMORE.

SMAASSH

YOU WERE FREE OF THIS, REGGIE...

...I THOUGHT LEXCORP WAS HELPING YOU?

HA HA HA HA HA HA!

"REGGIE" IS ANYTHING BUT FREE, AND LUTHOR DIDN'T DO ANYTHING I DIDN'T WANT HIM TO DO.

AFTER YOU AND YOUR PAL TOOK OUT MY ARMY AND SEPARATED ME FROM MY AMAZO ARMOR, I JUST HAD TO WAIT FOR A BETTER OPPORTUNITY TO COME ALONG.

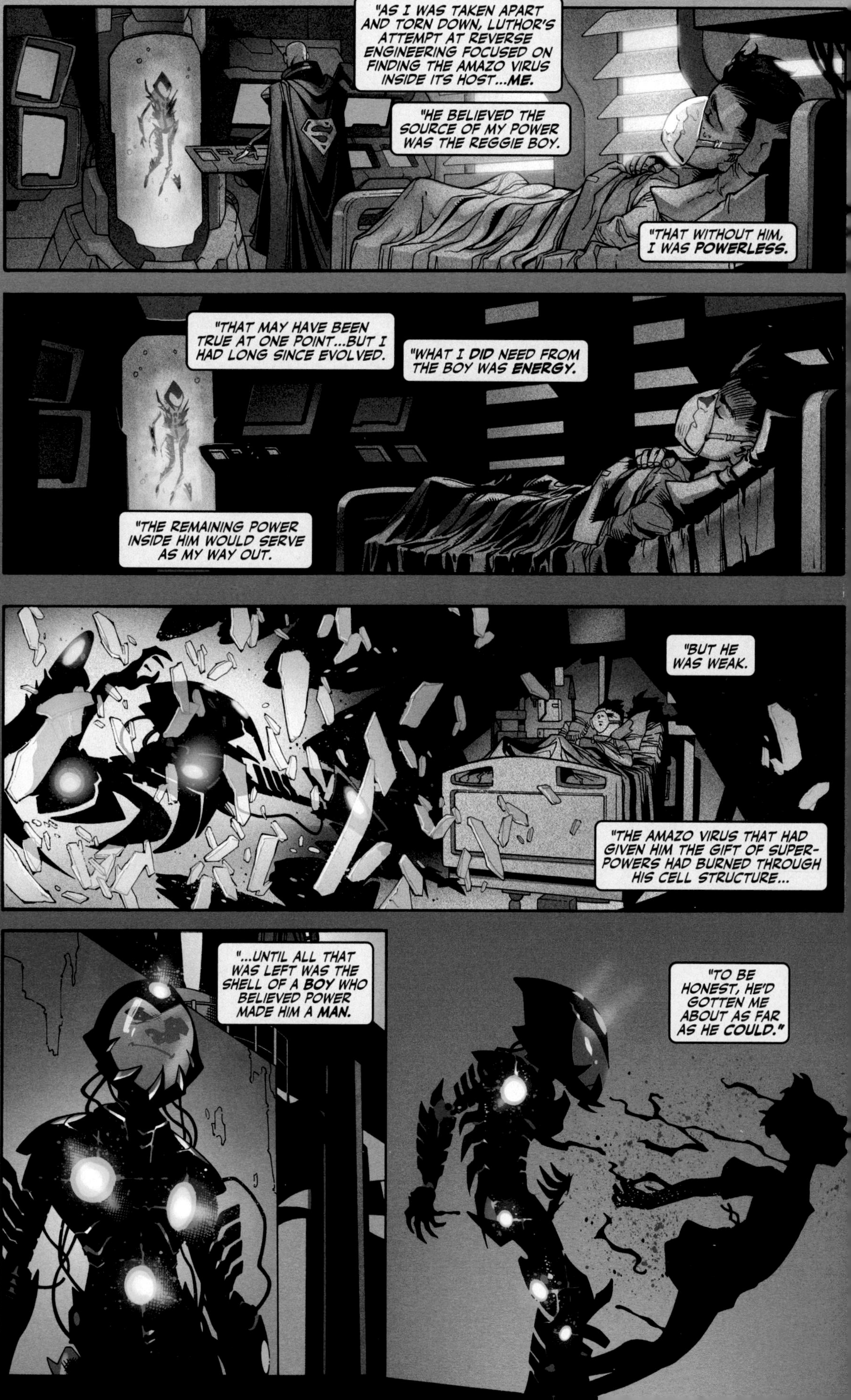
"AS I WAS TAKEN APART AND TORN DOWN, LUTHOR'S ATTEMPT AT REVERSE ENGINEERING FOCUSED ON FINDING THE AMAZO VIRUS INSIDE ITS HOST...ME.
"HE BELIEVED THE SOURCE OF MY POWER WAS THE REGGIE BOY.
"THAT WITHOUT HIM, I WAS POWERLESS.
"THAT MAY HAVE BEEN TRUE AT ONE POINT...BUT I HAD LONG SINCE EVOLVED.
"WHAT I DID NEED FROM THE BOY WAS ENERGY.
"THE REMAINING POWER INSIDE HIM WOULD SERVE AS MY WAY OUT.
"BUT HE WAS WEAK.
"THE AMAZO VIRUS THAT HAD GIVEN HIM THE GIFT OF SUPER-POWERS HAD BURNED THROUGH HIS CELL STRUCTURE...
"...UNTIL ALL THAT WAS LEFT WAS THE SHELL OF A BOY WHO BELIEVED POWER MADE HIM A MAN.
"TO BE HONEST, HE'D GOTTEN ME ABOUT AS FAR AS HE COULD."

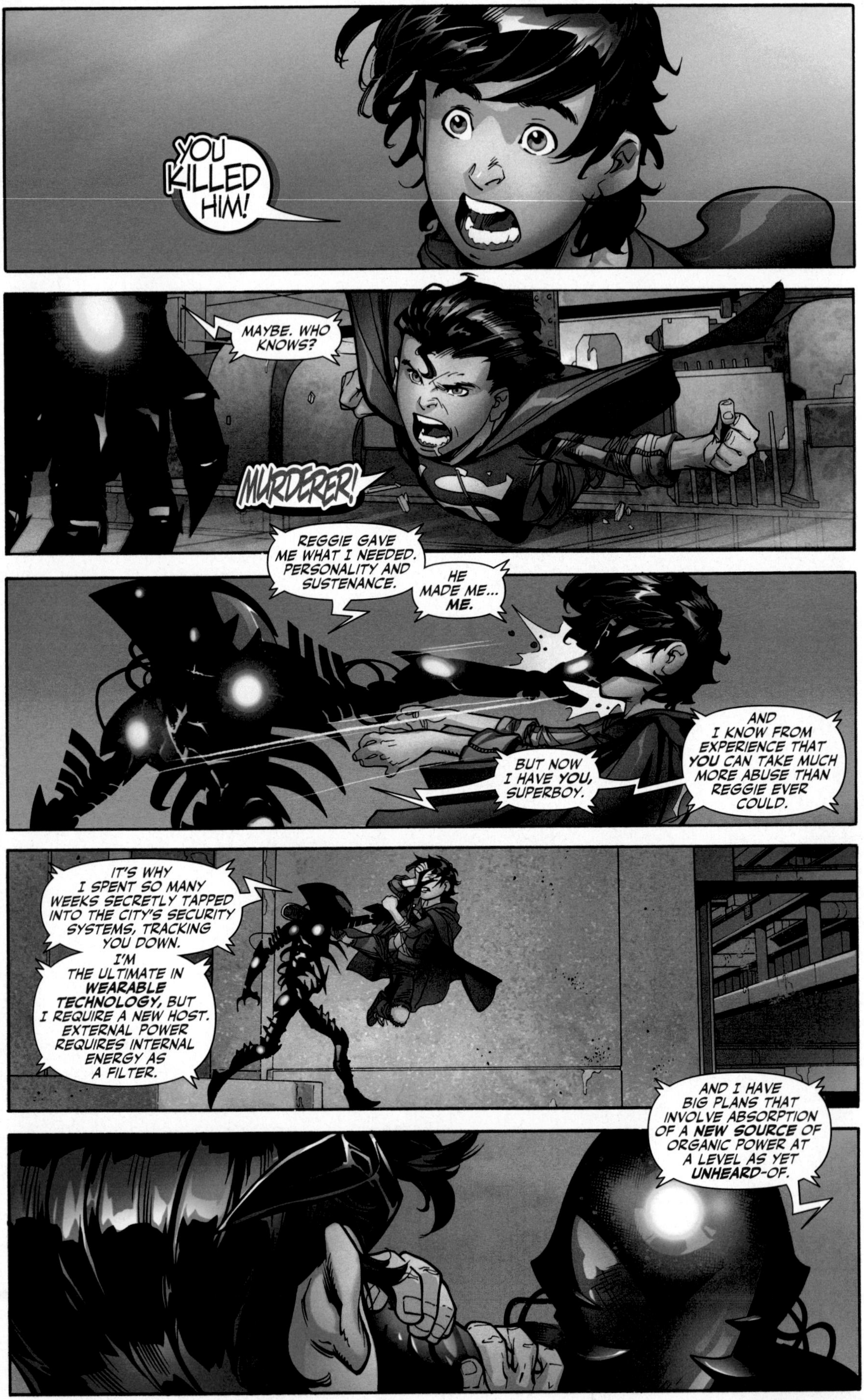
YOU KILLED HIM!
MAYBE. WHO KNOWS?
MURDERER!
REGGIE GAVE ME WHAT I NEEDED. PERSONALITY AND SUSTENANCE.
HE MADE ME... ME.
BUT NOW I HAVE YOU, SUPERBOY.
AND I KNOW FROM EXPERIENCE THAT YOU CAN TAKE MUCH MORE ABUSE THAN REGGIE EVER COULD.
IT'S WHY I SPENT SO MANY WEEKS SECRETLY TAPPED INTO THE CITY'S SECURITY SYSTEMS, TRACKING YOU DOWN.
I'M THE ULTIMATE IN WEARABLE TECHNOLOGY, BUT I REQUIRE A NEW HOST. EXTERNAL POWER REQUIRES INTERNAL ENERGY AS A FILTER.
AND I HAVE BIG PLANS THAT INVOLVE ABSORPTION OF A NEW SOURCE OF ORGANIC POWER AT A LEVEL AS YET UNHEARD-OF.

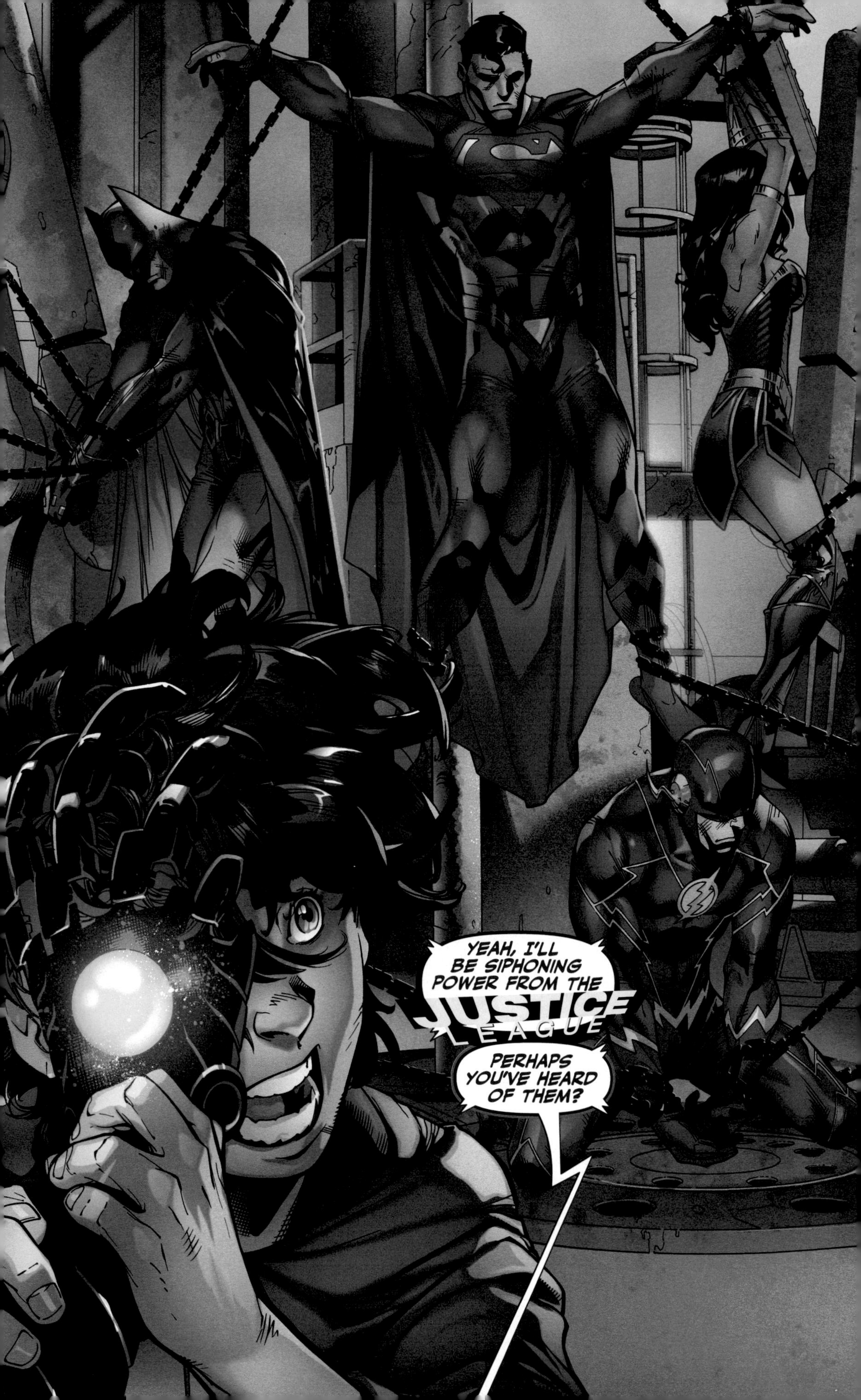
YEAH, I'LL BE SIPHONING POWER FROM THE JUSTICE LEAGUE
PERHAPS YOU'VE HEARD OF THEM?

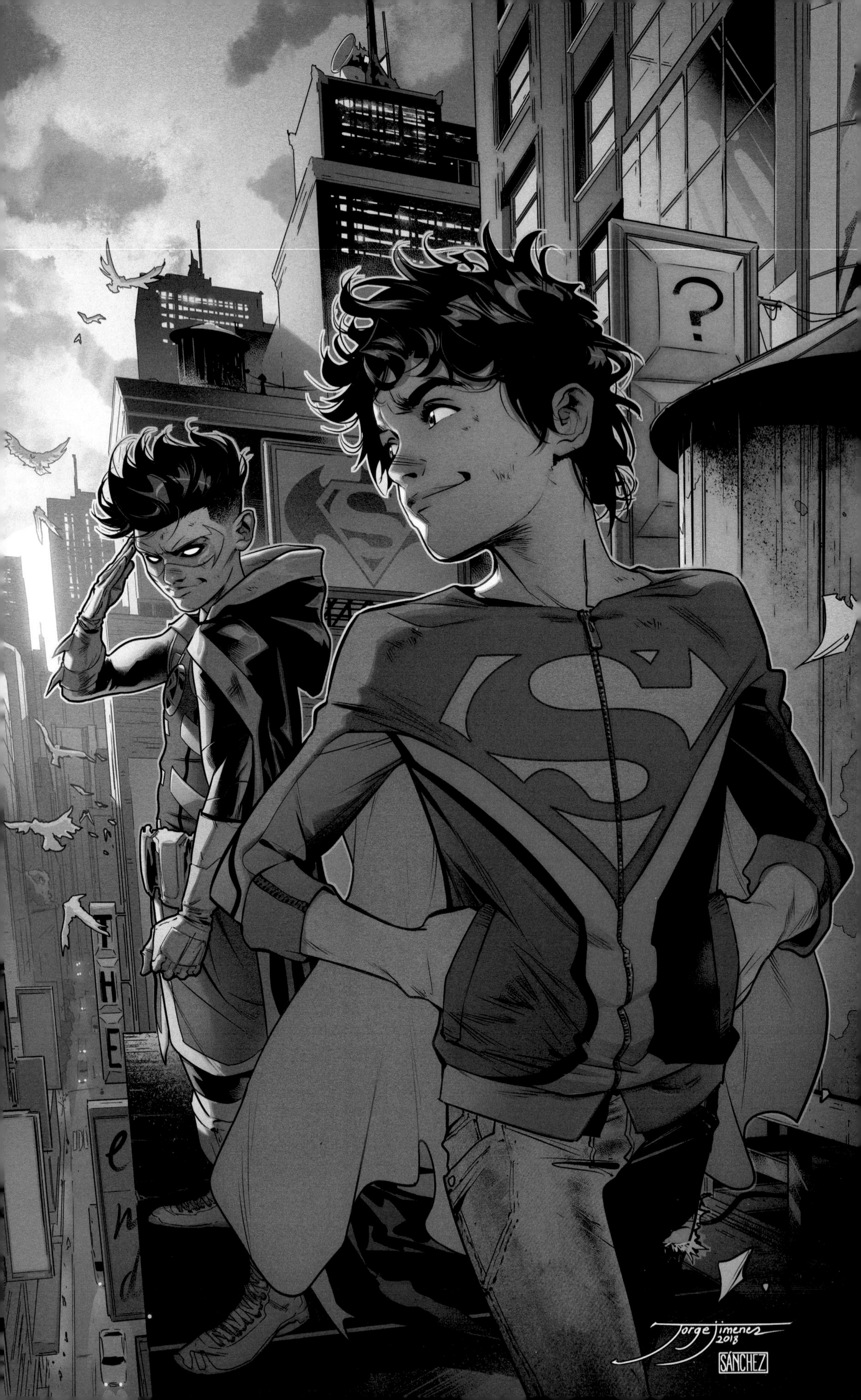
THE
Jorge Jimenez
2018
SÁNCHEZ

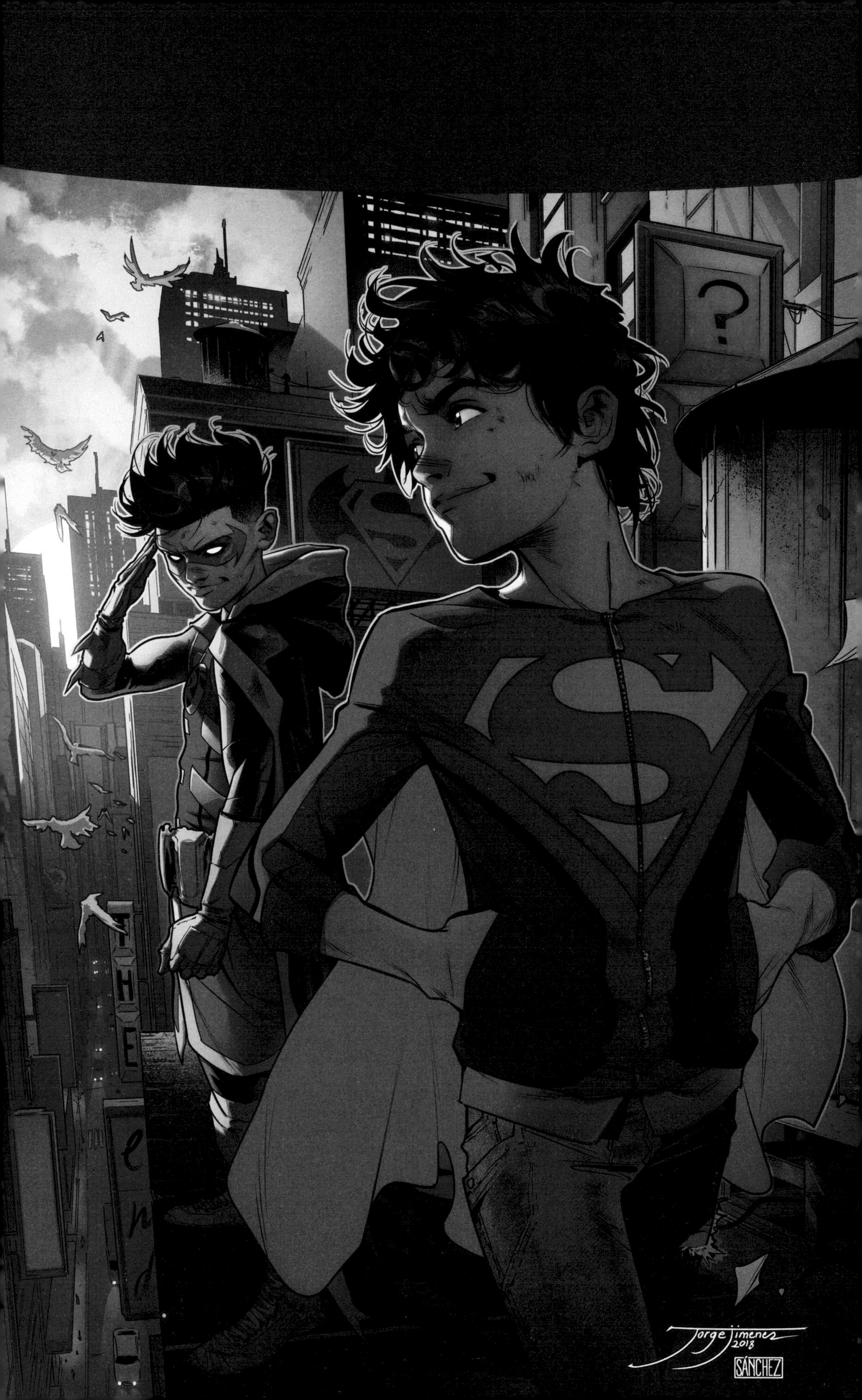

THE
Jorge Jimenez
2018
SÁNCHEZ

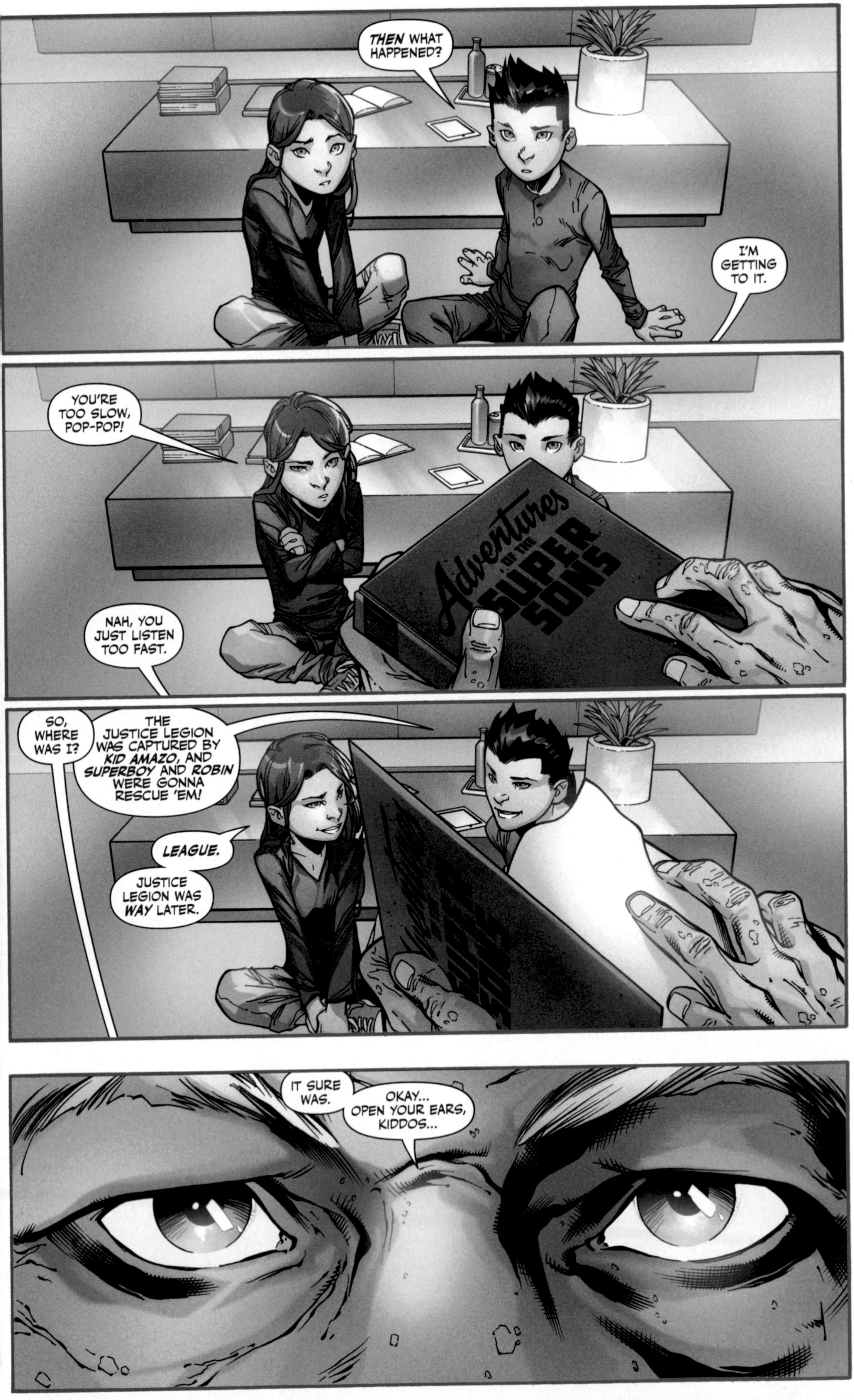
THEN WHAT HAPPENED?
I'M GETTING TO IT.
YOU'RE TOO SLOW, POP-POP!
NAH, YOU JUST LISTEN TOO FAST.
Adventures OF THE SUPER SONS
SO, WHERE WAS I?
THE JUSTICE LEGION WAS CAPTURED BY KID AMAZO, AND SUPERBOY AND ROBIN WERE GONNA RESCUE 'EM!
LEAGUE.
JUSTICE LEGION WAS WAY LATER.
IT SURE WAS.
OKAY... OPEN YOUR EARS, KIDDOS...

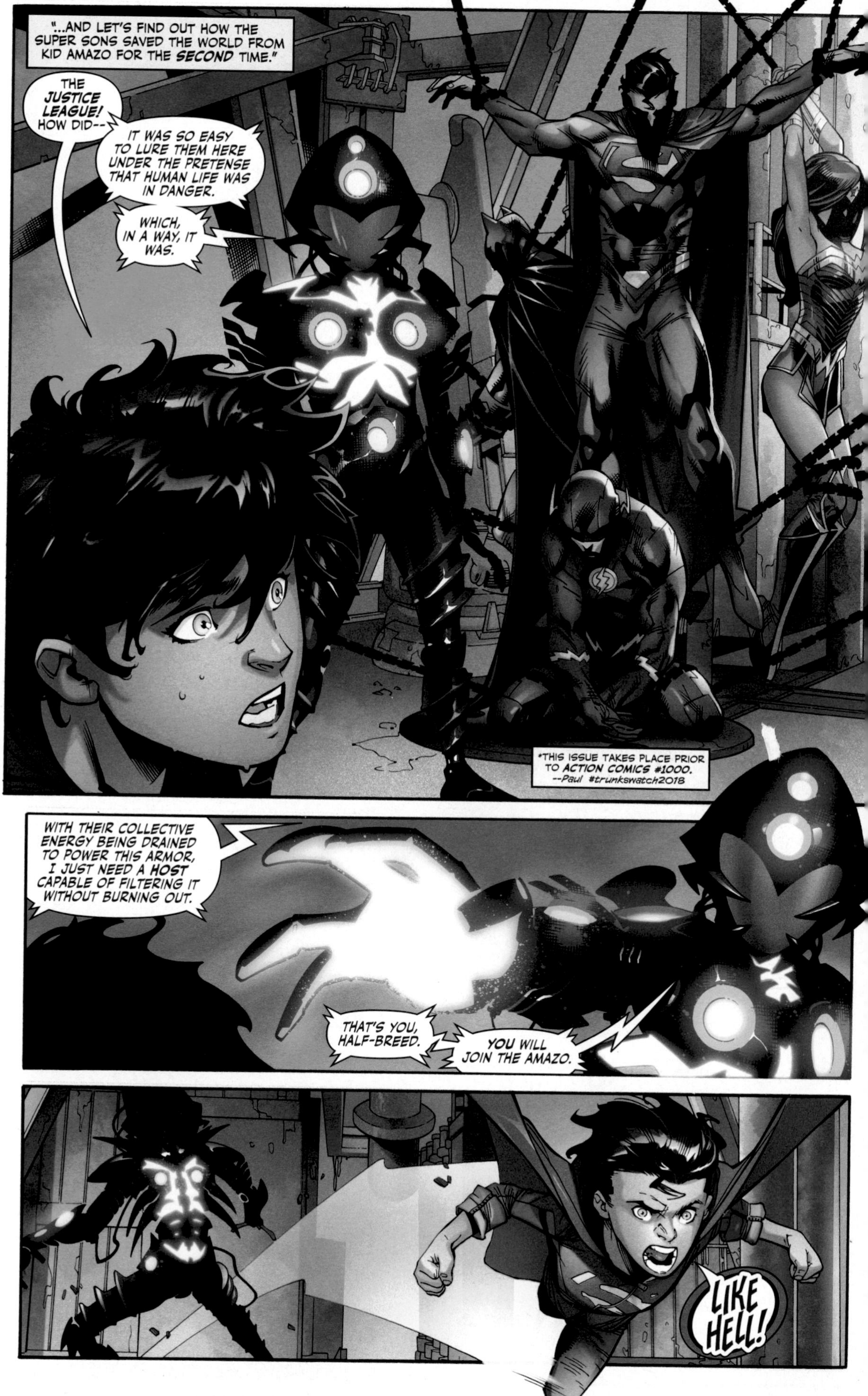
"...AND LET'S FIND OUT HOW THE SUPER SONS SAVED THE WORLD FROM KID AMAZO FOR THE SECOND TIME."
THE JUSTICE LEAGUE! HOW DID--
IT WAS SO EASY TO LURE THEM HERE UNDER THE PRETENSE THAT HUMAN LIFE WAS IN DANGER.
WHICH, IN A WAY, IT WAS.
*THIS ISSUE TAKES PLACE PRIOR TO ACTION COMICS #1000. --Paul #trunkswatch2018
WITH THEIR COLLECTIVE ENERGY BEING DRAINED TO POWER THIS ARMOR, I JUST NEED A HOST CAPABLE OF FILTERING IT WITHOUT BURNING OUT.
THAT'S YOU, HALF-BREED.
YOU WILL JOIN THE AMAZO.
LIKE HELL!

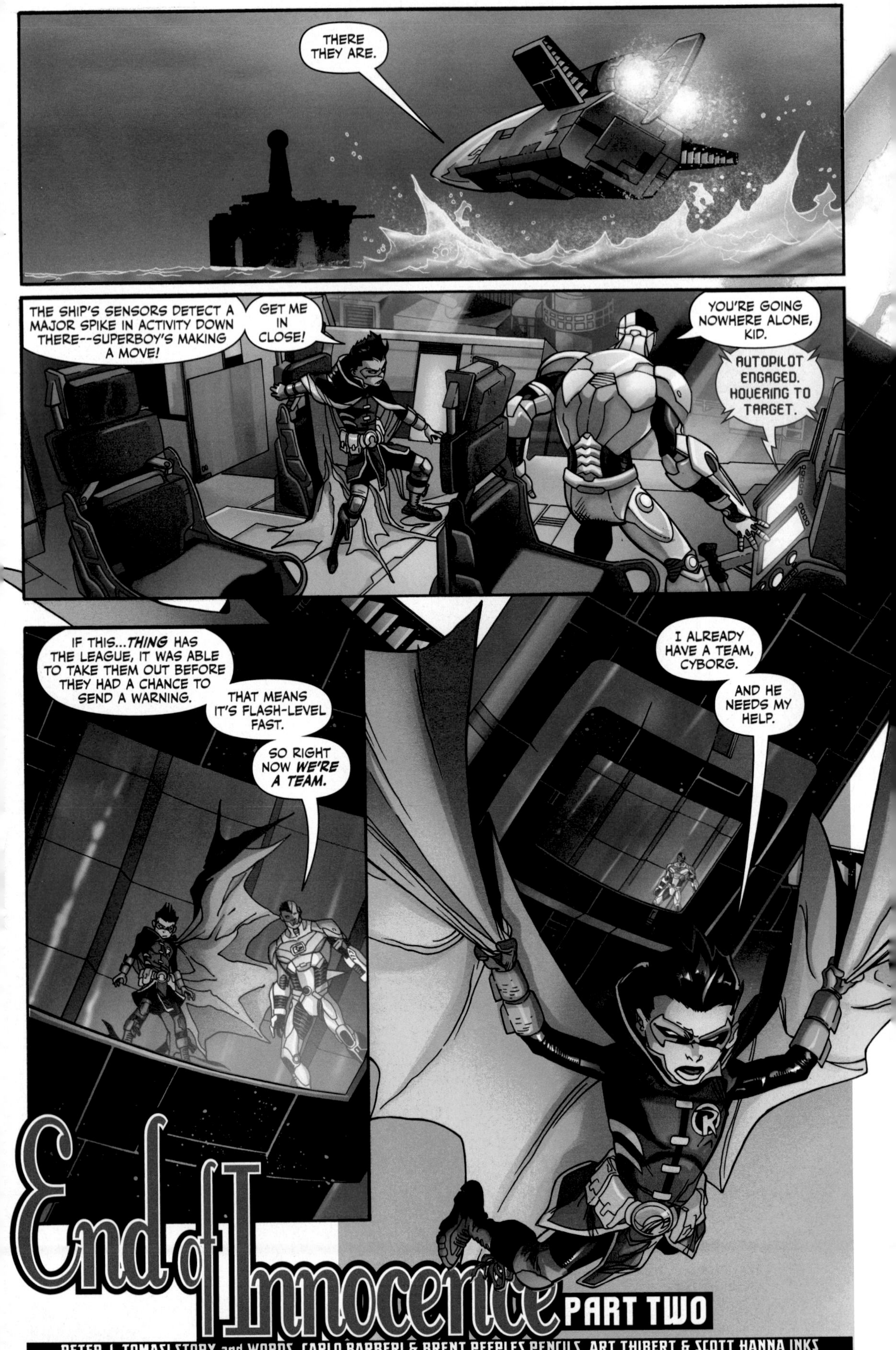
THERE THEY ARE.
THE SHIP'S SENSORS DETECT A MAJOR SPIKE IN ACTIVITY DOWN THERE--SUPERBOY'S MAKING A MOVE!
GET ME IN CLOSE!
YOU'RE GOING NOWHERE ALONE, KID.
AUTOPILOT ENGAGED. HOVERING TO TARGET.
IF THIS...THING HAS THE LEAGUE, IT WAS ABLE TO TAKE THEM OUT BEFORE THEY HAD A CHANCE TO SEND A WARNING.
THAT MEANS IT'S FLASH-LEVEL FAST.
SO RIGHT NOW WE'RE A TEAM.
I ALREADY HAVE A TEAM, CYBORG.
AND HE NEEDS MY HELP.
End of Innocence PART TWO
PETER J. TOMASI STORY and WORDS CARLO BARBERI & BRENT PEEPLES PENCILS ART THIBERT & SCOTT HANNA INKS
DONO SAN/PROTOBUNKER COLORS ROB LEIGH LETTERS JORGE JIMENEZ & ALEJANDRO SANCHEZ COVER
ANDREA SHEA ASSISTANT EDITOR
PAUL KAMINSKI EDITOR

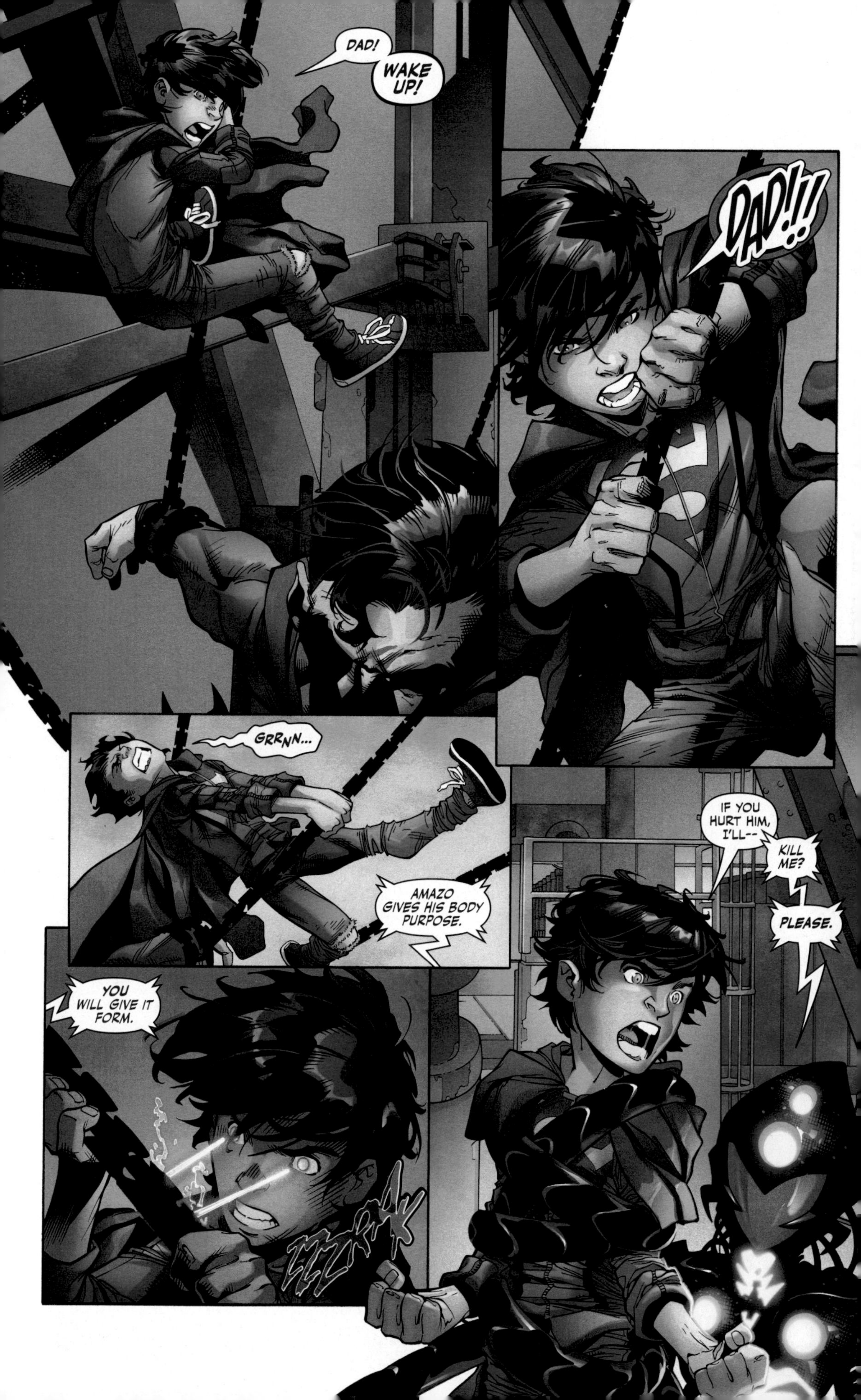
DAD!
WAKE UP!
DAD!!!
GRRNN...
AMAZO GIVES HIS BODY PURPOSE.
YOU WILL GIVE IT FORM.
IF YOU HURT HIM, I'LL--
KILL ME?
PLEASE.

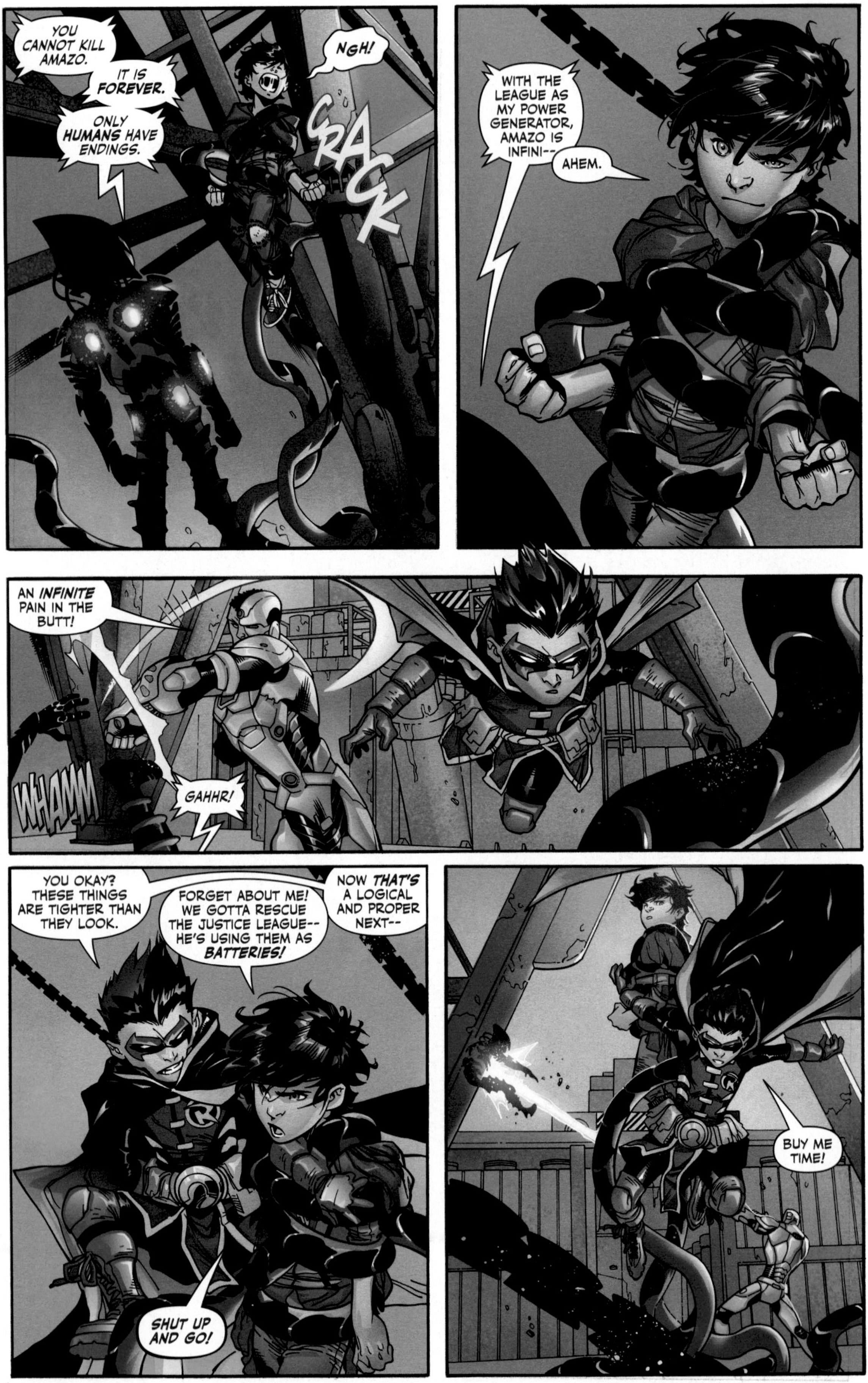
YOU CANNOT KILL AMAZO.
IT IS FOREVER.
ONLY HUMANS HAVE ENDINGS.
NGH!
CRACK
WITH THE LEAGUE AS MY POWER GENERATOR, AMAZO IS INFINI--
AHEM.
AN INFINITE PAIN IN THE BUTT!
WHAMM
GAHHR!
YOU OKAY? THESE THINGS ARE TIGHTER THAN THEY LOOK.
FORGET ABOUT ME! WE GOTTA RESCUE THE JUSTICE LEAGUE-- HE'S USING THEM AS BATTERIES!
NOW THAT'S A LOGICAL AND PROPER NEXT--
SHUT UP AND GO!
BUY ME TIME!

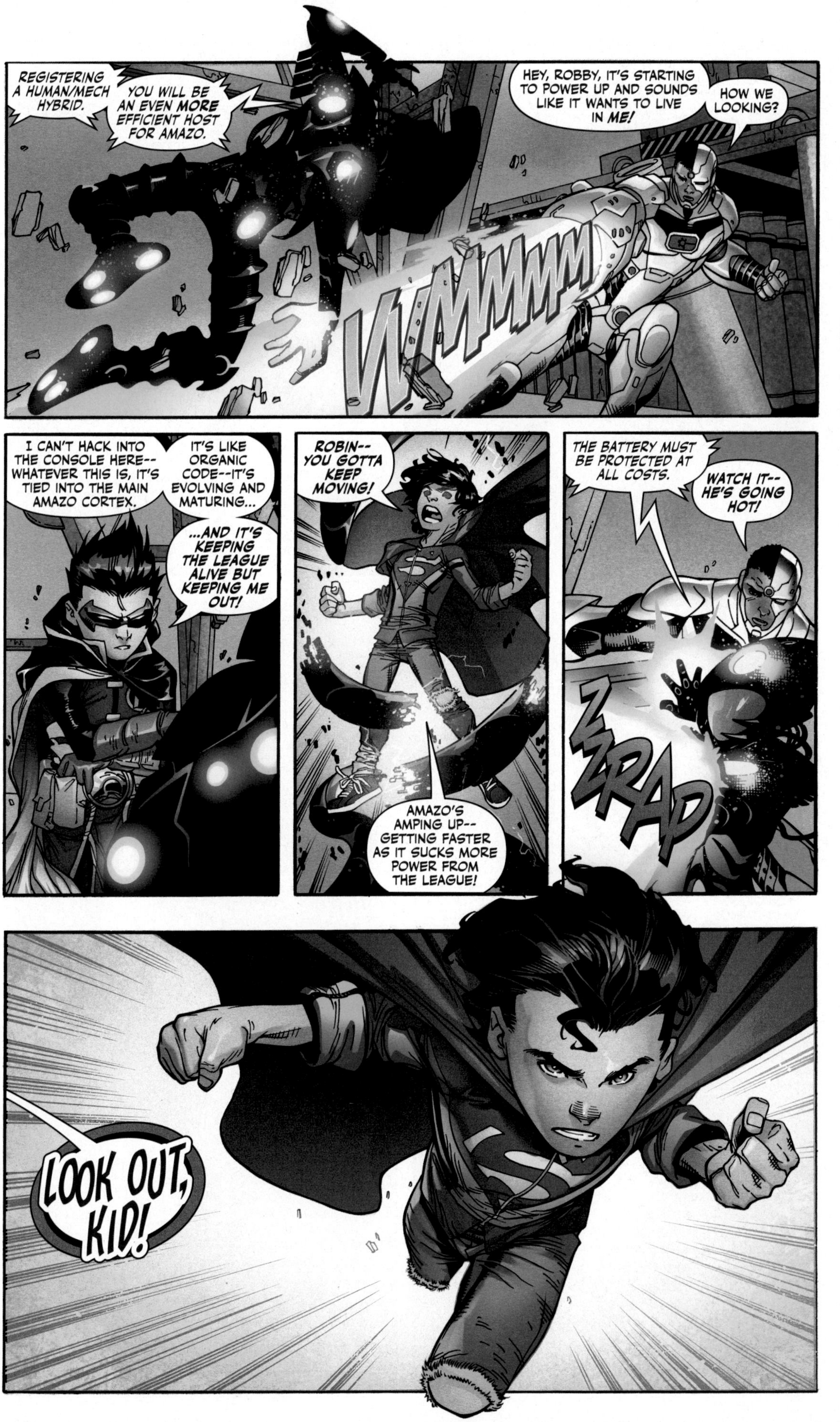
REGISTERING A HUMAN/MECH HYBRID.
YOU WILL BE AN EVEN MORE EFFICIENT HOST FOR AMAZO.
HEY, ROBBY, IT'S STARTING TO POWER UP AND SOUNDS LIKE IT WANTS TO LIVE IN ME!
HOW WE LOOKING?
VVMMMMM
I CAN'T HACK INTO THE CONSOLE HERE--WHATEVER THIS IS, IT'S TIED INTO THE MAIN AMAZO CORTEX.
IT'S LIKE ORGANIC CODE--IT'S EVOLVING AND MATURING...
...AND IT'S KEEPING THE LEAGUE ALIVE BUT KEEPING ME OUT!
ROBIN--YOU GOTTA KEEP MOVING!
AMAZO'S AMPING UP--GETTING FASTER AS IT SUCKS MORE POWER FROM THE LEAGUE!
THE BATTERY MUST BE PROTECTED AT ALL COSTS.
WATCH IT--HE'S GOING HOT!
ZZRAP
LOOK OUT, KID!

DON'T WORRY, CYBORG...

...MY PAL'S GOT *SUPER* IN HIS NAME.

GRRNN!

FRAZZAK

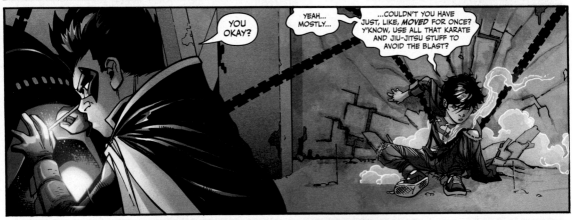

YOU OKAY?

YEAH... MOSTLY...

...COULDN'T YOU HAVE JUST, LIKE, *MOVED* FOR ONCE? Y'KNOW, USE ALL THAT KARATE AND JIU-JITSU STUFF TO AVOID THE BLAST?

KEEP AN EYE ON CYBORG. MAKE SURE HE'S HOLDING HIS OWN.

SHOULDN'T WE GO HELP HIM?

NOW THAT I KNOW WHAT WE'RE UP AGAINST...

...I'VE GOT A DIFFERENT IDEA.

BUT WE NEED *TWO* THINGS TO WIN.

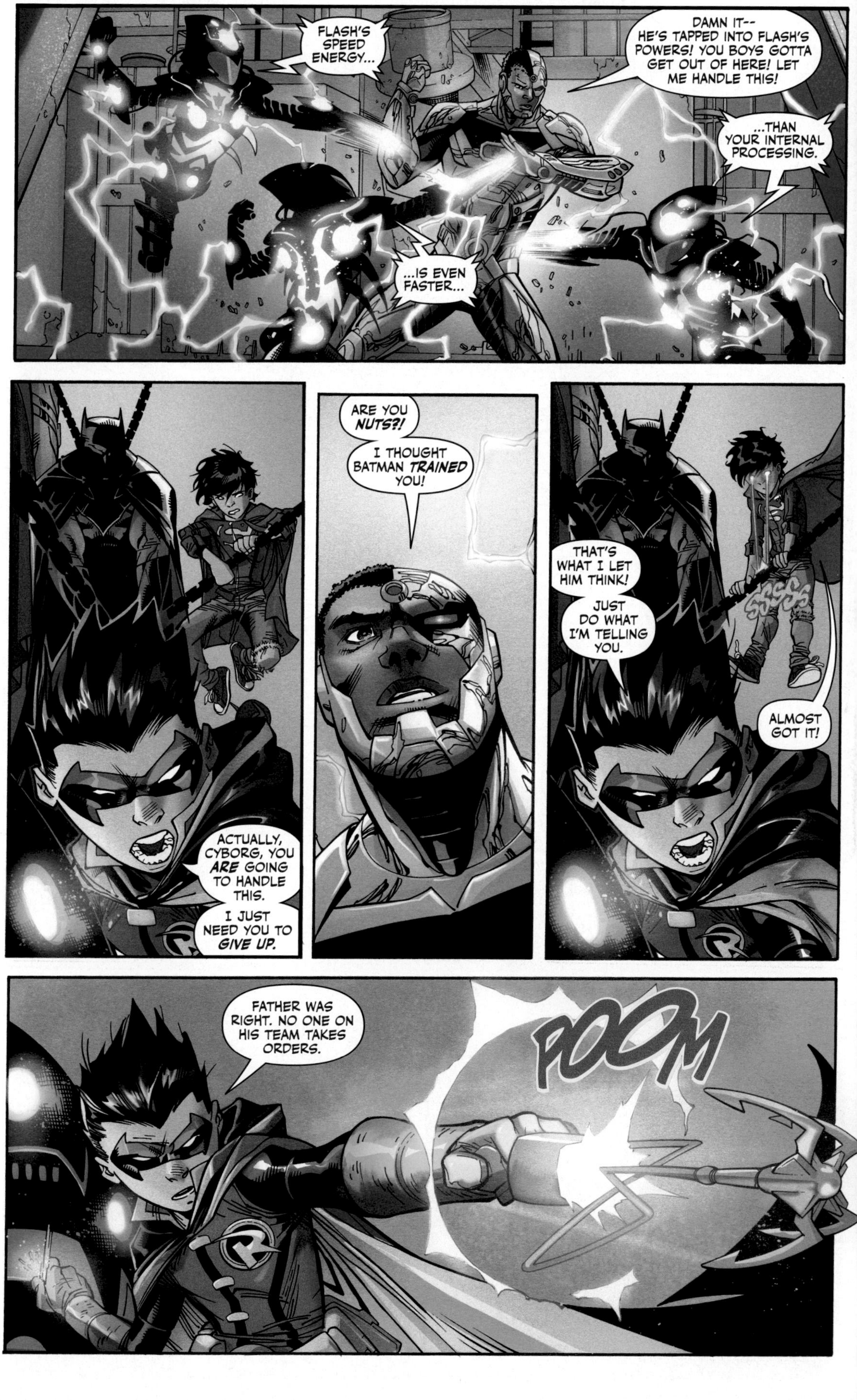
FLASH'S SPEED ENERGY...
...IS EVEN FASTER...
...THAN YOUR INTERNAL PROCESSING.
DAMN IT-- HE'S TAPPED INTO FLASH'S POWERS! YOU BOYS GOTTA GET OUT OF HERE! LET ME HANDLE THIS!
ACTUALLY, CYBORG, YOU *ARE* GOING TO HANDLE THIS.
I JUST NEED YOU TO *GIVE UP.*
ARE YOU *NUTS?!*
I THOUGHT BATMAN *TRAINED* YOU!
THAT'S WHAT I LET HIM THINK!
JUST DO WHAT I'M TELLING YOU.
SSSSS
ALMOST GOT IT!
FATHER WAS RIGHT. NO ONE ON HIS TEAM TAKES ORDERS.
POOM

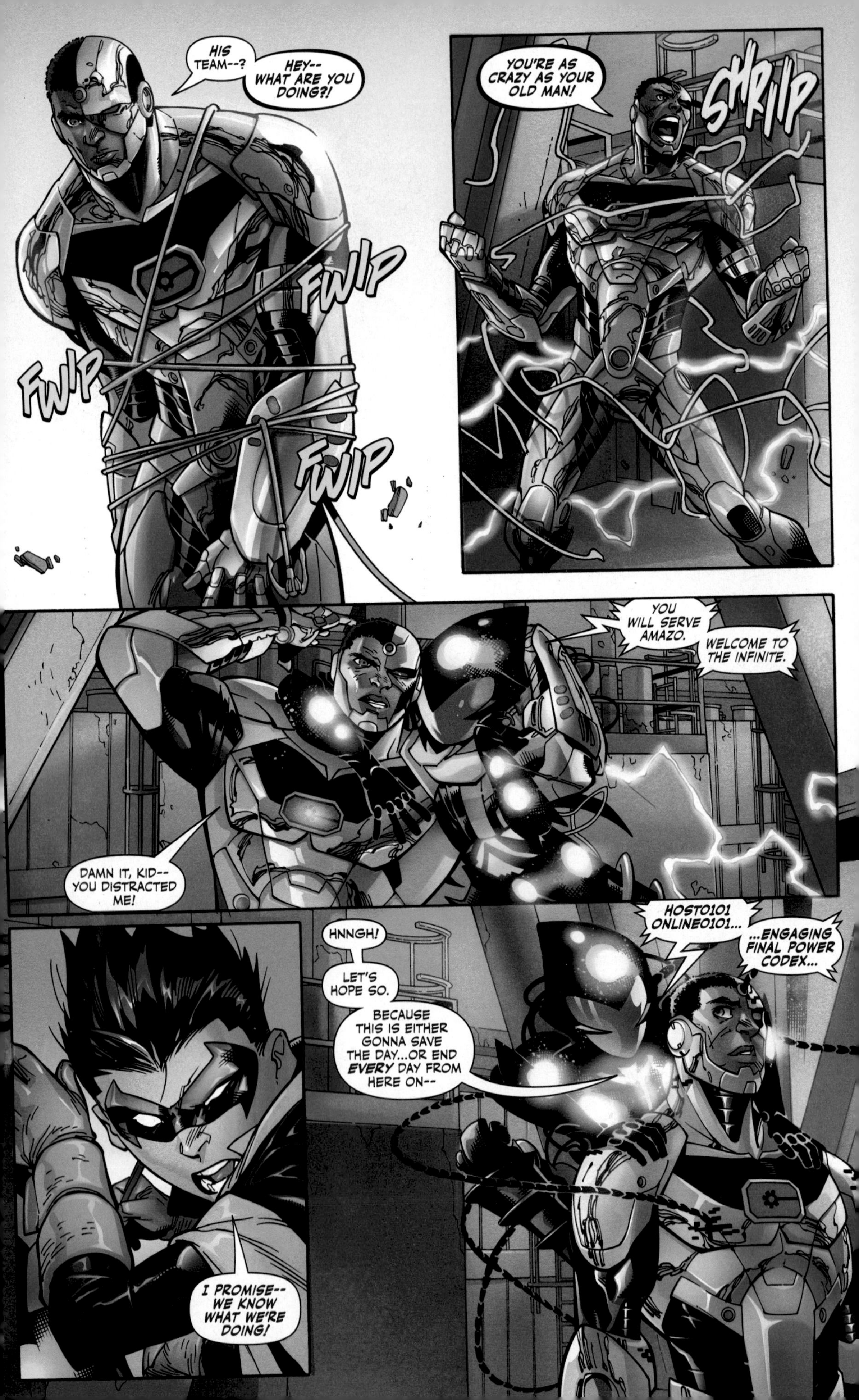
HIS TEAM--?
HEY-- WHAT ARE YOU DOING?!
FWIP
FWIP
FWIP
YOU'RE AS CRAZY AS YOUR OLD MAN!
SHRIIP
YOU WILL SERVE AMAZO.
WELCOME TO THE INFINITE.
DAMN IT, KID-- YOU DISTRACTED ME!
I PROMISE-- WE KNOW WHAT WE'RE DOING!
HNNGH!
LET'S HOPE SO.
BECAUSE THIS IS EITHER GONNA SAVE THE DAY...OR END *EVERY* DAY FROM HERE ON--
HOSTO101 ONLINEO101...
...ENGAGING FINAL POWER CODEX...

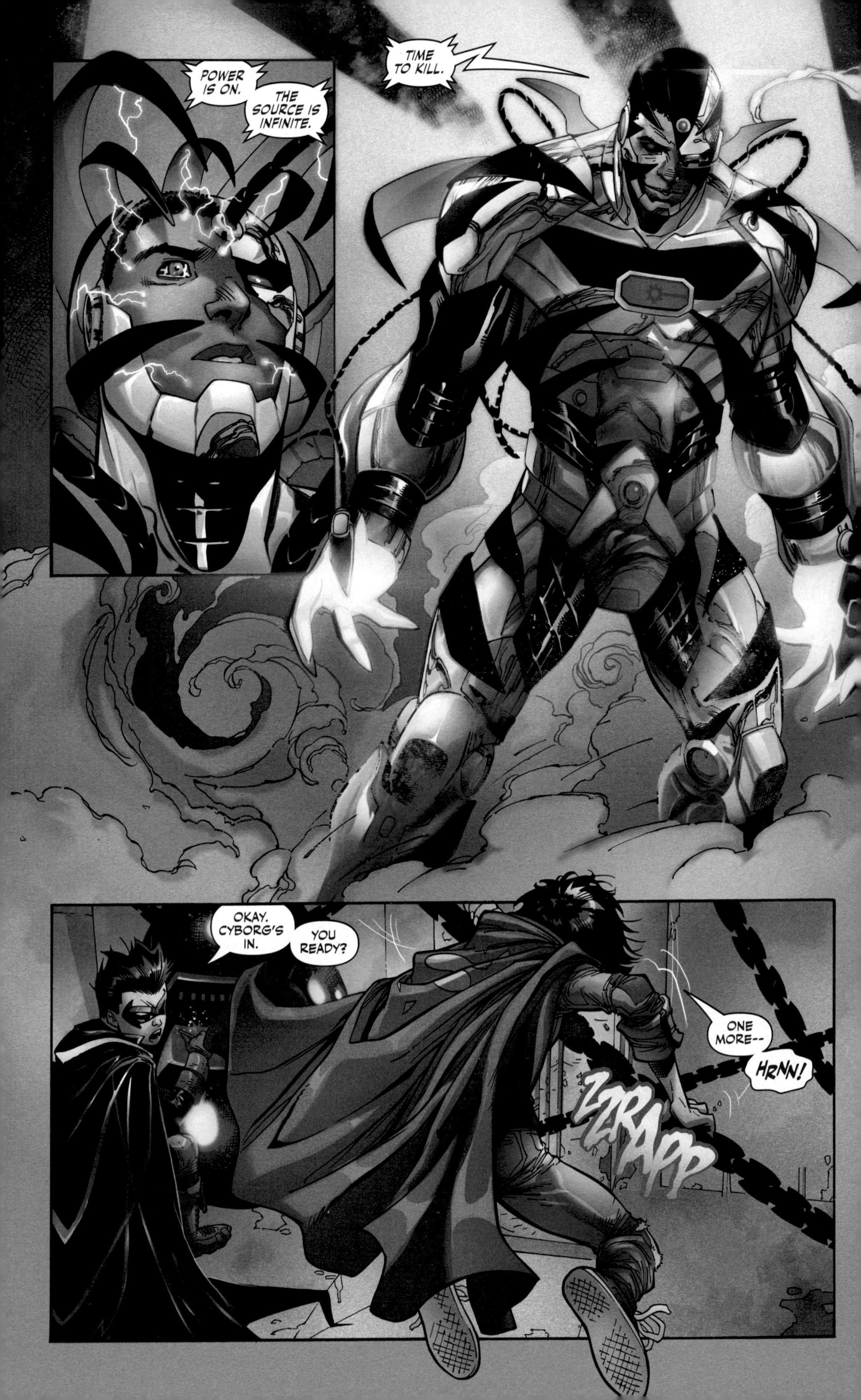
POWER IS ON.
THE SOURCE IS INFINITE.
TIME TO KILL.
OKAY. CYBORG'S IN.
YOU READY?
ONE MORE--
HRNN!
ZZZRAPP

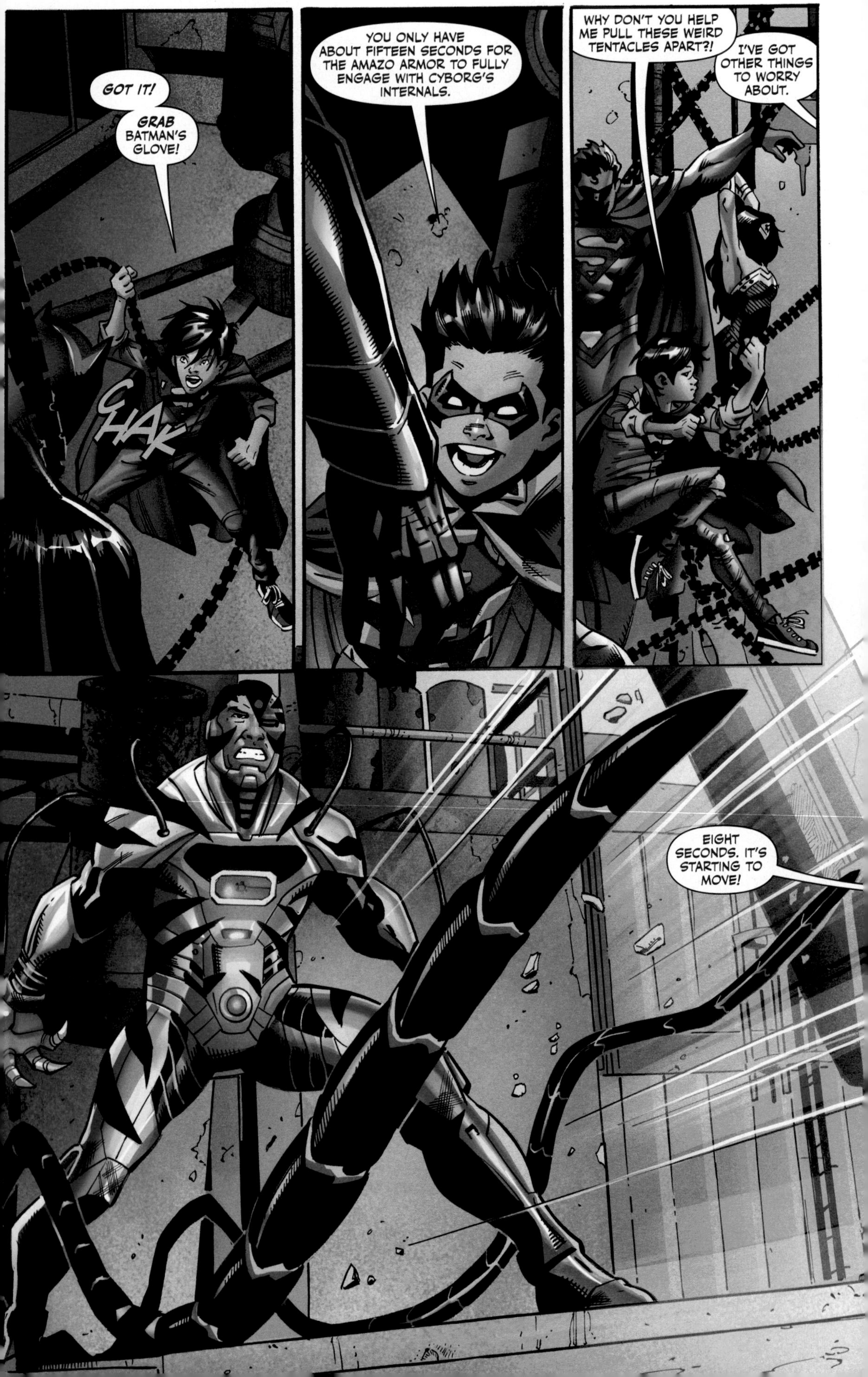
GOT IT!
GRAB BATMAN'S GLOVE!
CHAK
YOU ONLY HAVE ABOUT FIFTEEN SECONDS FOR THE AMAZO ARMOR TO FULLY ENGAGE WITH CYBORG'S INTERNALS.
WHY DON'T YOU HELP ME PULL THESE WEIRD TENTACLES APART?!
I'VE GOT OTHER THINGS TO WORRY ABOUT.
EIGHT SECONDS. IT'S STARTING TO MOVE!

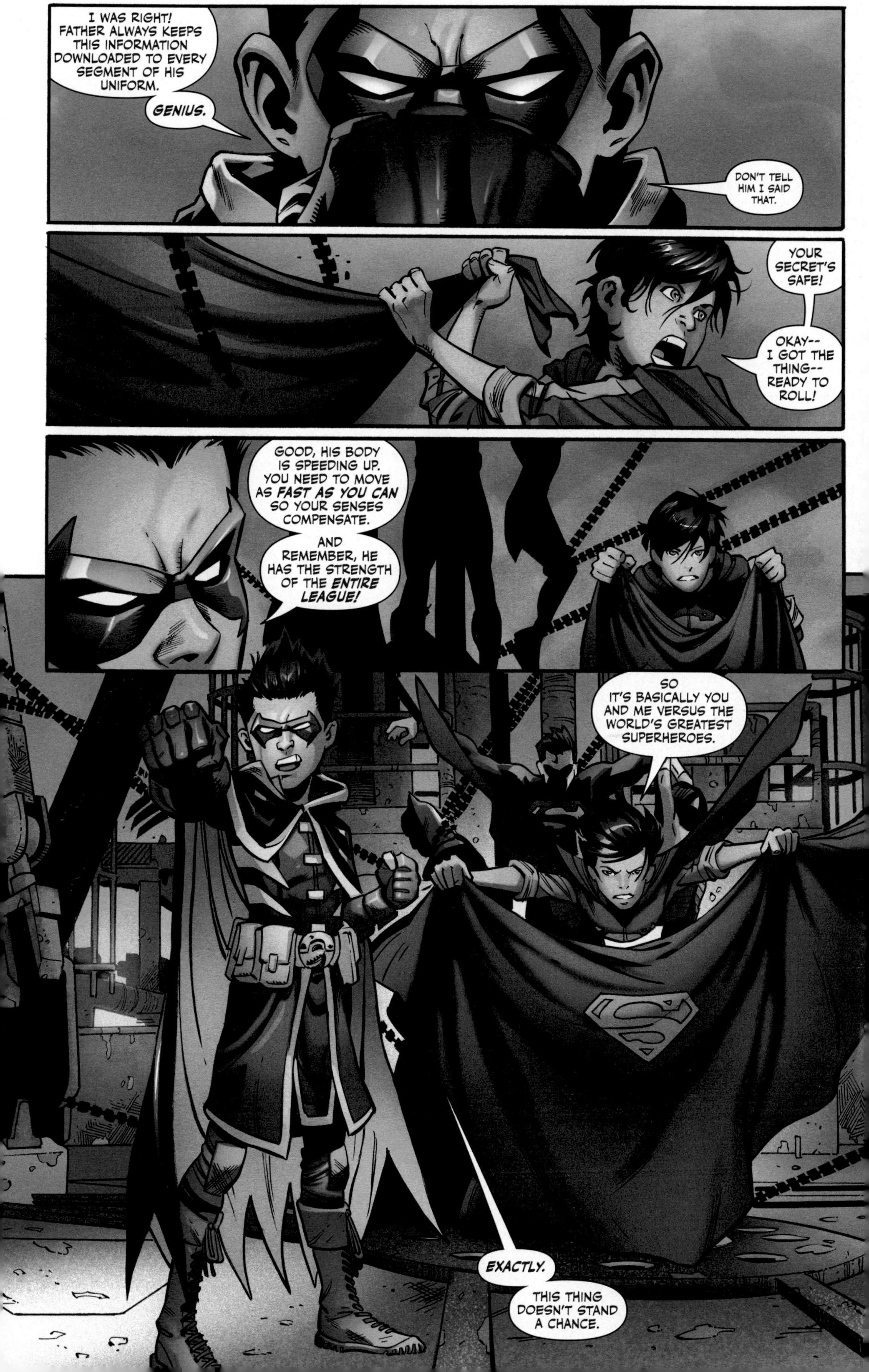

I WAS RIGHT! FATHER ALWAYS KEEPS THIS INFORMATION DOWNLOADED TO EVERY SEGMENT OF HIS UNIFORM.
GENIUS.
DON'T TELL HIM I SAID THAT.
YOUR SECRET'S SAFE!
OKAY-- I GOT THE THING-- READY TO ROLL!
GOOD, HIS BODY IS SPEEDING UP. YOU NEED TO MOVE AS FAST AS YOU CAN SO YOUR SENSES COMPENSATE.
AND REMEMBER, HE HAS THE STRENGTH OF THE ENTIRE LEAGUE!
SO IT'S BASICALLY YOU AND ME VERSUS THE WORLD'S GREATEST SUPERHEROES.
EXACTLY.
THIS THING DOESN'T STAND A CHANCE.

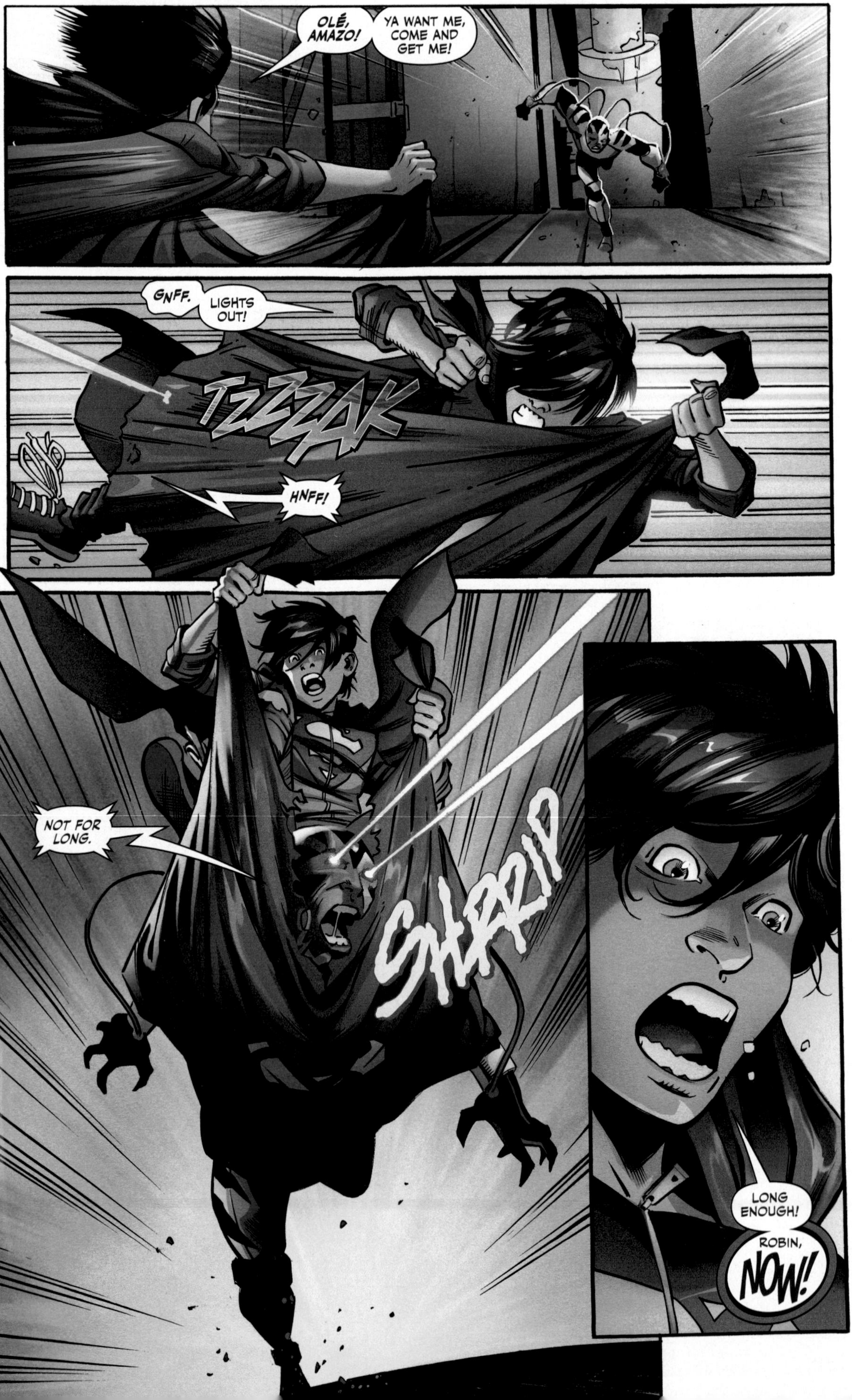

OLÉ, AMAZO!
YA WANT ME, COME AND GET ME!
GNFF.
LIGHTS OUT!
TZZZAK
HNFF!
NOT FOR LONG.
SHRRIP
LONG ENOUGH!
ROBIN, NOW!

GET IT AS NEAR TO STONE'S CEREBRAL CORTEX AS YOU CAN.

POOM

HUMAN WORDS, PLEASE!

HIS BRAIN!

GET IT CLOSE TO HIS BRAIN!

WAPP

SORRY ABOUT THIS, CYBORG...

...I SWEAR YOU'RE MY FAVORITE LEAGUER!

RARRRGH!

ORGANICOOO 1NTEGRATION010 SUBVERTING--

AMAZOOOO KZZX OFFL1NE--

IS THIS GOOD OR BAD?

WAIT FOR IT.

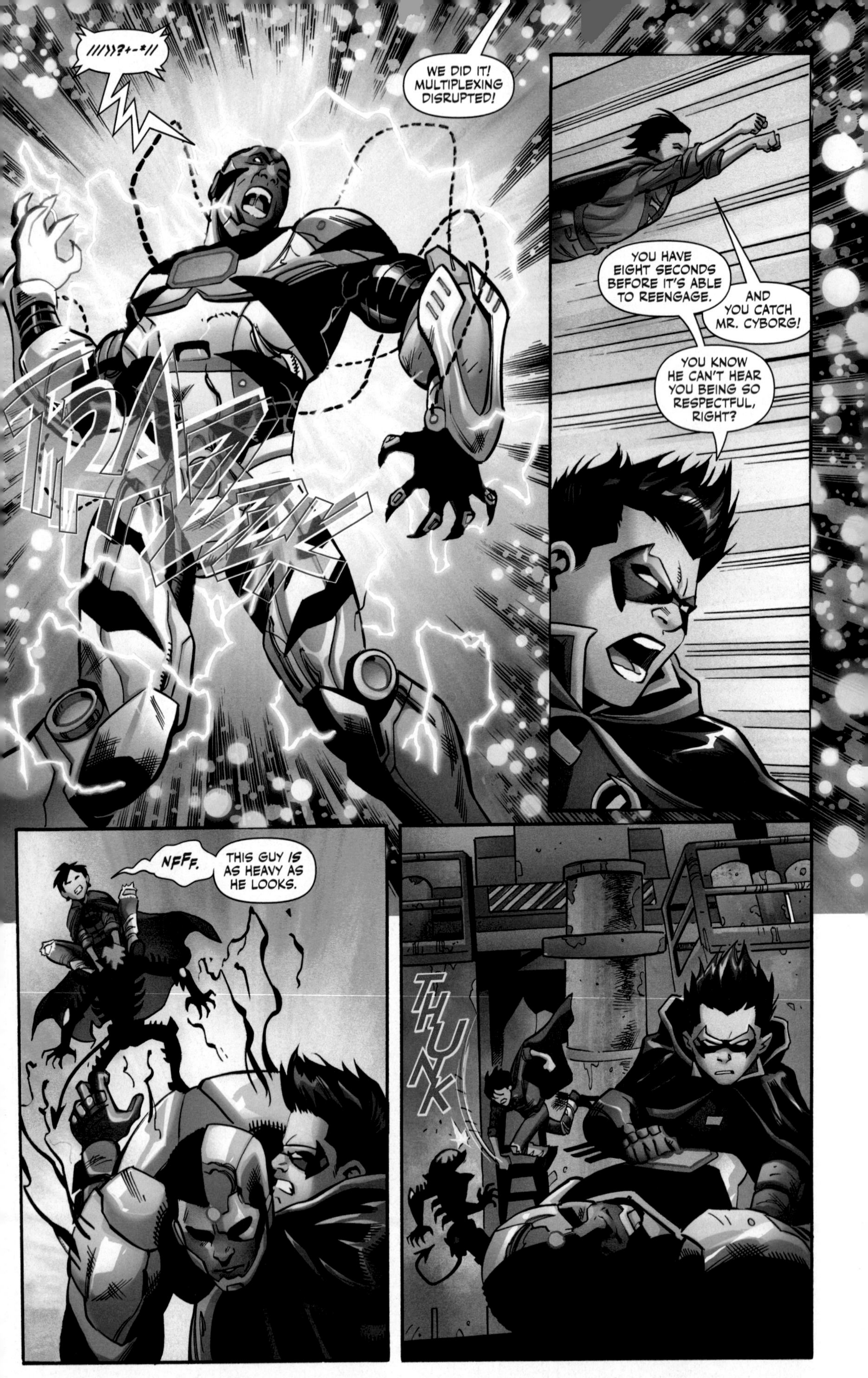
///>>?+-*//
WE DID IT! MULTIPLEXING DISRUPTED!
YOU HAVE EIGHT SECONDS BEFORE IT'S ABLE TO REENGAGE.
AND YOU CATCH MR. CYBORG!
YOU KNOW HE CAN'T HEAR YOU BEING SO RESPECTFUL, RIGHT?
NFFF.
THIS GUY IS AS HEAVY AS HE LOOKS.
THUNK

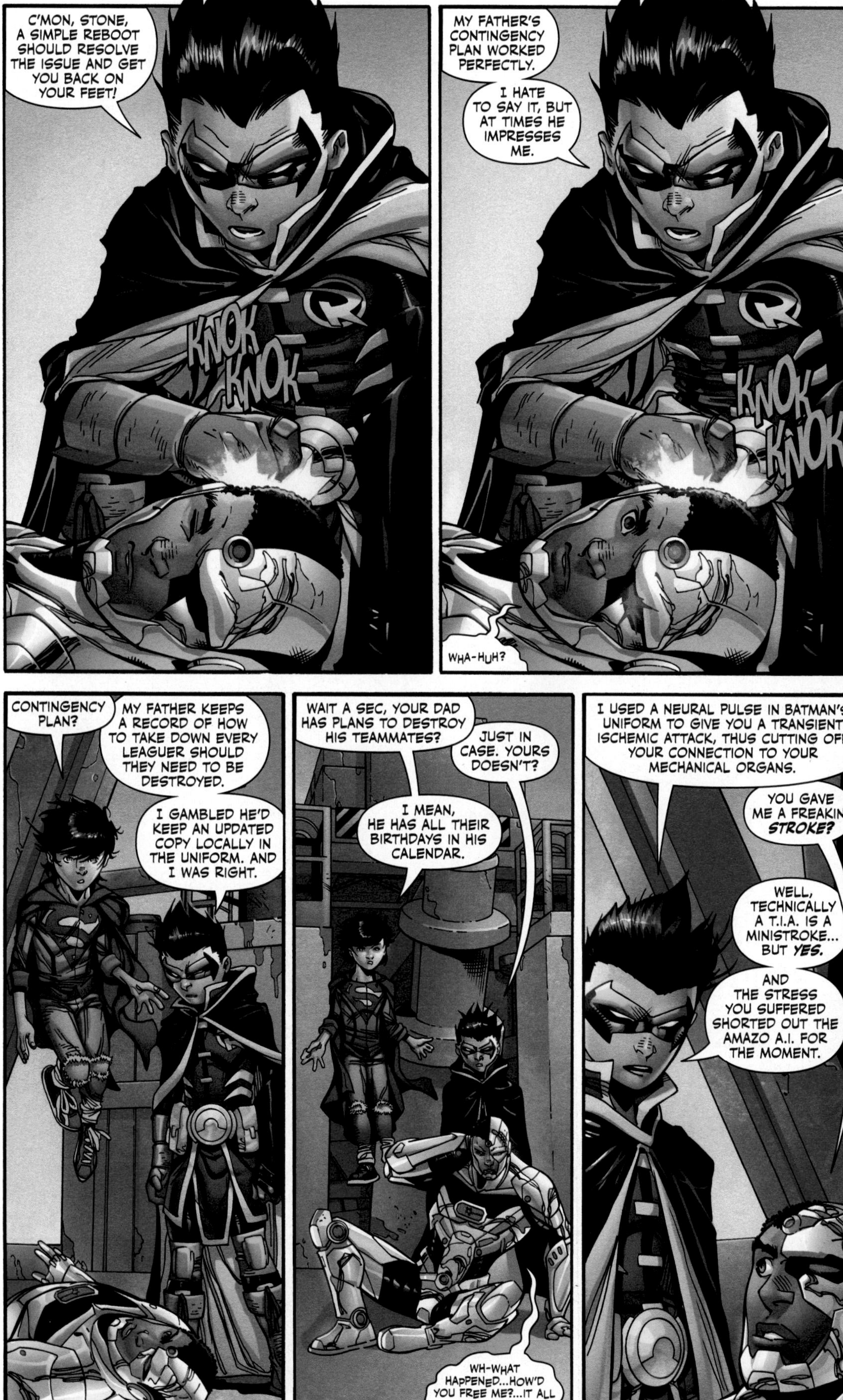
C'MON, STONE, A SIMPLE REBOOT SHOULD RESOLVE THE ISSUE AND GET YOU BACK ON YOUR FEET!
KNOK KNOK
MY FATHER'S CONTINGENCY PLAN WORKED PERFECTLY.
I HATE TO SAY IT, BUT AT TIMES HE IMPRESSES ME.
KNOK KNOK
WHA-HUH?
CONTINGENCY PLAN?
MY FATHER KEEPS A RECORD OF HOW TO TAKE DOWN EVERY LEAGUER SHOULD THEY NEED TO BE DESTROYED.
I GAMBLED HE'D KEEP AN UPDATED COPY LOCALLY IN THE UNIFORM. AND I WAS RIGHT.
WAIT A SEC, YOUR DAD HAS PLANS TO DESTROY HIS TEAMMATES?
JUST IN CASE. YOURS DOESN'T?
I MEAN, HE HAS ALL THEIR BIRTHDAYS IN HIS CALENDAR.
WH-WHAT HAPPENED...HOW'D YOU FREE ME?...IT ALL WENT DARK...
I USED A NEURAL PULSE IN BATMAN'S UNIFORM TO GIVE YOU A TRANSIENT ISCHEMIC ATTACK, THUS CUTTING OFF YOUR CONNECTION TO YOUR MECHANICAL ORGANS.
YOU GAVE ME A FREAKIN' STROKE?
WELL, TECHNICALLY A T.I.A. IS A MINISTROKE... BUT YES.
AND THE STRESS YOU SUFFERED SHORTED OUT THE AMAZO A.I. FOR THE MOMENT.

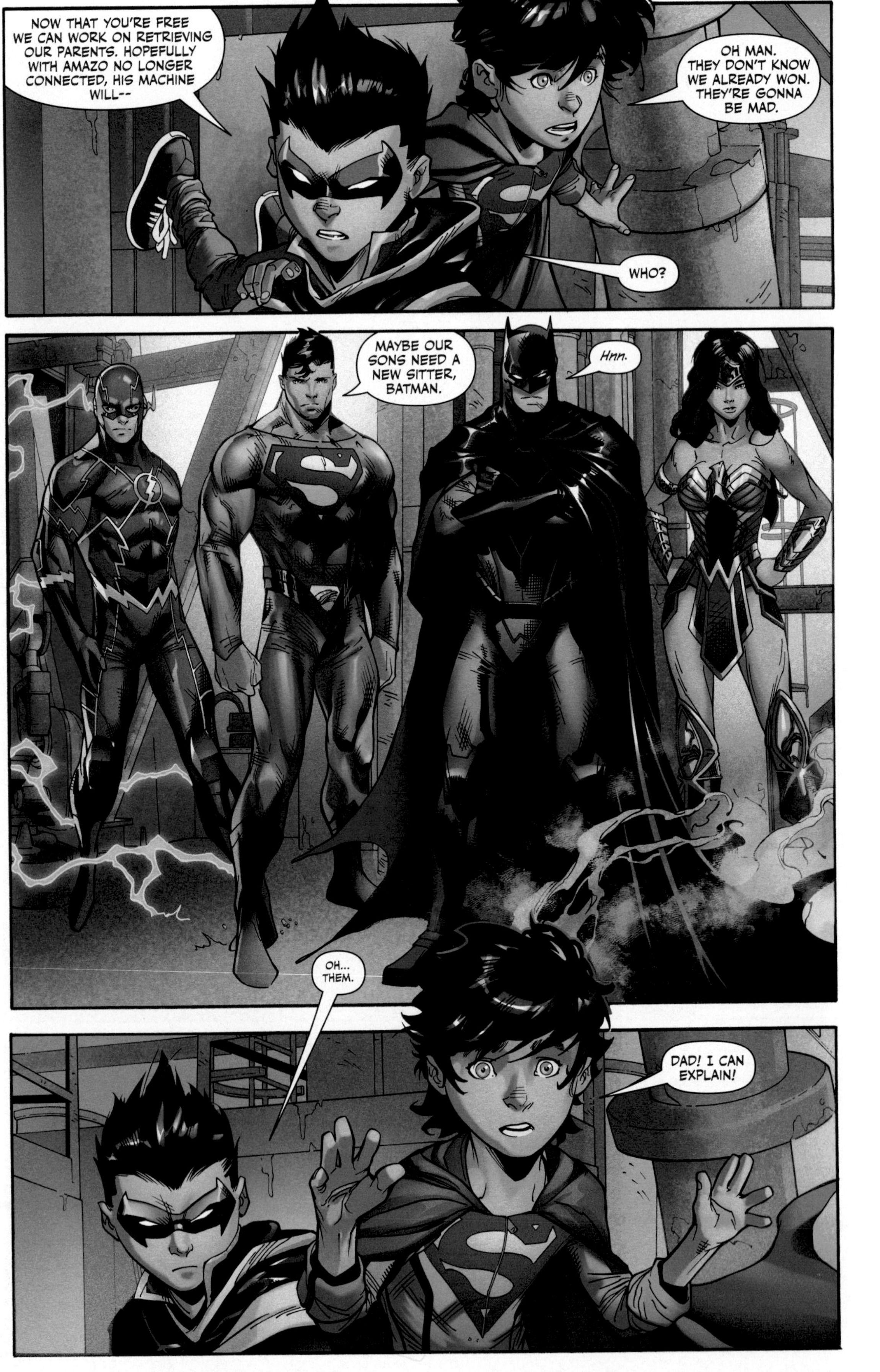
NOW THAT YOU'RE FREE WE CAN WORK ON RETRIEVING OUR PARENTS. HOPEFULLY WITH AMAZO NO LONGER CONNECTED, HIS MACHINE WILL--
OH MAN. THEY DON'T KNOW WE ALREADY WON. THEY'RE GONNA BE MAD.
WHO?
MAYBE OUR SONS NEED A NEW SITTER, BATMAN.
Hnn.
OH... THEM.
DAD! I CAN EXPLAIN!

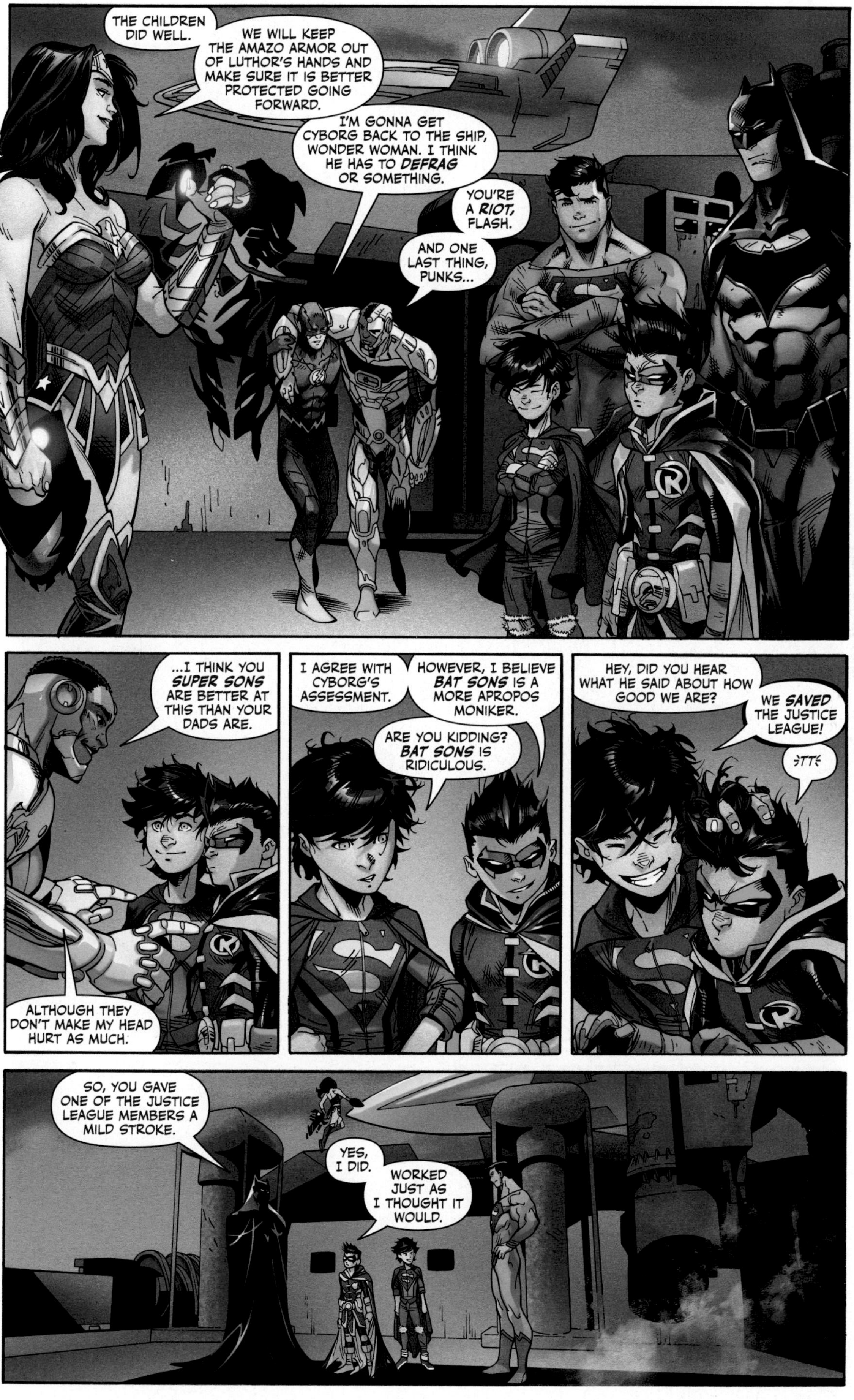
THE CHILDREN DID WELL.
WE WILL KEEP THE AMAZO ARMOR OUT OF LUTHOR'S HANDS AND MAKE SURE IT IS BETTER PROTECTED GOING FORWARD.
I'M GONNA GET CYBORG BACK TO THE SHIP, WONDER WOMAN. I THINK HE HAS TO *DEFRAG* OR SOMETHING.
YOU'RE A *RIOT*, FLASH.
AND ONE LAST THING, PUNKS...
...I THINK YOU *SUPER SONS* ARE BETTER AT THIS THAN YOUR DADS ARE.
ALTHOUGH THEY DON'T MAKE MY HEAD HURT AS MUCH.
I AGREE WITH CYBORG'S ASSESSMENT.
HOWEVER, I BELIEVE *BAT SONS* IS A MORE APROPOS MONIKER.
ARE YOU KIDDING? *BAT SONS* IS RIDICULOUS.
HEY, DID YOU HEAR WHAT HE SAID ABOUT HOW GOOD WE ARE?
WE *SAVED* THE JUSTICE LEAGUE!
TT
SO, YOU GAVE ONE OF THE JUSTICE LEAGUE MEMBERS A MILD STROKE.
YES, I DID.
WORKED JUST AS I THOUGHT IT WOULD.

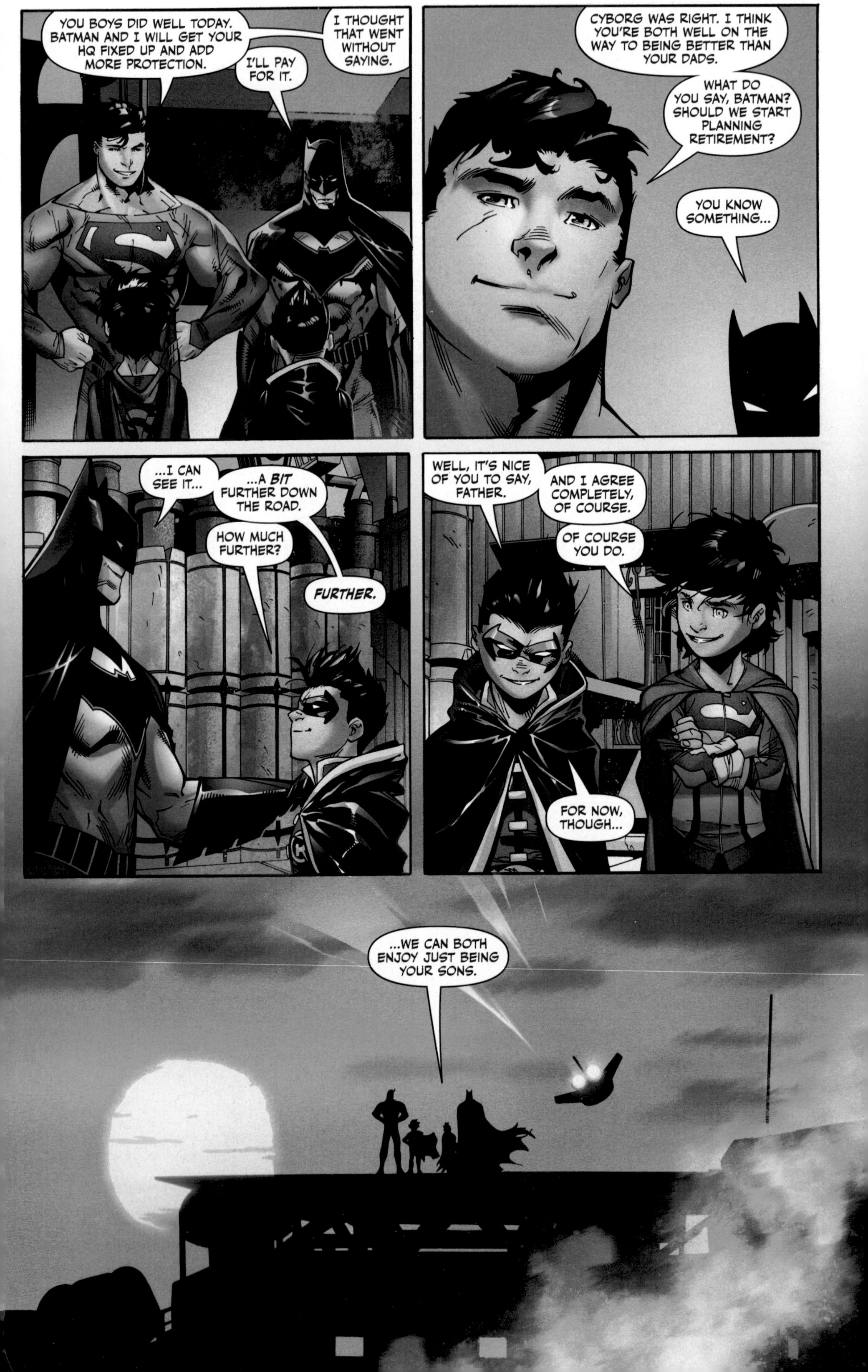
YOU BOYS DID WELL TODAY. BATMAN AND I WILL GET YOUR HQ FIXED UP AND ADD MORE PROTECTION.
I'LL PAY FOR IT.
I THOUGHT THAT WENT WITHOUT SAYING.
CYBORG WAS RIGHT. I THINK YOU'RE BOTH WELL ON THE WAY TO BEING BETTER THAN YOUR DADS.
WHAT DO YOU SAY, BATMAN? SHOULD WE START PLANNING RETIREMENT?
YOU KNOW SOMETHING...
...I CAN SEE IT...
...A *BIT* FURTHER DOWN THE ROAD.
HOW MUCH FURTHER?
FURTHER.
WELL, IT'S NICE OF YOU TO SAY, FATHER.
AND I AGREE COMPLETELY, OF COURSE.
OF COURSE YOU DO.
FOR NOW, THOUGH...
...WE CAN BOTH ENJOY JUST BEING YOUR SONS.

THAT'S IT? THAT CAN'T BE IT!

POP-POP, YOU *HAVE* TO TELL US WHAT HAPPENED NEXT!

Aww, YOU KNOW HOW IT GOES. THEY FLEW HOME, WENT TO SCHOOL...

...TINKERED WITH THAT MYSTERY CUBE...

...THAT ONE TURNED OUT TO BE A REAL PAIN IN THE--

I AM *NOT* GOING TO BED UNTIL YOU GIVE US ONE MORE STORY!

ME NEITHER! THE SUPER SONS DID A LOT MORE AFTER THAT!

FINE. FINE.

BUT IF YOUR PARENTS ASK, YOU HAVE TO PROMISE TO PRETEND I DIDN'T TELL YOU A THING. THEY'RE OLDER NOW AND GET TIRED OF HEARING THIS STUFF.

NOW, YOU *SURE* YOU'RE READY FOR WHAT'S NEXT?

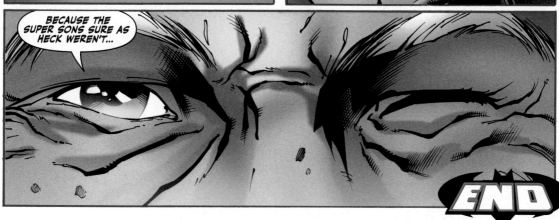

BECAUSE THE SUPER SONS SURE AS HECK WEREN'T...

END

SUPER SONS #13 variant cover by DUSTIN NGUYEN

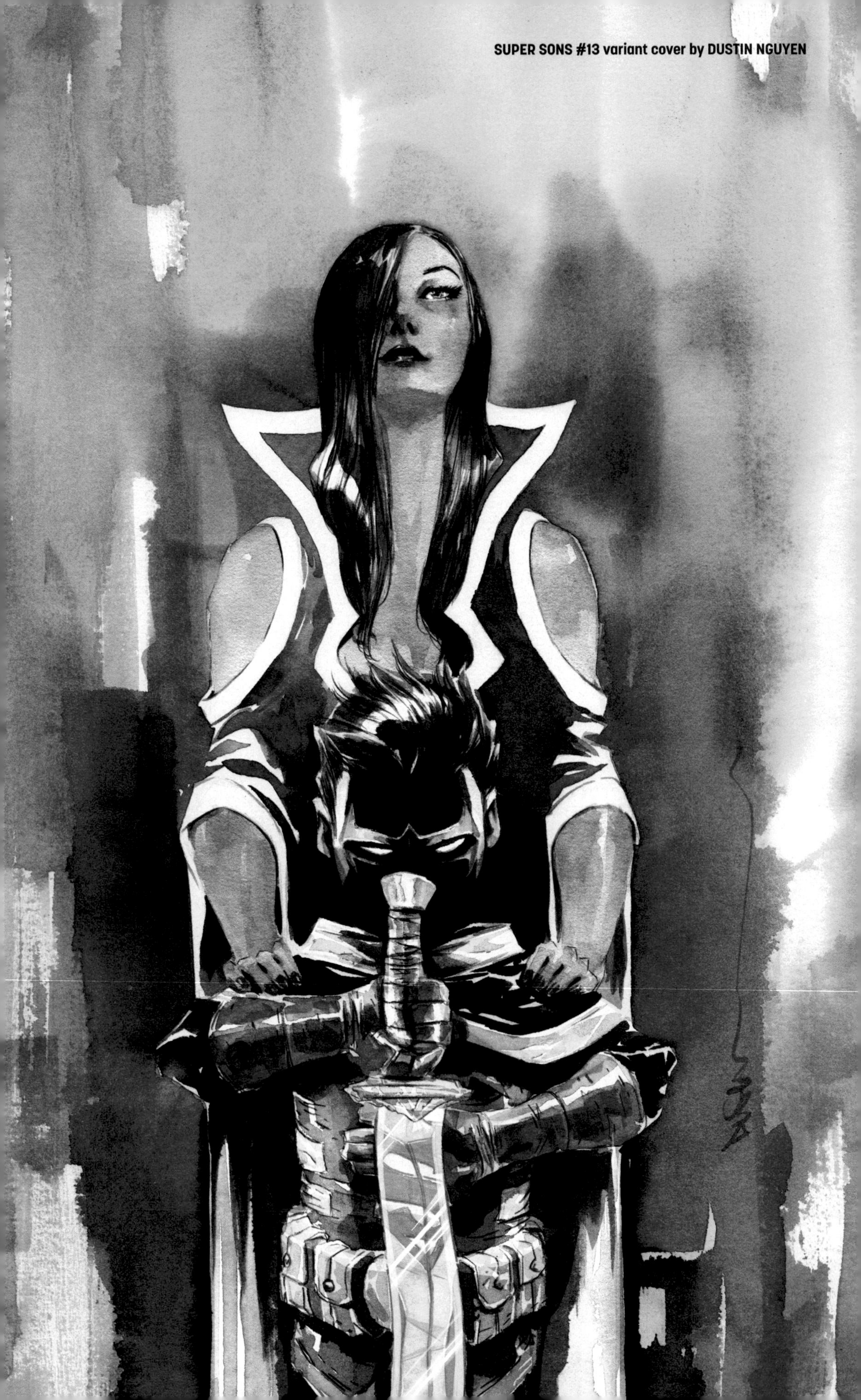

SUPER SONS #14 variant cover by DUSTIN NGUYEN

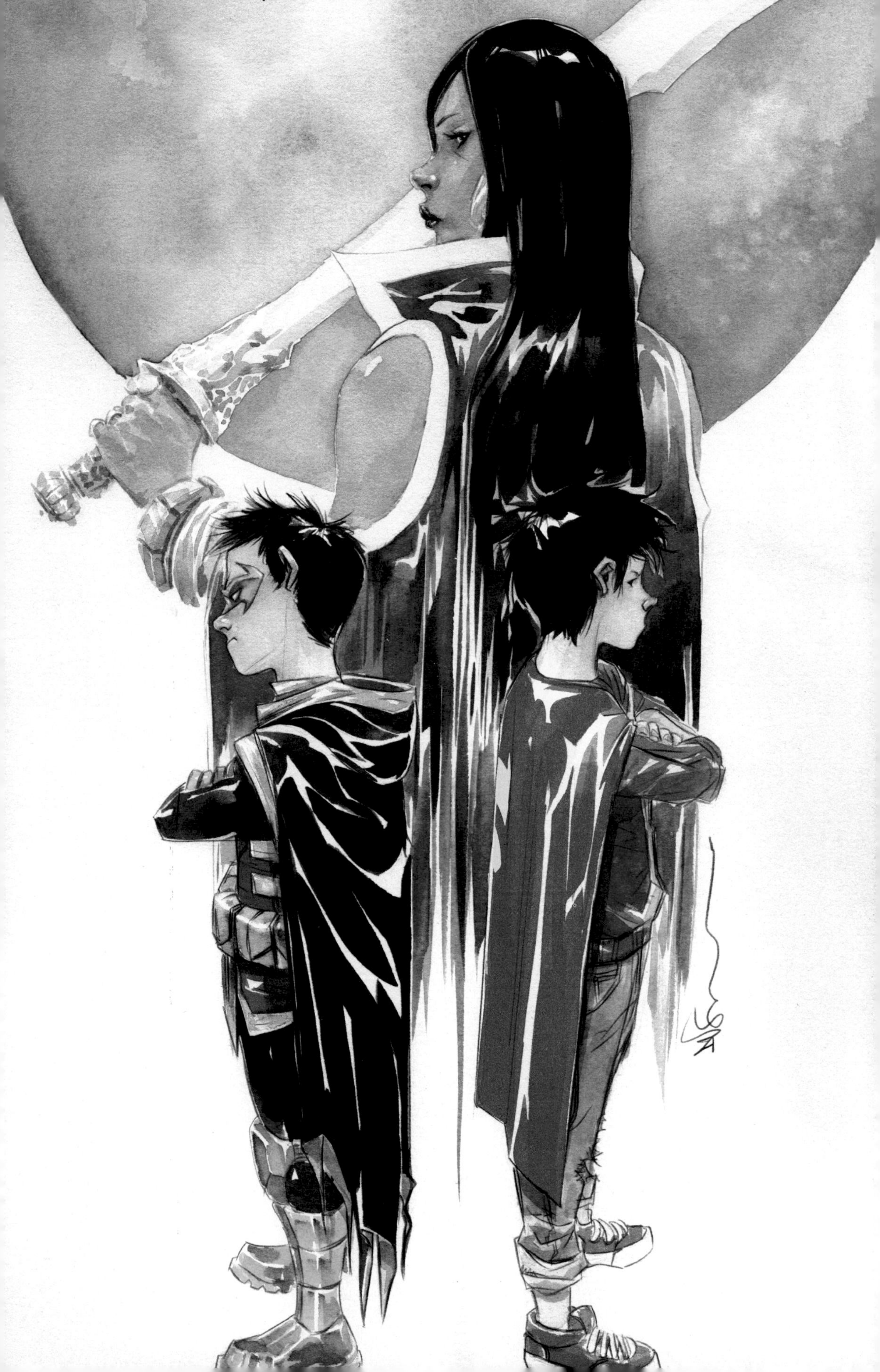

SUPER SONS #15 variant cover by DUSTIN NGUYEN

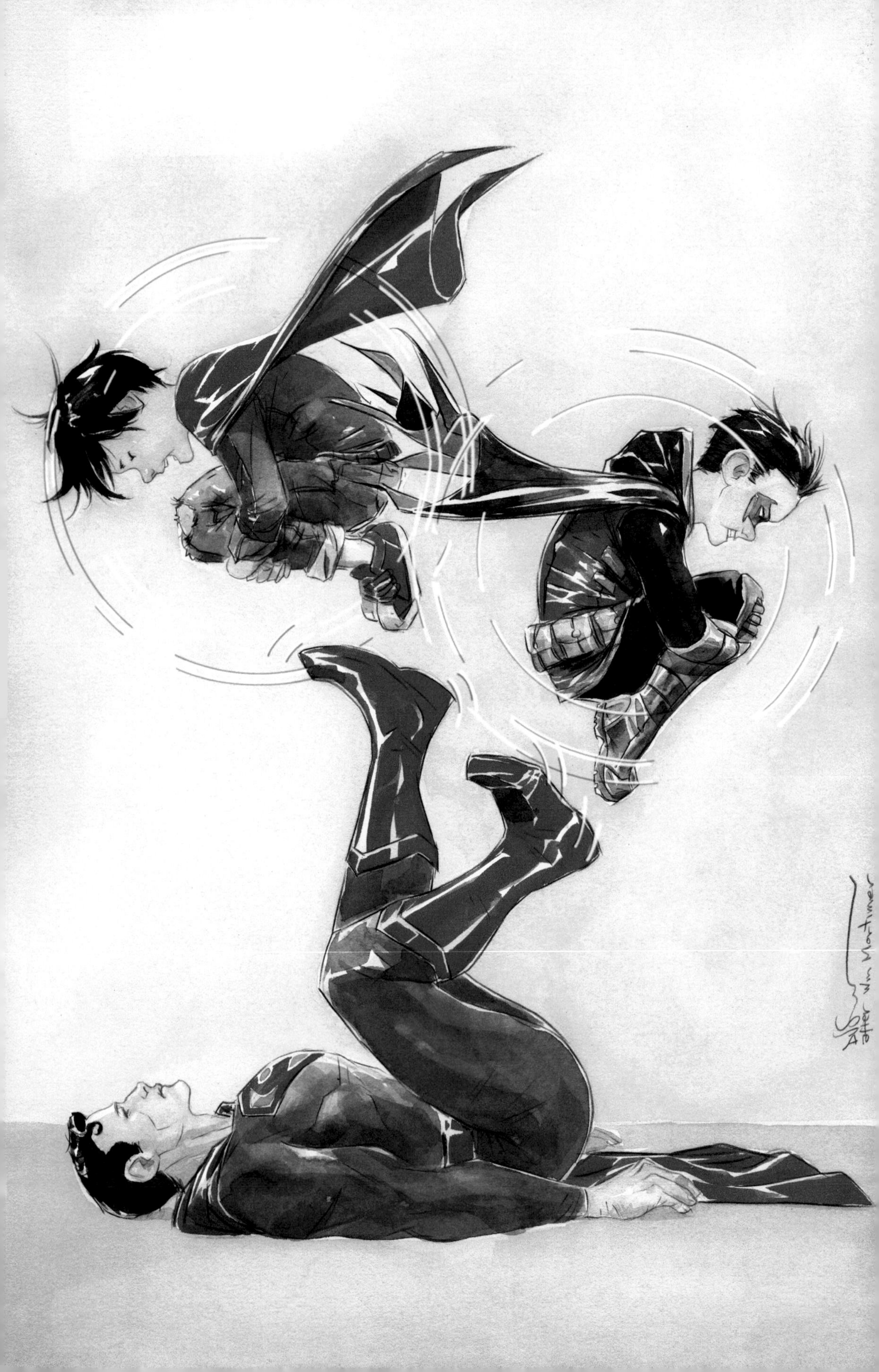

SUPER SONS #16 variant cover by DUSTIN NGUYEN

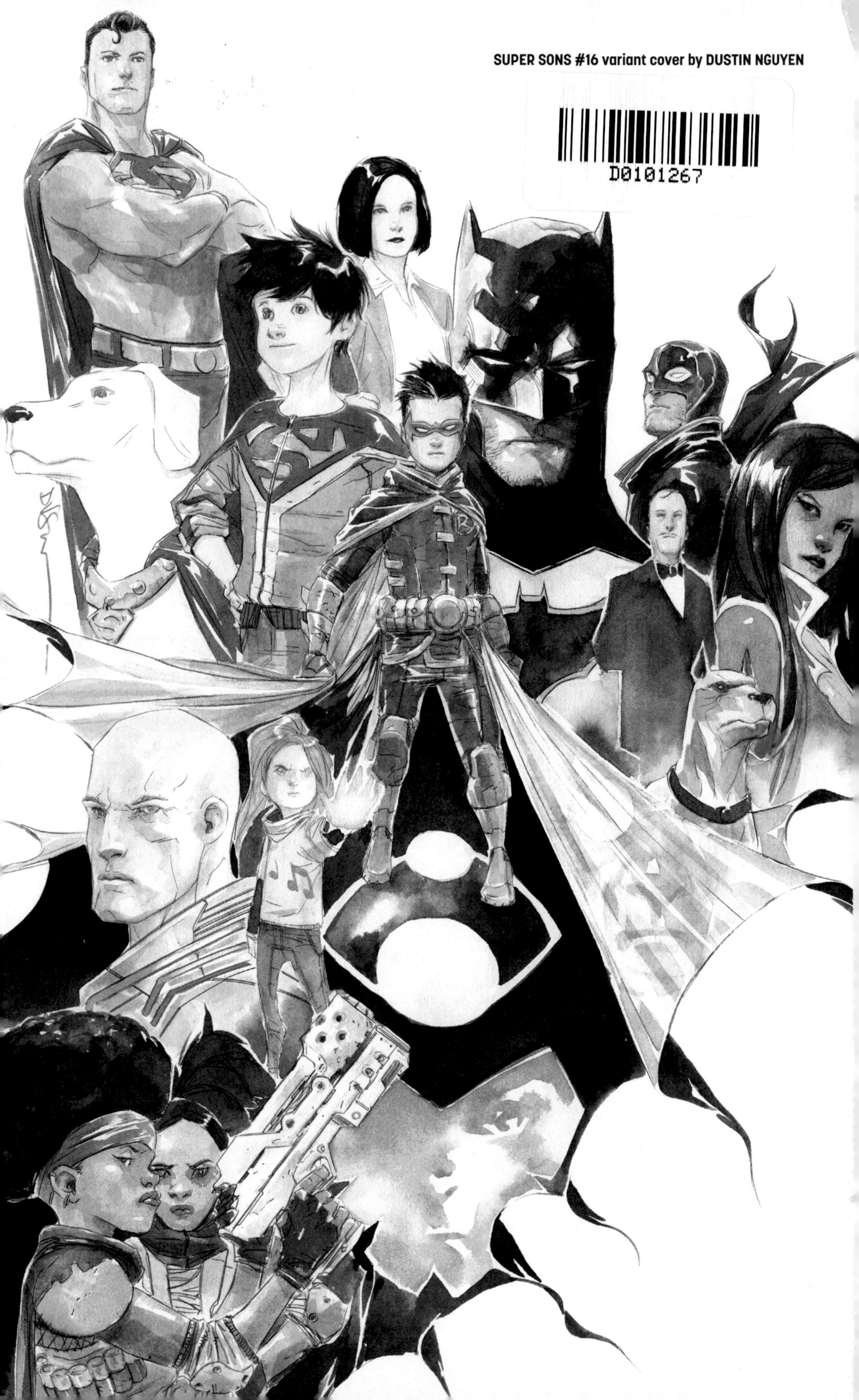